REA

FRIENDS
OF ACPL

W9-DGE-406

MAR 0 4 2005

Embracing the Mystery

Embracing the Mystery

The Sacred Unfolding in Ordinary People and Everyday Lives

Meredith Jordan

Copyright © 2004 by Meredith Jordan.

Library of Congress Number:		2004103383
ISBN:	Hardcover	0-9749535-1-2
	Softcover	0-9749535-0-4

All rights reserved. No part of this book may be reproduced or transmitted in any form or by any means, electronic or mechanical, including photocopying, recording, or by any information storage and retrieval system, without permission in writing from the copyright owner.

This book was printed in the United States of America.

To order additional copies of this book, contact:
Rogers McKay Publishing
P.O. Box 46
Biddeford, ME 04005
http://www.rogersmckay.org

Contents

This book is dedicated, with great love, to Bob Whalen,
whose love and support opened my life
and my heart for the words to flow.
He has been my full partner in every step of this work.

And to my community of beloveds,
whose unwavering support casts a circle of love around me:

Sarah and Josh Jordan, Deborah Pfeffer, Katherine Stiles,
Ellie Mercer, Marvin Ellison, Susan Doughty, Daya Carpenter,
Lisa Barstow, Christina Baldwin, Ann Linnea, Libbet Cone,
Jim Kellar, Cheryl Conklin, Michael Dwinell, Anna Birch,
Paloma Sylvan, Susan Tully Young, Barbara Hopkins Dulac,
Marilyn Danis, Alexis Teitz, and Diane Dunton.

Every journey has a secret destination of which even the traveler is unaware.

—Martin Buber

Introduction

Many years ago, early in my spiritual journey, I read a story about Uncle Frank Davis, a Pawnee elder. He told two young journalists that as a boy he had asked his mother how a person becomes wise. His mother explained that each of us follows the path through life that the Creator makes especially for us. Along our unique path, the Creator drops "little slips of paper" to provide us with instructions on the right use of our lives. *It's our task,* she told her son, *to notice the scraps of paper as they fall around us, to pick them up and to put them in our pockets. When we need guidance along life's way, all we have to do is reach deep into our pockets and pull out the slips of paper that, pieced carefully together, comprise our particular map.*

We all need a map. God is wildly unpredictable and mysterious. When good things happen, we often credit them to divine intervention. When bad things happen, we find we cannot grasp how God could cause us to suffer or leave us in despair. In our greatest moments of need, we assume God has failed us *personally.* These concerns have haunted our hearts even more since the tragic events of September 11th, 2001. Perhaps the larger question begging consideration in our present world-turned-upside-down is this: *Who then, or what, is the one we call God?*

Most religious traditions teach that God is a living being—the Father or Mother of us all—who lives outside us, takes personal interest in each of us, and has a direct influence on the events of our lives. Is it possible this is an outdated conceptualization of the magnificent Mystery that lives at the exact epicenter of all life? Possible that, in our attempts to maintain the illusion of order in a troubled and turbulent world, we try too hard to force the Mystery of God into names, forms, images, or even belief systems? And while these attempts to pin God down may offer small measures of comfort, they may also fail to convey the complex nature of Ultimate Reality. Both theologians and scientists are concluding simultaneously at this point in human understanding that the Mystery of God—both wondrous and baffling—is almost impossible to proclaim.

For many traditionally religious people, this news is unsettling. It shakes the foundations of all they believe. For individuals who are less traditional in their search for a meaningful relationship with the sacred, the possibility that God is a complex, inexplicable, unpredictable *mystery* explains their lifelong discomfort in the presence of religious dogmas that don't correspond with their own personal encounters with God. Many quiet, unassuming everyday mystics choose to remain silent because religious traditions and leaders discount their personal experiences of God for failing to substantiate a doctrine.

Early in my own religious upbringing, I was startled to discover that church doctrine explained God in terms that departed wildly from my personal experiences of That-Which-Is-Sacred. Even then I knew my direct relationship with the Sacred communicated information far more authentic, more embodied, and thus more *believable* to me about the unpredictable, unexpected, changing nature of God than what I learned in church. I adopted a belief that God is more mysterious than I would ever understand and began to address God simply as *Mystery*. This belief led me to perhaps the most important of my questions: *Are we failing to experience the wonder of the Sacred Mystery in our midst—and to learn from it—because we foolishly and mistakenly believe God has already finished revealing its holy nature to us?*

It seems plausible that we're being challenged to revise our understanding of God. Could God be something other than what religious doctrine tells us? Could God be evolving and changing in the same way humanity is evolving, and therefore be different today than God was two thousand years ago? Questions like this fascinate me.

I take the position that God's nature is always changing, continually growing and revealing itself to us in new ways. In my opinion, we have to remain on our toes for whatever (borrowing from my colleague Michael Dwinell) "God is up to" in our lives and in the world today. This means I cannot assume someone else—for example, the world's clergy—knows God better than I do and can interpret God to me. I alone am responsible for paying attention to how the Mystery of God continually reveals itself in and through my life. No one else can do this for me. *I'm the one who must develop my own relationship with, and understanding of, the nature of the Divine Mystery.*

As we go through life picking up our little scraps of paper, we quickly learn that no two people are given the same set of instructions, nor are they intended to follow the same path through life. The greater design alive at the center of All That Is includes a unique blueprint for every one of us. These blueprints provide all the directions we need to build a life suited to our soul's highest learning and purpose. Wisdom lies in comprehending that the Mystery Among and Within Us is forever offering little slips of paper to guide us as we compose our lives.

Think about it: *If no two people receive the same set of*

instructions, it's also possible that no two individuals are meant
to experience the One of Many Names in exactly the same way.
Although I strive to be honest and real with the people I love,
I rarely reveal myself in the same way to any two of them. Each
person draws out a slightly different aspect of the many parts
of my complex nature. It's as we elicit different "threads" in the
intricate tapestry comprising each of us that we actually help one
another to grow into all we're meant to be.

ᵣ Isn't it possible that the One of Many Names is even more
complex and intricately designed than we human beings are,
never revealing itself in its totality, but rather revealing its many
different aspects to each of us at different times and in different
ways? Our human need to conceptualize God in specific images
or forms may ultimately *limit* our grasp of God's complexity,
just as a friend who knows one part of my nature very well
would be misguided if she assumed to know all parts of me
well. Further, in healthy relationships, it's a mark of *respect*
to allow the people we love to teach us who they are as they
change and grow through life's many challenges. It's a mark
of *disrespect*, however unintended, for us to behave as if we
know them better than they know themselves. In a similar way,
perhaps it's our spiritual mandate to wait for God to tell us
who—or what—God is. If so, doesn't it make sense that our
job is to listen, experience, and learn as we encounter the
Mystery for ourselves?

It's said throughout the great wisdom traditions that God
names God by saying only: *I am that I am.* This statement
points strongly to the possibility that the Sacred Mystery is
consciousness or *essence* rather than *person* or *being.* By using
names for God that, while comforting, may limit the depth
and breadth of our experience of this Mystery, we may
unintentionally close our eyes and hearts to that which is
attempting to reveal its ever-developing nature to us. Striving
to find and experience God, we may fail to see the holiness

blooming in the garden, the suffering throes of anguish staring at us through the face of an enemy, or hear the simple knock at the door of our own hearts.

Who, or what, is God? Are we prepared to allow traditional images to fall away and our personal encounters with the Mystery to teach us something of God's ever changing, ever expanding, ever disclosing nature? It's been the most consistent experience in my spiritual life to have things—a relationship, a belief, a way of understanding myself, my possessions—stripped away just at the moment I grow complacent with them. I strongly suspect I'm not alone. As a therapist-witness for others making earnest efforts to live in spiritual integrity, I see this *stripping away* process all the time. We just draw a bead on God . . . and God changes.

In order to come to terms with a more fluid view of God, one I hope is actually more authentic, I've spent the last dozen years of my life quietly paying attention to what's right in front of me, revealing something about the nature of spiritual reality. I gave up trying to comfort myself with answers. In place of that, I began to ask questions that challenged me to mature as a spiritual seeker, and gave those questions room to roll around in me. I joined in hundreds of conversations with other seekers who want, as I do, to have a real relationship with the Sacred, whatever that might be and wherever it might lead. I tried to remain open to a Presence of Mystery teaching me about itself in small moments, through ordinary people and everyday events. Some of these events have been so imperceptible as to almost escape notice. Others set off tremors in the bedrock of my life. The stories in this book reflect some of those life-changing moments and offer up many of the questions that pursued me in the simple process of paying attention.

The net effect is that I am changed in my relationship with God, and I have come to believe that God, the one I call *Mystery*, is also changed by its relationship with me. I have no way to prove this belief so that you, the reader, might believe it along with me. Yet it's consistent with all we as a people are learning about the interactive nature of reality. Everything changes as a result of our paying attention. It's just common sense that there exists a great feedback loop operating throughout all of creation. In the way a friend's insight suddenly inspires an insight in me, I wonder if we grow more conscious in spiritual tandem with God-Consciousness, and if God-Consciousness expands because we make efforts to awaken.

Can it be that God and humanity assist each other in the process of expanding, transforming, and ultimately evolving into more of what we are intended to be? Perhaps as the Sacred Mystery widens, broadens, and deepens its experience of reality, there's a corresponding expansion in human awareness. And as human awareness or consciousness grows, it's possible there is a corresponding flutter in the heart of God-consciousness.

God may be growing along with us as we evolve humanity into greater consciousness, and we may be growing along with God as the Mystery expands its ever-changing, ever-evolving ability to be conscious of itself and life. This concept seems to stretch us beyond any present theology. The far reach of this thinking appears to be that God may not know answers to our worries and concerns in advance. That God is as confounded and uncertain as we are by what might happen next. That God is waiting on the actions of the human family, just as we are, to see what future we will choose.

I see this possibility as *good* news. It suggests to me that *each of us greatly matters* to the future of existence. Each of us participates in determining if, and how rapidly, the consciousness that infuses life will expand or will, conversely, contract. This idea presumes we are not victims of a random universe: I make a difference to the Unfolding Mystery in the way I live my life, and so do you. From this perspective we can begin to see ourselves as *partners with the Mystery* in shaping the future of life on this planet and throughout the cosmos. Although some people may call this view arrogant or heretical, I call it humbling. The thought that I am called upon to live my ordinary life in such a way that I enable humanity to move forward in consciousness, and perhaps help God make leaps of consciousness as well, touches me profoundly and has me considering every step I take more thoughtfully.

This leads me back to those "little slips of paper." Just as we might partner with the Mystery in the evolving experience we call life, so might the Mystery be partnering with us, as we become what a number of prominent theologians call "God bearers" and others call "bearers of light." Such a proposition suggests that we are on this path with a map, although we often seem not to be. The map is actively constructed of all those clues to the Mystery that are dropped in our way. As in this book, many of those clues come to us in the form of stories, some personal and some transcending the personal to become universally applicable. We find these clues and piece them together until the puzzle begins to form a recognizable shape and direction. In this way, the Mystery we call God is a not a being, but an *internal compass* that points us toward true north, or home.

The essays in this book are some of the little scraps of paper that have fallen on my path. I began writing them as inspirational letters in an outreach project that was developed in collaboration with Ellie Mercer—a dear friend who is both minister and colleague—though it would be more accurate to say they wrote themselves in a timing over which I had little control. Participants in this project appreciated the letters so much they would forward them to friends and family nationwide. We discovered people weren't just reading the letters for inspiration but were actively using them as a means to examine and challenge their lives. Many of our readers acknowledged being moved, shaped and re-shaped by the letters. They asked me to publish them as a collection of short stories so others struggling to develop a relationship with the Mystery, to discern and follow their own instructions, would be sustained in what is often an arduous trek.

I have long believed in the power of story to sustain, encourage, heal, and empower us in times of struggle and need. I am a psychotherapist of more than twenty years, before that a nurse, and I have listened to stories from people of many ages, from many places, struggling with many kinds of issues. *It is my belief that listening to one another's stories is a holy act.* Listening with reverence to the stories each person places before us creates a sacred container where that person may release physical, psychological, and even spiritual burdens. Holy listening, I have learned, is balm for a wounded or broken heart and surcease for a troubled spirit. Every time I sat in witness to a struggling person's story, I tried-without-truly-knowing to answer the question loosely paraphrased from German writer-poet Rainer Maria Rilke: *Who, among all the choirs of angels, will hear me when I cry out?*

I have been gathering stories—little scraps of paper—for a long time. Stories of love and loss, stories of strength and weakness, stories of fear and courage, stories of faith and despair, stories of trust grown and trust broken. Stories told from the hearts of people at their best and worst junctures. Over time, as I heard them repeated by others in only slightly modified form, it became clear that certain stories belonged to more than the teller of the story, but to all people who have embarked, willingly or reluctantly, on the adventure called life.

In my own emerging journey, the listener became a teller of stories. One story, then another, would fall on my path or catch my ear, and I'd turn it over as the gardener turns the soil before planting until I had gleaned the universal truths contained in each one. The universality of these stories fascinated me; I wanted to pass them on to others. Thus, this collection of essays, which originated with a group of sixty people and grew to more than a hundred participants, comes to you now. Through them, I invite you to enter the awe and wonder of the Mystery revealing itself in and through the lives of ordinary, struggling people.

There's no particular order to this book. You can start anywhere and move forward or backward at will. Some essays will speak to you; some will not. Those that are useful to you can be viewed as little scraps of paper on your spirit-walk through this life. At the conclusion of each essay, you will find questions and meditations to encourage you to explore your own unique encounters with the Mystery, recognize the design of your own blueprint, and value the one life you've been given to tend.

May the indwelling Mystery guide your life to its true purpose.

Meredith Jordan
January 2004

Pay Attention

*The real miracle is not
to walk either on
water or in thin air
but to walk on earth.*

—Thich Nhat Hanh

When the demands of the outside world are not intruding upon my life, there is a summer rhythm by which I love to live. In the evening, as the sky begins to change color, I stop whatever I am doing and watch the heavens slowly take on a pastel luminosity. I notice subtle color changes in the clouds as day ends and night falls. The time bridging day with night is my silent time. I often pray or meditate. Sometimes, if I'm sufficiently moved, I will sing my prayers. And if I am truly brave, I may even dance them.

When I follow this rhythm, I am usually ready for sleep just before full dark sets in. I wake at first light, about 4:30 am, as the birds begin their morning chorus. This world-not-yet-awake time is mine to walk in the gardens, to see which new buds will burst into blossom that day, to listen for the whispers of wisdom in the dreams of the previous night's interior journey. This is the time of day when I'm happiest writing. It is a post-children life, one that contains both the pleasure and the loneliness of solitude.

One morning, awake as usual at 4:30, I was writing and listening to a soft tap-tap-tapping sound somewhere in my house. Since living alone, I've become intimate with the common noises of my home. This was not a familiar sound: *Tap-tap-tap*. All would fall briefly quiet, only for the sound to begin again several minutes later. Absorbed in my writing at the time, I didn't move at first to explore the source of the noise. When I heard the sounds for the third or fourth time, *so insistent*, my curiosity piqued and I went off in search of the muffled *tap-tap-tapping*.

I followed the sound to my dining room. This room looks like a miniature solarium: big windows; bright natural light; bushy green plants; orchids in bloom; colorful posters on the wall. It attracts immediate attention as people enter my home.

This particular morning, there was a small brown sparrow hovering against one of the windows, beating its wings on the pane, intent upon getting inside. This was not what happens when a bird mistakes an indoor plant for a tree and flies accidentally into a window. This sparrow wanted to get *in*! She hovered mid-air at the small glass pane, insistently flapping her wings until she exhausted herself. Then she flew away to rest a while, and came back to try again. Back and forth, the little sparrow came and went.

Concerned the sparrow was going to be injured in her futile attempt to get into my house, I stood on the opposite side of the window and talked to her. I explained that she was a bird and needed the freedom of the open skies to fly: a freedom she would lose if she succeeded in entering my house. "Fly away, little bird," I commanded, as if I actually had command of such matters, "Go back to the open sky, where you belong!"

Despite my strong entreaties, the sparrow continued to flutter at the window, persisting. I gave up before she did, and returned to my writing. Several hours later, I was ready for breakfast and sat down at my dining table to eat. There was no bird at the window. I assumed she had finally moved on to other important sparrow activities. Suddenly, there was a sharper *tap-tap-tapping* against the pane. To my astonishment, the bird was now hopping on little sparrow feet across the sill of my window, looking directly at me and pecking her beak against the glass. She hopped the entire distance across one windowsill, jumped onto the next, and repeated her action: *Tap-tap-tap.* Watching me all the while. If this wasn't enough to give me pause, she then turned and hopped back across all three sills, still tapping her beak against the pane.

I have never seen such a performance. I laughed at her antics and enjoyed what seemed like a small display of natural wonder put on just for my amusement. Finally, after more than four hours of fluttering, hovering, hopping and tapping, she disappeared into the flock of sparrows that frequent my bird feeder. I wouldn't recognize her again. She quickly became another small, brown sparrow in a family of many.

I was telling this story to my friend Ellie the next day when she asked, "Well, what do you make of all this? What do you think it was about?" I thought for a while about the Mystery in that tiny, nondescript bird—one of hundreds of sparrows, yet totally distinct—fluttering and tapping in an attempt to get me to look up from the self-absorption of my writing and simply *pay attention.*

How often am I sufficiently present in the moment, really paying attention to what is right in front of me? Not often enough. I am all too frequently caught up in thinking that lures me into the past, remembering something, or into the future, where I am anticipating something. Paying attention, though I know it to be the central spiritual practice of many traditions, has never been my strongest suit.

A day or two after my personal sparrow event, Ellie had one of her own, sitting on her deck, watching a pair of sparrow mates build a nest in the birdhouse of her backyard. As she sat silently—both observer and participant on a glorious summer day—one of the birds brought a single strand of grass and laid it on the deck rail beside her. She said, "This sounds silly, but I felt this was a gift given to me with such love." Not so silly if we hold to the truth that all of creation is interconnected and interactive. Thich Nhat Hanh, a Vietnamese monk and Nobel Peace Prize recipient known to thousands simply as Thay, speaks of this as evidence of our *interbeing*.

The indigenous peoples of this earth still live attuned to the rhythms I fall into only on occasion. They remember what it's like to live as if one is just another participant in the family of creation. To live as if the Mystery is revealed to us in everything and everyone we encounter along the path. They watch for signs of this in the world, recognize and honor them when they appear. They see the changing colors of the heavens, know when the birds come with messages to call the people awake. They attend to their encounters with the Mystery in a manner that's both humble and reverent.

There is a river of Mystery flowing through all of life in which the indigenous people have fully immersed themselves. Western modernity—or what we call *progress*—seems to rob us of the experience of being immersed in this river, if we've ever experienced it at all. Perhaps we are our own bandits. Perhaps we have voluntarily surrendered our birthright connection with the Mystery to worship the little gods of worldly achievement, over-activity, and the accumulation of material goods that provide such transitory pleasures. Are we forgetting that one day we'll have to slip through the eye of the needle and leave everything we've accumulated behind?

I don't own a thing that can give me the delight of that brief encounter with a sparrow dancing across my windowsill. Not my house, which, although small, is lovely. Not my gardens, lovelier still, and a source of constant joy through the seasons of their birth and death. Not the precious objects I have gathered in my travels to many places, all of which enrich my life by their beauty.

For a few brief hours one summer morning, I was privileged to witness God-at-work in the most ordinary of creatures, and to be conscious and awake in the now of that experience. I don't know why. I still have no idea what this encounter meant, or if it meant anything at all. I know only that something mysterious hovered at my window until I stopped long enough to pay attention.

Paying attention is the most profound of spiritual teachings. How will we notice the evidence of wonder and the reasons for awe in our lives if we're too caught up in the activities of daily living to pause, to notice, and to understand what is being placed before us to assist in our awakening? Like so many of us, I busy myself with what I insist are the important activities of everyday life. I actively distract myself from the activities or spiritual practices I consider truly important and that benefit me in the process of maturation as a seeker of wisdom and truth.

Don't we all get in our own way much of the time? We say we want a meaningful spiritual life and generate endless excuses for why that doesn't happen or go to great lengths to sabotage our own best efforts. If we're paying attention, after a while we start to recognize the patterns by which we interfere with the good intentions that prompted us to set out on the spiritual path in the first place. If we are able to be ruthlessly honest—of course, this is a big "if "—we might eventually acknowledge that we are the ones obstructing the way.

I could so easily have missed the moment when that sparrow arrived at my window, seemingly intent on teaching me to open my eyes to behold the Mystery. *Tap-tap-tap.* That could, of course, be my projection. The bird was, after all, just an ordinary sparrow. If she was there to "teach" me about where I do, or do not, place my attention, she was certainly unaware of being the teacher, even of being observed. I made the choice to stop what I was doing, notice her, and assign to her actions a spiritual significance.

We are given these choices hundreds of times in a single day. This bird lesson was simply more insistent than most.

Tap-tap-tap. Flutter-flutter-flutter. Hop-hop-hop.

Such soft sounds, so easy to ignore. But what delight becomes available when we listen, when we rouse from our "busy forgetfulness" to go in search of holy surprises, and when we finally remember to give honor and reverence to the One who taps insistently, waiting for us to notice!

𝒢

- What is it like for you when you able to be in the present moment, paying attention only to what is right in front of you: to each person, each task, each conversation, each sensation, each new breath that is breathing you?

- Try that now. Look around you. What do you see as your eyes scan the room? What textures do you feel against your skin, what scents do you smell, what sounds do you hear?

Just for the moment, let the world go on its way without you, and keep your attention in the here and now. Is there anything you would have missed if you had not brought your attention into this moment?

- Has there ever been a time when you discovered a "holy surprise" waiting for you, like the sparrow at the window? How did that experience touch you, change you or enrich you?

Waking the holy heart

In compassion,
justice and peace kiss.

—*Meister Eckhart*

Sister Joan Chittister, a Benedictine nun who dares to stand as a courageous and challenging presence in the contemporary Catholic Church, speaks loudly and wields a big stick. Without flinching, she tells us this: "Compassion is the soft and bottomless well of the holy heart." That singular statement tweaks the good intentions of every spirit-centered person, from each religious tradition, who seeks to embody the teachings of his or her faith. And she poses this challenge not in the best of times, but in a time of unprecedented uncertainty and worldwide political turmoil.

What, then, does it mean for us to flounder in this messy human soup and nevertheless live as a compassionate people embodying a "holy heart?"

Fears sweep into our lives like the bitter winds of winter. We wake in the morning, tune in to the news, go to work, retrieve our children from school or soccer practice, return home, make dinner, go to bed. We are advised to maintain "normalcy" while anticipating the next catastrophic event. Terrorists strike without warning and leave bone-chilling, heart-stopping loss in their wake. In a fraction of a heartbeat on a bright fall day in September, 2001, the world altered dramatically, and changed us in ways we Americans could never have imagined. We are no longer able to retreat into the illusion that we are somehow insulated from the horrors of war that have been visited upon others. That horror has reached our shores.

This is not the vision I had imagined in the first brightly dawning hours celebrating the birth of the millennium. For that brief time, there was a great upwelling of optimism and creativity in the human spirit, hope rising in us that we might, at last, move toward a new way of sharing this earth together. So much of that optimism collapsed as we watched in horror while two doomed planes plunged into the towers of the World Trade Center, transforming them into a funeral pyre for thousands of unsuspecting people and a place of mourning for their surviving friends and loved ones.

After the events of September 11th, we were mercilessly flooded with images of planes setting off a free-fall of the World Trade Center buildings; photographs of weeping children doubled over the flag-draped caskets of their mothers or fathers; news reports of Afghan and Israeli youngsters whose arms or legs were amputated by land mines buried deep in their playing fields; stories of lives snuffed out too soon by suicide bombers blowing themselves up on the crowded streets of Israel's cities. Because of the wonders of modern technology, we even had the questionable privilege of watching the minute-by-minute bombing of Baghdad.

One relatively peaceful winter morning two years ago, curled up in the warmth and comfort of my living room and briefly on retreat from news of the war efforts in Afghanistan, I opened the Sunday newspaper. Staring at me from page eleven was the face of an Afghan woman who had lived the last decade of her life in a refugee camp under the harshest of circumstances. She had survived the deaths of her husband and her children, starvation, unimaginable cold, living with no shelter but a tent. If she was lucky, she had been given a blanket as protection from the brutality of a winter endured in an unforgiving land. I was utterly transfixed by her face. This was a woman's strong face, a fierce face furrowed with evidence of a hard life. Perhaps it was the first time she had lifted her face to the world since Taliban leaders decreed all women must remain under cover of the burka. This Afghan woman was neither beaten nor defeated.

That was what mesmerized me. Her eyes commanded me to see what war looks like on another woman's face. As I forced myself to look at her more carefully, I saw what I had failed to see at first glance: one eye was blind, clouded by an untreated cataract that had stolen her ability to see. As the hard reality of her life pierced my comfortable existence, an Afghan widow, a childless mother, became a mirror and an unlikely spiritual teacher.

In such terrible times as these, troubling questions rise up in the minds of spiritual seekers everywhere: *Where is God in all of this? Where will we find the holy heart?* The leaders of warring parties, political and religious, claim that God is on their side, is fighting their fight, and is supporting their might. It does not seem to matter if the claim is made in the name of Allah or Yahweh or in the name of Christ. Others claim God has retreated from the fighting, waiting patiently for the evil to end so that God can return to our world.

But I wonder other things. I think other thoughts. I ask questions others might call heretical: *What if the holy heart is present in the exact epicenter of this horror? What if that is God's ferocious and penetrating face looking out at the world through the blinded eye of an Afghan woman, calling the attention of the world to the plight of a poor and exiled people? What if the holy heart has taken form in the child bent broken-hearted over the coffin of a murdered mother or father? What if I am witness to the holy heart as I hear the story of a man whose leg has been ripped from his body by a land mine, or in the terrible grief of a woman cradling the body of her child, dead by starvation?*

What if the holy heart is right in the center of the suffering, crying out, "See it! Feel it!" What if it is in those moments of *seeing and feeling* that we are actually participating in the holy heart?

How different it all might be if we deeply and truly believed that the holy heart is alive and at work in absolutely everything that is happening, here and now, in our world. That God or Allah or Yahweh is not separate from us, not located outside us . . . not even outside the suffering we willingly cause one another. How might it be different if we were to retire the belief that God, the Mystery of Mysteries, is *outside* waiting to be called in, and adopted—in one extravagant human experiment—the belief that the Mystery is *inside*, waiting to be called out?

How different it might be if we believed that—in the midst of confusion and uncertainty, in the presence of a sorrow deeper than our hearts can sometimes bear, in the fear and rage sweeping across nations like a fierce storm cloud, in the haunted dreams that may pursue the women and men digging rubble from the crater of the World Trade Center to the end of their days—*this is exactly where the holy heart is at work?*

All the cards have been tossed into the air, and we have no idea how they will fall next. Maybe it is at the pivotal moment of not knowing where to find God in our horror or fear that the Mystery is hardest at work. What if we trusted this possibility?

What if we stopped resisting the upheaval but cooperated with it instead? What if we did not polarize into sides at war with one another but stood shoulder-to-shoulder in the uncertainty and confusion? What if we allowed the not-knowing to pass through us, de-constructing our hardened certainties of opinion, softening our positions of right and might and power?

Don't get me wrong. I'm not advocating a do-nothing response to an act of aggressive violence against innocent people. Bullies who intentionally hurt others must be stopped with the best means at hand. We are playing in a high stakes game, one in which rogue nations and leaders have the capacity not just to threaten other countries but to destroy them in one swift, decisive touch of a finger. These are certainly dangerous times. Even the Dalai Lama, surely among the gentlest of men, has said that there are times when violence must not be tolerated.

But too much of the harm being rendered in these fearful times is perpetrated under the false names of God. Keith Morrison, an NBC journalist reporting on the hijacking of the Islamic religion for the political purposes of a small number of Muslim fundamentalists suggests that the most troubling of all questions raised by recent acts of terrorism is the one about God. How can we believe that God wanted or commanded such obscenities? This is a question only historians and religious scholars should attempt to answer. The religious and social culture of the Middle East is far more complex than most Americans comprehend. Inside the Muslim jihad movement, there is a pervasive rage toward America. While there may be justifiable reasons for their rage, this does not justify their rageful actions.

This rage could be enough to stop us dead in our tracks, immobilized by powerlessness, if it were not for one thing: *we are not powerless.* As a people of conscience and a people of spirit, we are called to more than a military response to terrorist rage and action. This is a time of "both/and" rather than a time of "either this/or that." There is serious work to be done on our insides . . . even as political leaders make difficult calls about what is to be done in world affairs. They are doing their part as best they know to do, though I may not always agree with their actions, and so must we. *There is power in each individual life choice.* It is up to every one of us to determine where that power resides and bring it to bear upon these times.

Somehow we must awaken *the holy heart* among us and turn a terrible tide of events toward the good. We can start simply, right now, with you and with me. I have little influence over public policy, but I do have the capacity to awaken the holy heart within me. Every day, by the personal actions I take or I decline to take, I decide how I walk inside my family, my circle of friends, my community, my world.

I determine how I will impact others by actions only I can choose. It is within my power to embody compassion or to embody indifference. What I choose to embody, through right use of my life, makes a difference to those I encounter as I go my way. I can look through a lens of merciful God-eyes into the ferocious face of an Afghan widow and mother. I can reach over the chasm of culture and experience that separates us to better understand the relentlessly harsh life that carved those particular lines into her face. If I do this, I will most certainly notice that her God-eyes glare harshly back at me. I could ignore her penetrating look and turn my face away, shutting her out of my awareness, making her *other* in my mind and heart. Or I could stretch to comprehend her suffering. Which choice will I make: an open heart, reaching for understanding in the midst of catastrophe, or a heart that's closed in self-justification or self-righteousness?

The humbling truth is that we all have blood on our historical hands. At other times, even in the present time, Christians have been perpetrators of crimes at least as serious as the ones being committed against them now. Crusaders once moved through

Europe mercilessly slaughtering innocent Muslims. Anglo-Saxons settling the North American continent killed untold millions of indigenous people whom we called savages despite the fact that many tribal nations were gentle, intelligent, civilized, advanced people. Hitler killed more than six million Jews and Christians, lesbians and gays, and gypsies during his terrible reign of power in Germany. Saddam Hussein has tortured and murdered hundreds of thousands of Iranians and Iraqis. Hard as we try, we can never escape the reality that we are a species capable of brutality beyond the imagination.

Joan Chittister tells us, "Time changes nothing: people do. We must all look at the qualities of soul that need to be carefully cultivated in each of us if we are to become a different kind of people in this rapidly different kind of world. Cultures, countries and communities are not made by institutional figures. *They are created by us.* The question I ask of us is this: what do we need to develop in ourselves if we hope to become a positive presence in our changing world?"

This is a concept we too rarely consider. That it is *up to us* to develop qualities in our individual spirits that will impact those around us positively, that will ignite in them a desire to develop themselves with a similar intention, and that will hopefully create "a different kind of people" and a different kind of future for the children and grandchildren of the human family.

Isn't this our spiritual responsibility? Native Americans understood this a long time ago. Every decision taken under consideration by their elders was examined for its anticipated effect on the children seven generations into the future. This is a reasonable paradigm in a world thrown repeatedly, and sometimes carelessly, into catastrophe by the power needs of a few to control the many. In these times, many of us are wrestling with the question of what to do. Is fighting ever a compassionate act? Is living a loving and compassionate life *enough*?

The truth is that none of us holds the answers to the big questions. The only action we have the power to control is the one we take in this minute, with this life.

We start with developing the "soft and bottomless well" of a compassionate and holy heart. It is really a simple enough place to begin. We have already received our instructions from the sacred texts of all the wisdom traditions. There is nothing new to learn . . . and a lot to put into practice.

We can walk through this uncharted, often terrifying, terrain with our hands and hearts held out to each other. We can steady one another when we falter, and we will. We can tell the truth when it's difficult to know who and what to trust. While we sort out our confused and churning insides, we could actually listen to each other instead of arguing or disputing. We could pay attention to our dreams, from which a greater collective wisdom often emerges. We can make certain that all children—not just our own—are fed, clothed, sheltered, kept safe, healthy and loved. We could generate a genuine concern for those whose struggles to survive are more difficult than most. We could speak in clear, strong voices for what is good and just.

We can start anywhere. There is no place on this earth that does not need goodness spread from one of us to another. We would all be more content if we lived from "the soft and bottomless well" of the holy heart. Nor do we need to wait for tragedy to strike us before we awaken and come forward. Just offering compassion to someone who has not known much of it, is a generous and holy act.

Small gestures, practiced and offered with clear intention, help to cultivate the holy heart . . . and help us in making the evolutionary leap to become a new and different people.

Spiritual masters have pleaded with us throughout the ages and across spiritual traditions, "Oh, my people, awaken!" The twentieth century Spanish schoolteacher-poet Antonio Machado wrote of Jesus: "All your words were one word: *Wake up!*"

The time is fast bearing down upon us when we must either rouse the holy heart from its long slumber or destroy the sanctity of life on our fragile planet. Those who wait for God to intervene or our political leaders to chart the course fail to realize that, having been suddenly thrust onto the world stage, we all have a part to play in this unfolding drama. *None of us is here by accident.* We have each been located at this time in human history by, and for, a purpose greater than we might ever understand.

We are called to awaken, to recognize, and to cultivate the Mystery as it lives in us and as it attempts to work through us. We are asked to cooperate, to collaborate, to take up our parts as midwives at the birth of a constantly emerging, ever-expanding God-consciousness in the world. If it is imperative to generate a new world order, *and it certainly seems to be*, then we are the partners with God in that creation.

We must begin by closely examining the innermost regions of our individual hearts, the beliefs we hold and the actions we make toward good or harm, for it is deep within our own souls that the Sacred truly resides. Isn't it time to stop waiting for God-Out-There to rescue us with divine intervention and invoke the intention for God-In-Us to manifest through our choices and actions?

We can do this. The battle for a compassionless or a compassion-filled world starts with the next breath we draw and the next step we take. Everything I do—or you do—*counts* toward building a world for the children of tomorrow, the one we will hand off to them when we leave at the end of our earthly sojourn.

What will we do? If we do nothing, the compassionless future rests assured. We must do something, anything at all, that will move us in the direction of an awakened holy heart residing at the center of the human family. The decision lies with you, and with me. This decision is bearing down upon us . . . sooner, not later. The bill comes due today.

The holy heart is located *inside* each one of us . . . longing to be awakened and put into action. Seek its soft and bottomless well there. Frankly, there is no other place left for us to turn.

℥

- Who or what stands in the way of you coaxing open your own *holy heart*?

- Are you afraid of something? Where does that fear originate? Does fear serve you in some way or does it hold you back from being all that you are here to be?

- How might your life change if you surrendered to the power that comes in truly living from the *holy heart*? What would you have to give up? What do you imagine you might gain from doing this?

- What qualities do you want to develop in yourself so that you may serve as a conduit for the *holy heart* or as a positive presence in your family and community of friends?

- Who can you reach out to, or what action might you take, to help open the *soft, bottomless well* of compassion in you?

The children shall lead us

Our children are like flowers to us.
Each one different.
Each one beautiful.
Each one growing strong with us.

Our children are like stars to us.
Each one sparkles.
Each one moves through the universe.
Each one closer to the heart of us.

—Nancy Wood

One Christmas Day, after a leisurely morning of breakfast and gift opening with my young adult children, we drove west to join my extended family of elderly parents, sisters and brother, their spouses and children—nineteen of us—for Christmas dinner. Our drive through Maine and New Hampshire had been very quiet, as we listened to an extraordinary program of Christmas music on National Public Radio. By the time we arrived at my brother's house, there was already noise and activity everywhere.

Most of the grandchildren in my family are now teenagers or young adults, and because of this, the decibel level on Christmas Day has actually dropped many points. Even the youngest boys, eleven and ten that particular Christmas, played quietly. Almost all the noise and excitement of Christmas was generated by the two smallest family members, Jillian and Rachel, then ages five and six. They were full of imagination and full of life. With these energetic little girls, anything goes.

Jillian had been very busy this day with her new baby doll, Katie Rebecca, who had been "born" that Christmas morning. As a newborn, Katie Rebecca required a lot of attention and care. Jillian devised a clever way of providing that care and attention while still being able to loose herself of the burdens of new motherhood. She proclaimed she was Katie's "sister" and, over the course of that afternoon and evening, she took her doll to one family member after another. She handed over Katie Rebecca's care, showing each caregiver how to hold her when she was awake, how to hold her when she was asleep, how to pat her back when she needed to be burped, and how to stroke her back when she needed to be comforted. Then Jilli would disappear into another part of the house to play, leaving Katie Rebecca in the arms of an aunt or uncle, one of her grandparents, or one of her many cousins.

I was actually first up for babysitting duty, though Katie Rebecca was handed back to me several times before our family gathering came to an end. But, throughout the afternoon, I would look up from lively conversations with various family members to notice that my twenty-six-year-old son or my six-foot-five-inch-tall nephew held Katie Rebecca tenderly in his arms. Sometimes this tiny doll was being rocked or burped by my twenty-eight-year-old daughter or my fifteen-year-old niece. Jillian always found a family member willing to join in Katie Rebecca's care.

And she never had a moment's hesitation that there were

sufficient arms and sufficiently big hearts in her family for her "baby sister" to be well cared for while she bounced happily from one activity to another all day. She had unshakable trust in an extended family of grandparents, aunts, uncles, and cousins to be a large and loving "village" or "tribe" for her doll.

That same confidence emerged from Jillian one more time that day. Once we finally strung together a hodgepodge of tables and chairs to seat nineteen people in my brother's not-quite-large-enough house, once we had put the potluck Christmas dinner on the not-quite-large-enough table and called everyone for the meal, my mother quietly asked to begin with a grace. She was struggling for breath—this would be her last Christmas—and no one heard her over the din of family chatter. I raised my hand, called for attention, and asked if anyone would like to lead us in a prayer.

With no hesitation, Jillian—the smallest and youngest member of our family—spoke up and said, "Yes! I would like to do that!" Not missing a heart beat, this blond, blue-eyed whirling dervish of a little girl with a huge imagination and a solid sense of who she is in this world, led her family in a lovely, spontaneous Christmas prayer.

I have thought a lot about this since that Christmas Day. The words that come to me again and again are these: *and a little child shall lead us.* It is possible that this scene was repeated in many other homes and families just like ours. If so, that is a welcome sign of the growing good in our world. A five-year-old child with enough trust to believe that *everyone* in her family would love her cherished new doll. Enough trust to believe that her "instructions" would be heard and carried out, even by her grown boy cousins. Enough trust that, when the time came to lead her entire family in prayer, she sat tall in her seat, two pink hearts painted on her cheeks, and proudly announced, "I would like to do it!" She proceeded to create a prayer at least as moving, probably more so, than any of the adults could have done.

There is hope in this story. Hope for the children of the world, and—through them—for the rest of the human family. Jillian's very precious spirit remains mercifully intact. Thanks to the careful nurture of her mother and father, she has not been taken hostage by cultural, community, or even family, pressures to influence her to become someone other than who she truly is.

This child has a big, wise and trusting spirit. The human family needs children like Jillian and every one of her cousins who held Katie Rebecca without embarrassment: big-hearted, big-spirited, wise and trusting children from many nations, races, cultures and all kinds of families to remind us of the ways of wide-open love. Children who still remember what too many adults have forgotten: why we are here on this earth.

Even more recently, my brother reached his fiftieth birthday, and our family gathered again to surprise him with a celebration. It was a terrible day in the middle of a long and dreadful Northeast winter: rain mixed with snow made the roads slick and the driving near to impossible. Many families who love him as much as I do came despite the weather . . . but my brother did not want to come to his own party. He had been caught up all day in the grueling task of shoveling heavy, wet snow from the roof of his house and was exhausted, to say nothing of sweaty. He resisted when his wife went home to trick him into coming to the town hall, where all of us, also exhausted from decorating an old gymnasium to resemble a festive party, were waiting to greet him.

When he came through the door, he took the surprise with his usual good grace, but privately he whispered to me, "I'm so exhausted! This is the last place I want to be. Can I go home now?" He quickly got swept into the spirit of the party and appeared to have a good time. Late that night, as we poured our weary bodies onto the sofa at his home, he opened birthday cards that were left at the party for him. One after another bemoaned the aging process or poked fun at how old he was. Then he came to the card I gave him. It showed the picture of a handsome young man and read, *"You were wild once. Don't let them tame you."*

My beautiful brother's eyes misted, and we laughed together, as only an older sister and younger brother can, remembering the antics of his youth. But that night, as I fell asleep in the loft of his house, I heard my tired brother pick up a guitar and begin to pick out a tune. He told me later that he hadn't played the guitar in years. I enjoyed thinking, as I drifted into sleep to the sound of his music, something I'd done dozens of times when we were living in the converted attic bedrooms of our family home, that I'd reminded him of his original nature. His own divine blueprint . . . lost somewhere in his efforts to be a husband, a father, a provider. Something else of his true nature rose out of his exhaustion that night and reclaimed itself, if only for a moment. I like to imagine that he'll go on playing the guitar while his own children fall asleep, just as I did many years ago, to the soft sounds of their father making a little night music.

Where is God in this story? In the hearts of the people who love my brother, and in the music he makes as he sits alone late at night. In the trust of a child that her family will embrace her beloved doll, or that she will be able to create a prayer for her entire family on a moment's notice. In the whispered request of a beloved grandmother who could barely draw a breath and would not live for another Christmas. In the memories my brother and I share of the days when his spirit was wild, and his adventures were bold. In our aging bodies, worn from efforts we once took for granted, reminding us now that every day left to us is a precious gift. In each experience that is authentic and true, the Mystery is born again and again.

The wonderment of Jillian is that she has not lost sight of her true nature. We should all be so blessed, although few of us are. In that place where this little girl knows just who she is created to be, lives the Mystery. Lives the one we call God.

That place is present in each of us, buried deep in some. It can be resurrected, if we open to that possibility. Ask my brother. He will tell you how simple it was to pick up a guitar after ten years and begin to make music again. On a night that he had good reason to collapse into the peace of an exhausted sleep, he chose to pick out the notes of a song he'd nearly forgotten in the relentless pace of his ongoing life. He chose to incarnate the music that lives in his spirit, waiting to be born through him.

Or you can look around for the Jillian in your life. There is one, if you have eyes to see. Learn from her; learn from him. Learn from each other that it is possible to give birth to the Mystery that lives inside our individual souls. This is some of the good news being revealed to us: that, to discover who we are here to be or what we are meant to do with our lives, we only have to follow our original instructions. Jillian knows this without being told. With nothing more than a birthday card to jolt him, my brother began to remember too.

One last, brief story. When my daughter was young, she loved to play with her dolls in a small, stand-up, walk-around closet off her bedroom in our century old house. She spent hours in that closet, making up stories for her doll families. She was happiest when she was left alone to follow her imagination, and to immerse herself in play. This troubled her father, who thought she should be outdoors, in the fresh air. But Sarah defended her closet as her sanctuary from the world, the one place where she could explore the growing, developing elements of her own essential nature without being scrutinized by anyone else: not her friends, not her teachers, not her parents. Here, the world did not intrude on her. In that closet, she learned some of her most important lessons about being true to herself.

Discovering your true self is one important reason you are here. Expanding your heart in wide-open love is another. Children do not have to be taught this: they only need to be reminded not to forget what they already know. The children will take us in hand to guide us back to our own God-given nature, as well as forward into the unknown, ultimately hopeful, future. Just slip your hand into a child's, and let her show you the way home.

Whatever you have forgotten, you can remember. Whatever you have buried, you can unearth. If you are willing to look deep into your own nature, if you are willing to peel away the layers of not-self you have adopted in making your way through the tribulations of life, you will find that your true self is not as far removed from you as you think. I know this to be so. Jillian has told me.

g

- Close your eyes and breathe all the way down to your lower belly. Feel the light rise and fall of your abdomen with each breath. When you are quiet inside, allow yourself to remember a time when you were most yourself, when no one expected you to be anyone but who you are here to be.

Let that feeling grow until it fills all of you. Let every one of your cells soak in the delicious feeling of being you, with no limits, no expectations but the ones you take on by choice or by the instructions of your divine blueprint. This is your natural state: the coming alive of your essential nature. No one can take this away from you without your permission. Remember that.

This quiet, true place is where God is alive in you, acting in the world through you. It is yours alone to discover, yours to cherish and care for once you have discovered it. You are here to live your true self to the fullest expression of its passions, its joys, its sorrows, and its delights. Your whole life is an act of ensoulment, of fully embodying the glorious and untamed spirit awakened by your birth, of sacred incarnation. It is a holy privilege for you to be you.

As you open your eyes and return to the world, come back with the certain knowledge that you are beautifully and wonderfully made: a unique participant in a great Mystery.

Circle of life

Old one, dying.
Young one, being born:
perhaps in the circle of life
you meet along the way.

—*Meredith Jordan*

Some years ago, I had an unusual dream in which a Voice, the Speaker never visible in the dream, was instructing me about the way souls depart the earth upon their deaths and new souls enter embodiment at the time of their birth. The Voice meticulously explained that each soul carries a particular energetic "vibration," the result of that individual's psycho-spiritual development though his or her years of earth time. At the time of death, as the departing person discards the physical body like an outgrown suit of clothing, there is an "energetic vacuum" created by that death that draws into incarnation another soul at an equivalent level of psychological and spiritual maturation.

My mother died three years ago. She grew increasingly

debilitated through seven years of her battle with chronic obstructive pulmonary disease. Her breathing was compromised to such an extent that her normally active life had grown limited and limiting. She had an especially hard time drawing breath in the relentless heat of the last summer of her life. Her death was both long anticipated and, paradoxically, sudden.

She fell and fractured her pelvis two weeks before her death. Oddly, although I was in Salzburg, Austria, at the time, I knew this had happened. The last morning of my trip, I had a dream that showed my parents' home tilting abruptly on its foundation, hanging dangerously in mid-air at an angle that put them both in peril. In the dream, I called to my mother as I crawled slowly on my belly across the tilted house, trying desperately to reach her. "Don't move!" I called out repeatedly, "Or you'll fall!" I learned when I returned to the United States late on the day of the dream, that I dreamed of this accident at the precise hour, accounting for time zones, my mother fell from her bed.

At the rehabilitation hospital, she was regaining strength and recovering physical ability when she was exposed to a virus. Within two days, she died. I think she simply had nothing left in her fragile body with which to fight. She had just said goodbye to one of her grandchildren and had several goodbyes still ahead, as other grandchildren prepared to leave for distant places. I believe she couldn't stay behind and watch them leave, suspecting as she did that she wouldn't survive to see them again.

We had enough warning that death was approaching to reach the hospital and sit vigil with her in the last twenty-four hours of her life. My father, my brother, my sisters, my daughter and I all gathered. Though she was frail and had an oxygen mask on all the time, helping her to draw each labored breath, we could not stop her from talking. She had thoughts left unspoken and she was determined to speak them, even if only some made sense through her morphine delirium and oxygen deprivation. We rotated turns to sit with her, to hold her hand, and to tell her we loved her. One of my sisters delicately fed her tiny bits of graham cracker. When she asked my mother if there was anything else she wanted, my mother wryly responded, "Where's the cheese?" She could scarcely draw the next breath, but her sense of humor remained intact, untouched by death.

My mother was afraid of dying, so afraid that she had resisted it ferociously for years. As it became clear that death had a hand on her shoulder, intending to claim her before long, none of us wanted her to die in a state of fear. We made plans for teams of two to rotate with her during the last hours of her life, so the others could eat, sleep, shower, and return for another round of the vigil. My father and brother sat with her through the last night of her life, calming her if she became frightened. My sisters returned the next morning to relieve them. They sang her favorite hymns until she drew her last breath, and beyond. She died to the sounds of their sweet voices, just a few hours before it was my turn to relieve them.

My mother gave as much love as she could possibly give in her last hours of life. She died surrounded by love. This is the way we all wanted it to be for her. At her funeral service later that week, her family and many friends, some of more than fifty years, laughed and cried and loved and blessed her on her way to the next world. Three of her four children and four of her nine grandchildren delivered the eulogy. Surely, this is as good a death as we can hope to have, given the indignities of aging and dying. Death is not a pretty sight, and has never claimed to be. But we were reassured that she had been given the best shot at dying well we could offer her, and a loving remembrance of the value of her life.

The afternoon that my sister called me to say that Mom had died just minutes before, I wandered around aimlessly, wondering: *What do I do on the day that my mother dies? What am I supposed to feel?* I watched the sun set that night, soft peach-colored sky, luminescent, and I thought: *The sun sets on the last day of my mother's life. There will never be another day like this in my lifetime.*

Shortly after that thought, the telephone rang, and I received the joyous news that a very special person in my life, a dear young woman, was going into labor with her first child. Already, there was another kind of vigil.

My mother died at two in the afternoon. Before the day was finished, a new life was on his way to being born. Not just any baby, but a little boy I will know and love. The dream from a long time ago came back to me then. I don't know whether the dream spoke truth or was a projection, the reflection of my own hope that life is an enduring circle. I'm not sure it matters. When I ask where God was in all of this, I have to speak the truth: that dream throbbed, pulsated, vibrated with a penetrating sense of the *mysterium tremendum.* Of the Unseen Ones, coming to speak of a world beyond our sight. Whether or not God was present in the dream, you will have to judge for yourself. I lean toward *yes.*

And there was, if not proof, then *evidence* of the dream's credibility. Not long after my mother exhaled for the last time in her life, a tiny boy inhaled for the first time in his. Releasing breath, releasing body. Intake of breath, inhabiting body.

To fully embrace life, we also have to embrace the reality that life will end, and we will die one day. This is a bittersweet truth that makes each day more precious, each new birth more joyful, each child more welcome, each love more of a gift, and each loss more of an arrow to pierce the heart. One soul departs this world. Another enters on that energetic stream. As one life closes its final chapter, another begins in hours. Such is the nature of the Mystery that unfolds before us. In our grief, there is always joy. In our joy, there is always grief. Life and death are all one river, all one stream, all One.

❡

- Is there anything you have left unspoken or unfinished as you move through your life? Anything you want your loved ones to know but have held back from telling them?

- How might it change your life if you didn't postpone saying these things to the ones you love but said them now?

- Are there any rituals you would like your loved ones to hold in your honor when you die? Write them down or let someone know.

- Imagine the possibility of life and death as a continuing stream of souls embodying and leaving their bodies behind: An endless cycle of souls arriving and souls departing. How does this image from the dream change your understanding of the Mystery, and how it works?

- When has the Mystery revealed something of its God-nature to you in the form of a dream? Are you receptive to the possibility that we are most available to be touched, and taught, by the Spirit as we sleep? What have your dream encounters with the Mystery revealed to you?

Is it okay if we talk?

Go for a slow and mindful walk.
Show the children every little thing
that catches your eye. Don't look for
lessons or seek to teach great things.
Just notice. The lesson will teach itself.

—*The Parent's Tao Te Ching*

One night, after a long and stressful day, I settled in to sleep. My daughter was leaving early the next morning for a new job in North Carolina, and we were devoting some time to our goodbyes. We went to dinner at a favorite restaurant and drove around the beaches where she had run headlong into the wind since she was eleven. This was a precious time for us, deepened by the death of my mother (her adored grandmother) a week before. The delicate balance of life and loss weighed heavily on each of our minds and hearts.

Somewhere around 1 am, the sound of the telephone pierced the peace of the night. I'd been on a call late into the evening with a friend who was also in a delicate place of loss, so I answered the phone still half asleep. A soft voice asked, "Are you awake? Is it okay if we talk?" Thinking it was the friend from my late night conversation, I sleepily agreed, "Sure." The caller abruptly hung up. Then he called again. This process went on four times before I came to full realization that I wasn't talking to my friend but to a stranger. The phone would ring, and a soft voice now identifiable as a child's would ask, "Are you awake? Is it okay if we talk?" As soon as I agreed, the caller would hang up the phone.

On the fourth attempt, an hour after the first, the child escalated into a full-blown crank caller, mumbling something incoherent, but definitely intending to frighten or intimidate me. I buried the phone beneath a pile of pillows so I wouldn't hear it again and fell back into a troubled sleep. When I woke the next morning, cranky, there were four more calls on my answering machine. The last was recorded at three a.m. By then, my caller was out of control. His mutterings were frantic. One message involved music containing the sound of a gunshot.

Despite being rattled by events of the long and broken night, I had sufficient presence of mind to retrieve the caller's phone number. It was listed in the name of a person who has done work around my house, a lovely man with whom I have had a good working relationship for years. I had grown to depend on him for any handiwork I was not able to do alone. I was aware that he had remarried recently, and I thought there was now a child in his home, but I wasn't sure of this. Debating what to do, I decided that anything was better than doing nothing.

I called this man's home. When he answered, I identified myself and explained what had happened. He had a young stepson who had disappeared with the portable phone the night before. When confronted, the boy burst into tears and admitted he was my caller. His worried parents talked with him, decided upon consequences that were appropriate to his actions, and told him he would have to meet with me to apologize and learn something about how his calls had affected me. They called to ask for my cooperation. Still suffering from sleep deprivation and more than a little irritable, I agreed to meet this boy. I was prepared to give him what folks would once have called "a good tongue lashing."

A short while later, a skinny little kid with long, luscious eyelashes, delicate features, and rivers of tears pouring down his face, got out of his mother's car and stood—absolutely frozen—in my driveway. He could not move. He could not look at me. He could not speak. He just stood there, scared to death, his head turned away and down. He did not move a muscle. I couldn't even tell if he was breathing.

This was a little boy with a heavy heart.

I watched him briefly from the sanctuary of my kitchen, and then I went outside and held out my hand. He looked away, didn't take my hand. He smelled of sweat-drenched little boy fear. "So!" I said, "This is the guy who frightened me so badly last night?" He couldn't have weighed eighty pounds, soaking wet. He did not even reach my chin. He was a *little boy.*

"Yes," he whispered, "I'm sorry." The whisper was barely audible. His mother prompted him to look me in the eyes as he apologized. Hard as that was for him to do—and it caused him no end of anguish—I think she was right. It was important that he look directly into the face of the fear he had generated, right into the eyes of the person whose life he had impacted. In that moment, I became more than a disembodied voice on the other end of a telephone connection. I was now a real person to him.

And I looked into his eyes. They were the eyes of a child who was lost, frightened and lonely. I heard his voice whisper from earlier that night, "Are you awake? *Is it okay if we talk?*" I wondered about this child who had needed to talk so desperately that he had called a random number in the dark of the night and found a person who just happened to counsel people with troubled hearts. *Who was this boy, and what was breaking his heart?*

He is a child with a good mother and a fine stepfather. They were right on top of the problem, and quite appropriately. The boy and I talked about why he had called me. He claimed that he hadn't known who I was, that it was just a coincidence that I knew his stepfather. If that was true, the wild unpredictability of God had certainly intervened. This boy, in an act of random desperation, reached someone who was able to hear a plea for help in his voice and to act on what I heard. Someone who did not permit this incident to pass without notice. How easily it could have been otherwise.

We talked for just a few minutes. I told him he was courageous to be willing to meet me and to apologize in person for what he'd done. "You did a brave thing by coming here, and I thank you." With those words, his eyes flickered with just the tiniest bit of life.

This little boy needed to be loved, no matter how troubling and serious his misdeeds. He needed to talk to someone—anyone—so badly that he called out to a stranger in the middle of the night, hoping for a response to his question, "Are you awake? Is it okay if we talk?" He needed to know that he wasn't alone in the world. He needed to believe that someone would listen as if he mattered. *Who among all the choir of angels will hear me if I cry out?*

His mother and his stepfather got a big wake-up call themselves and paid attention to this boy's needs in a deeper, fuller way. In the end, not a bad resolution to what was certainly a bad night.

But this leads me to wonder how many other children wander

out there—lost and unattended—in the middle of the night? Full of the confused feelings that come with growing up, and no one to listen. No one to pay attention or to give love when love is what's needed. This question haunts me, and well it should. There are too many of them, and not enough adults who are listening when they cry out.

My late night caller frightened me. I could have spun all kinds of stories or projections about who he was and what he was up to. I could have called the police and sent them to his door. I didn't do that, and my heart rests more peacefully. I chose to set aside my irritation and go out to meet him instead. In making this choice, I found myself holding out a hand to a sad, lost, hurt and confused little boy. It was the right thing to notice his tear-filled eyes, to look into the downcast face of his shame, and to find compassion—mercifully, even love—for the heavy heart of a troubled child.

As I did this, I remembered nights when I too had been a child desperate for someone to know, and to understand, how scared and alone I felt. I had taken the opposite action of this boy, and stayed silent in my fears. No one knew about the terror in my heart, or how alone I felt with it. I was just a bit older, not much, when my innocence was stolen and desperation entered my world. How many times have I started out to be angry with another for injuries done to me, as I did with this child, and came to see the face of my own wounds reflected back to me? If I'm open to the lesson, every one of those times is an important opportunity to learn something about myself.

Is there any one of us who has not, at some time, done something terribly misguided in order to cry out for others to listen, to love us, no matter what we have done? Is there any one of us who has not been helped, or healed, often in profoundly ruptured places, when someone actually did?

Among other things, I teach communication skills to help those in relationships and families learn how to reach each other more effectively. One such useful skill is how to listen to one another *devoutly*. To underscore the point, I often call this *holy listening*. This is the art of putting our own needs aside for the period of time that someone else is trying to communicate something important . . . and focusing, intentionally and intently, on their message. This boy's telephone calls pierced the quiet rest of my night and accosted me in the most abrupt and unexpected way, but something greater than fear intervened and I was able to hear this child with a devout attention.

When I moved my own fears to the side and *listened devoutly*, I heard a distinct cry for help and responded. Had I given fear free run, I would still be afraid today, wondering about the caller and when he would return. Now I know that he was a skinny, scared kid, wanting someone to hear him, someone to pay attention to him, and someone to care about the state of his confused spirit. There is in all of us the universal need of *call and response*. If I call out and no one answers, I believe I am alone. If someone listens devoutly, then I experience God. The *response* is proof of God's existence in another.

I still see the boy's stepfather regularly. He doesn't say much about the boy, but when I ask, he will tell me that he's "doing all right." I listen for what is hidden in the message, and what I hear is a softness in his voice, a kindness for the boy, gratitude that I care enough to ask. Because of this, though I will never know for sure, I have a sense he really is doing all right . . . or will, once he passes through the hardships of growing up. I think of him fondly: that little guy standing in my driveway, so afraid he could not raise his head to look at me.

I think of all the scared little kids, trying to grow up in a world where not enough loving adults listen to them, let alone listen devoutly. I pray that this will change in time for them to know we care when their spirits are confused or hurt. As a wise rabbi once said: "If not us, then who? If not now, then when?"

ℊ

- With your eyes closed and your heart open, remember a time when you were in need of someone to listen to you with devout attention. To listen as if you were the only person who mattered, and they had all the time in the world for you to speak. What did you learn from that experience, and how are you carrying that lesson with you today?

- Is there someone in your life who needs you to listen to him or her in a deeper and more intentional way?

- When that person calls out, how will you answer? How will you prepare to *listen devoutly*?

- Take the risk to do that. Notice how you benefit from that experience as much, perhaps more, than the person who asks for your attention. Where do you find the Mystery, and what is it "up to," in an encounter like this? What is the opportunity for you to expand your consciousness in this encounter?

Breakthrough

How lovely the world becomes
in just that single instant
of seeing the truth about
yourself reflected there.

—*A Course in Miracles*

Woodchucks are the current blip on my radar screen. Several summers ago, a baby woodchuck made a bold end run from the edge of the woods to the gardens in front of my house. This small ball of fur was too cute for me to remove or destroy . . . so, with my tacit permission, it munched its way through my beautiful perennial beds on the way to becoming a very fat adult woodchuck before the summer was over. The following year, my woodchuck returned with a mate, tunneled under my front and back steps, and ate through the asphalt of my sidewalk in order to reach the garden beds unnoticed. Though I grumbled all summer, I had the sidewalk replaced rather than take serious measures to remove the woodchucks.

This summer, the woodchucks expanded their family to include four adorable babies, and all six of them spread across my lawn, devouring their way through another season of daisies, bee balm, cosmos and Echinacea. Trying to sound fierce, I would hiss at them and send them scurrying for their tunnels, only to have them creep back into view as soon as I moved on to something else. The woodchucks were not taking me seriously. My grumbling continued without ceasing.

Or it did until one summer day. I had a friend visiting for the week, and this friend had a front row seat to my woodchuck drama. I explained that my neighbor, also a victim of the woodchuck clan, was calling a trapper to come for the critters who plagued our gardens. "Any day now," I said with some authority, "he's planning to call the trapper." My friend nodded pleasantly and watched as I continued to throw windows open and make ferocious-sounding noises that would send the woodchucks for temporary cover, only to return as soon as I closed the window. There was no question that woodchucks were having their way in my gardens. It seemed a losing battle.

Then, one day, my friend and I left the house about the time my neighbor was cleaning up from work in his yard. I stopped to inquire if he had made the call to the trapper. He grinned with a kind of aw-shucks smile and said: "No. I saw two of the babies snuggling up to each other in the yard this morning, kissing each other on the nose, and I just didn't have the heart to do anything about them."

He was soon to become a daddy. I could tell that he was a lost cause: the woodchucks suckered him too. Once I understood that he was not going to rescue me from our common woodchuck dilemma, I had to take action on my own. But did I? Certainly not. As the days passed and I failed to call the trapper, the woodchucks had a field day. They chowed down on everything green, and I continued to grumble and sputter. I came to enjoy the sounds of the woodchuck story rolling off my tongue. It made interesting conversation with many people.

After watching me thrash about in the woodchuck dilemma for several more days, my friend finally cleared his throat and dared to say tactfully (which is always a good beginning): "Hmm, Meredith, I notice that you *talk* more about getting rid of the woodchucks than you *do anything* about it. Maybe you don't really want to get rid of them. Maybe the drama you're experiencing is exactly what you want. Have you thought about that?"

In a flash of oh-so-reluctant insight, I found myself staring a whole new truth in the face.

I really believed my own tale of woe. I had invested three summers in finely crafting the details of my woodchuck stories. I told them to anyone who would listen. It never occurred to me that it wasn't so much the wild creatures that were running rampant in my life as it was my own lack of consciousness. Suddenly, I became my own example of what happens if we consciously develop one plan but actually invest, unconsciously, in another. The unconscious plan wins, hands down, every time. I teach this to clients, as they struggle to understand why their lives are ricocheting around so unpredictably, but I had failed to see myself happily carrying out my own unconscious action. *I was having more fun telling the woodchuck stories than I was doing anything about them.*

I would like to justify my lack of action by saying this was just one small corner of my life, and it didn't matter much whether I was conscious or unconscious there. Asleep or awake. Truly, I would. I would also like to tell you this was no big deal. But the practical reality was that I'd lost hundreds of dollars worth of plants to a simple lesson: *I was the one responsible for the presence of woodchucks in my garden, and I was the one who*

*had to do something to change the situation, or accept the fact
that I'd already made my choice by default.*

I was the one who had to tell the truth about my choices. I was
also the one who needed to hear the truth. It was as if my friend
had pulled a switch and lit a room that was previously in the
dark. Now that I could see what I hadn't, or I wouldn't, see before
. . . well, then what? Would I finally wake up? Or would I stay
unconscious, continuing to spin woodchuck tales as if they were
true?

I finally called the trapper. He was a nice man, and I felt a lot
better as the babies were caught and taken off to someone else's
woods—for a hefty fee—by a *very nice person.* It soothed my
guilt. After all, the baby woodchucks were cute, and I am as
softhearted as my neighbor. But the lesson stands: I was caught,
even if kindly, in a moment of my own unconscious ambivalence.
I'm forced to wonder how many other unconscious niches remain
in me, yet to be illuminated? How many woodchuck stories have
I concocted that need to be challenged, compassionately, before
I am who I say I am?

No doubt, there are many. If I am particularly blessed, the person
pulling the switch in the future will be as thoughtful as my friend
was this time. Fortunately, he offered no judgment: just a gentle
comment to highlight the awareness that, while I was articulating
one reality, I was busily, smugly, creating another.

We all have woodchuck stories, tales that we tell ourselves and
others for the point of impact more than to reflect the truth. Often,
it's fun to make them up. I enjoy my own woodchuck stories,
and I have been known as a great audience for others'. But
oftentimes woodchuck stories are actually *obfuscations* on the
path. They may seem to be true when, in reality, we use them
to muddy the waters. I used the stories I had by then developed
to a fine art, to postpone responsibility.

Benedictine Sister Joan Chittister offers this thought: "'To live,' Antoine de Saint-Exupery once wrote, 'is to be slowly born.' The fact is that to be fully alive and cognizant is the task of an entire lifetime. There's so much in each of us that we have never touched, so much beauty that we've overlooked. Consciousness is what lifts the ordinary to the level of the sublime."

Waking up, getting conscious, is a slow process. Little by little, we challenge ourselves to notice what we have left undiscovered in our psyches and spirits. Little by little, we tweak ourselves to see truth, to tell truth as it is, and not as we would have it be. Little by little, we set out to locate in ourselves the "beauty that we've overlooked."

This is a lifelong journey, and surprising teachers wait for us at many locations along the way. Some of those teachers are woodchucks. I am tickled by the humor of that notion. I chuckle at my own mind-blindness, at the same time I strive to illumine it. We humans are the strangest species: given the tremendous gift of consciousness, we so frequently fail to develop it.

I have also learned a lesson. Woodchucks are capable of reproducing much faster than I might catch up with them, just like the stories I make up multiply faster than I can make them conscious. This is true for all of us. At some point, we have to stop running so furiously from truth and turn to confront the large or small deceptions we perpetrate on ourselves, on others, in the world. For only when we call ourselves to consciousness, do we become fully available for the Divine Mystery to put us to use as inhabitants of, as instruments for, its own evolution. The Mystery is also evolving along with us, also maturing . . . and calling itself to Consciousness.

Yes. That's what I said: we are the physical embodiment of the Divine Mystery, which is experiencing its own growth in consciousness each time one of us wakes up and turns toward the truth. The game we're playing has high stakes. This fragile planet on which we are perched so precariously right now needs all the consciousness we can lend to it. I play a part in growing that consciousness, and so do you. It's that simple, and simply that easy to ignore. Our woodchuck stories are tricks the mind can play in order to ensnare us in a *spiritual lethargy* . . . and to postpone answering the call for us to awaken.

Woodchucks. Imagine! Next summer, to be sure, the first call I make is to the trapper.

ℐ

- Where, in your life, are you actively telling woodchuck stories? Telling a story that allows you to put off taking full responsibility for your own process of awakening?

- What is the payoff? And what is the price tag attached to your staying unconscious about what you are doing?

- In what way might it change things for you to consider that the Mystery is awakening with us, and needs us—as incarnated beings—to awaken fully so that God can also grow its own God-nature?

Have mercy upon us

By compassion,
the soul is made blessed.

—Meister Eckhart

Far too many people in this world live in a state of perennial disconnect. Most of us don't even know we are doing this, until something dreadful happens. In the early morning hours of a winter day last year, in the city where I grew up safely roaming neighborhoods without concern, something dreadful happened. A young woman was assaulted while walking home from mailing letters at the post office. In full view of morning commuters, she was dragged across a park in the city, and was beaten and raped before anyone stopped to help her. Most of the morning commuters, busy juggling cups of coffee and thoughts about the day in front of them, ignored what they saw.

One brave person—another woman—stopped to help. She drove the terrified woman, who had by then escaped her attacker, to her home and came back later that day to check on her. In the aftermath of the attack, the shocking disregard of those witnessing the assault was raised to a community-wide forum of discussion and collective self-scrutiny. In those discussions, many people wondered if they could have mustered the same courage to stop and offer help.

This *perennial disconnect* is a symptom of the malaise that is quietly infecting the spirit of our people. The events of September 11th startled many of us out of that malaise into an experience of national unity, but I'm skeptical that this change is pervasive enough or long-lasting enough to lead us out of the moral stupor that's been overtaking us. We maintain the belief, perhaps more tenaciously than ever, that the reason for our concerns or worries must be located in someone or something *outside of ourselves*. Would that this was true, but it is just another woodchuck story, built on a bigger platform, and teetering badly.

Sooner or later, and my prayer is this will happen sooner, we must all look into the mirror of truth where the possibility is strong that we will see our own faces reflected back at us. We have grown lethargic, no longer willing to lend a hand to a faltering or struggling member of the human family. The woman who walked to the post office one morning and became a victim of rape asks, rightly so: *Why? How could this have happened? So many people watched as I was dragged away, screaming for help. What's wrong that we refuse to notice when a person is in trouble, when we refuse to stop and help?*

This story reminds me of others that have come to my attention recently. The first was told to me by a young woman who waitresses in a restaurant in a neighboring town. There is a young man there who arrives to begin drinking when the bar opens each morning and never leaves until it closes at night. He's exhibiting classic signs of end-stage liver disease. His friends, watching in horror as he kills himself with alcohol, have tried repeatedly to approach his parents about what they see. His family blatantly ignores the problem. In this story there is evidence of monumental *disconnect*. This young man may die of it.

In another story, there is a young mother of two babies—one an infant, the other barely toddling—who is in a relationship with a partner who physically and emotionally batters her. She is afraid to leave, and she's afraid to stay. Her parents avert their faces so they cannot see her bruises and broken bones. *Disconnect*. We have become immune to stories like this, so much so that they've become background noise in our lives. Substance abuse? Domestic violence? Ho-hum.

One last story, and a more recent one. This was told to me by a friend in her mid-twenties who lived in New York City at the time of the events on September 11th. This story occurred more than a year later, after she had moved from the city back to her rural hometown. She had gone into the city to visit a boyfriend, arriving shortly after one of the many snowstorms that struck the Northeast this winter. All over Manhattan, snow was piled many feet high, blocking sidewalks and curbs. She was waiting for a traffic light to change when she saw a woman, pregnant-to-term, stranded halfway up a bank of snow she was trying to cross in order to get home from work. On all sides of her, people pushed past to get to their own destinations, while this woman floundered helplessly.

My young friend dodged traffic to reach the other side of the street, climbed the snowbank, and held out a hand to the woman. At first, the woman refused, certain of the belief that help could not be trusted. As she tried again to mount the bank and slipped, she fell, spent, onto the snow. "Come on," my friend told her, "If you take my hand and I take yours, we can get over the bank together." Her approach made all the difference. The woman took her hand and they cautiously made the climb over the snow. Without a *goodbye* or a *thank you*, the woman was swallowed up in the tide of home-going strangers. *Disconnect.*

The heart of the human family is in trouble, folks, and we each play a part in that with our silence, with our foolish refusals to get involved with someone else's suffering, with the blind eye we have cast in the direction of people who are in need of our attention and love. Some of them are our closest friends and family. Some are strangers.

The alternative to this indifference and disconnect is difficult, and many of us never consider it. We are too afraid of what we might find. That alternative is to allow the shields we have built around our hearts to fall, to be broken open with our own—or another person's—suffering, so that a healing-restoring presence might flow through us into the world. What is so frightening about the prospect of giving up our defenses that we resist so adamantly?

It's this: opening our hearts to love will push every button in us, will test us beyond measure, will try our faith and challenge our souls. Love mandates that we become all we are meant to be ... and nothing less. Love does not allow us to settle for being a mere shadow of a human being. Not as individuals and not as a people belonging to the Mystery we call God. Love calls us to surrender the small anxieties and desires of the human ego—control of an outcome, image management, the insistent need to be right rather than to be reconciled—so that we make room for something greater to take place within us.

If we let love in—*really* let love in to the broken places in our hearts—we will have to face some of life's hideous truths. We might have to admit that we are capable of hurting each other. That we are capable of causing considerable pain even to those we hold dear. That we have cruelty in us sufficient to push a pregnant woman aside to get home a few minutes sooner. We'd have to acknowledge we don't always know what to do, and we certainly don't always do what is right. We all have our vulnerable (and sharp) edges, and most of us do not want them exposed to view. We go to great lengths to conceal the aspects of ourselves we don't like or don't know how to embrace. *In the act of disconnecting from our true nature, with our many confusing parts, we become capable of disconnecting from others.*

The solution to this disconnect is the hardest simple thing we might ever be asked to do: to let our hearts break open to one another in compassion and love. This is life's most difficult work, and yet also its most faithful and courageous. It's what the Mystery invites of us, and perhaps the only act that truly matters. The true religion is that of an open heart toward others. In the realm of sacred reality, there's no fuss over the particulars. We're requested only to make our hearts a portal, or a passageway, for love and compassion to be offered in this world.

This is the most significant challenge of our troubled times. No one but you and me and all of us working together will be able to connect these disconnected dots. The woman who was raped, the man drinking his young life away at the bar, the mother afraid to protect her babies or leave her abuser, the woman stranded on a high bank of snow . . . serve as reminders that we are called to *wake up* to the struggles and suffering of others. We must climb out of the stupor into which we have been lulled. The time is now, and the need never more urgent.

Madeleine L'Engle writes in *Walking on Water*: "We have to be braver than we think we can be, because God is constantly calling us to be more than we are, to see through the plastic sham to living, breathing reality, and to break down our defenses of self-protection in order to be free to receive and give love."

If you have amends to make to someone you love, make them today. If your heart has been closed to someone who counts on you, open it today. If there's a lonely friend or relation asking for your attention, offer it to them. If someone you know is anxious or afraid, take them into your heart without hesitating. If someone precious to you is struggling, find the courage and compassion to talk to that person before the day is over. Tomorrow is too late for hundreds of thousands of struggling people all over this world.

In his book *The Seat of the Soul,* Gary Zukav asks a question that shatters our excuses and calls us to be accountable for the quality of space we take up in the human family: *What choose you?*

When it's my time to make this choice—and, of course, this is a choice each of us makes repeatedly over the course of an examined life—I take a deep breath and go about my small efforts to change the world by quietly changing the state of my own heart. This is not an easy path to follow. It can be difficult to be accountable when the easier way is to blame others, judge them, or disconnect from them, but it's a whole lot better—don't you think?—than the alternative.

♌

- What does it mean to you "to be braver than we think we can be?" How is the Mystery inviting you to change the state of your heart toward yourself or someone else?

- Imagine for a moment that you have a choice to change how you relate to the struggles or suffering of others. What would you change, and how would you go about it?

- C.S. Lewis said that if we lock our hearts away from pain, they will not remain "safe" but will harden and die to everything that is throbbing and pulsing in life. Only in giving our hearts away can we feel the thrum of life in our veins. In what ways or at what times have you locked your heart away from pain, only to feel your spirit wither? In what ways or at what times have you made the choice for an open heart and felt your spirit blossom?

• When has another person made a difference in your life by reaching out to you when they could just as well have walked away? Close your eyes, take a deep breath and drop into your heart, and quietly acknowledge the support and love they gave to you when you were in need of it.

Look up

What occurs around you and within you
reflects your own mind
and shows you the
dream you are weaving.

—Venerable Dyhani Ywahoo

That particular Saturday had been a difficult one for me. It culminated with a deep conversation with my daughter, who was beginning to terminate her work with the children she had been seeing as clients for two years in her social work graduate school program. She had formed significant bonds with each child, and this period of closure was painful for Sarah and the children. In her anguish, she asked: "Mom, does the joy in life ever balance out the suffering?"

That question is almost impossible for an honest person to answer, and I was too drained from my own concerns to try. I wanted to tell her that yes, there is often great joy to be had throughout the living of our lives . . . and truly there is.

But that was not so for me—or for her—on the day she asked the question. Instead of saying something that fell short of the truth, I talked with her about what it means for us to help each other "bear the unbearable." I suggested, sadly, that bearing the unbearable is sometimes the best we can do.

Then I told her that earlier that morning I'd looked out my living room window to see the first red-tailed hawk of the season floating high above the trees at the end of the road. The hawk looped in wider and wider circles, swooping into the high branches of the trees and then diving back into the open skies. The sunlight fell upon the hawk in just such a way that the burnished red of its wing and tail feathers glowed like embers of a dying fire.

I watched as my neighbors hurried in and out of their homes, their cars, off to do errands, back from their errands, never looking up to see the miracle flying high in the sky over their heads. I ventured to guess I was the only person who saw the hawk in the fifteen or so minutes it circled our neighborhood. I was the one who noticed the hawk lift high onto currents of air far above the trees, glide majestically along those currents for a last breath-taking moment, and silently depart on the next leg of its long migratory journey.

That afternoon, as both of us reeled with exhaustion and sorrow, I told this story to Sarah and said: "At times, something magical and mysterious like this is enough to ease the suffering for just a little while. It's sometimes sufficient to remind us that beauty is all around us, even in the midst of the worst anguish." We can't always change what breaks our hearts; sometimes there's nothing to do but to bear it with as much authenticity as we can. At times such as these, we wear hearts on our sleeves, and that is an act of power and courage. An act of faithfulness to life and to love. If Sarah did anything less than bear the unbearable in quiet anguish, she'd have diminished the truth of her love for the children who revealed their stories to her waiting heart and changed her in the process. Her broken heart was evidence something meaningful had transpired between them. She was weaving the dream of love.

I tell myself, as I recount the story to you now, to remember that it's good to look up when I'm feeling most down. One never knows what wild and beautiful moment is waiting to be noticed.

℘

- What helps you to "bear the unbearable?" Where do you find your inspiration when times are difficult, and you haven't the energy to take another step or go another mile?

- In this short story, where do you find evidence of the Mystery we call God?

- Remind yourself of a time when beauty restored your spirits. Where do you go when you seek an encounter with beauty, wonder, and awe?

Beginner's Mind

To say that we abandon our will
to another's will
seems very easy
until, through experience,
we realize that this
is the hardest thing
one can do if one
does it as it should be done.

—Theresa of Avila

This is actually Ellie's story. I wish it was mine, it is that delicious, but it isn't. I am tempted to steal it for myself, but since it's a story of her humiliation and her resurrection, I will graciously step aside and allow her to speak for herself:

"About two weeks ago, I had an experience in humility that is reflected in the words of Theresa of Avila. When I told my yoga teacher-friend Deborah about this, she said, 'Oh, yes! Zen mind.

Beginner's mind.' That short phrase is a perfect way of describing what happened for me.

I decided that it was time, at the age of sixty-two, to try yoga. I had never done yoga before. I don't consider myself particularly agile, and I have never liked trying something new, especially if it involves going by myself to places where I don't know anyone, and I don't know what to expect. While we are growing up, we have ample opportunity to 'be new,' to go to places we have never been, to show up in social situations that challenge us, to enter new schools and to make new friends. There are plenty of opportunities for 'being new' in the younger stages of our lives.

As far as I was concerned, I had completed that course. I was done, finished, and graduated. No more work needed. As the time for my new yoga class approached, I became aware of excuses I was making to myself about why my schedule would not allow me to go. I told myself I could not afford to take the class, I did not have the right clothes to wear. I was quietly lining up one excuse after another. Excuses or no excuses, like it or not, the day of the class arrived.

I had planned my outfit the night before. I didn't want to stand out more than I already had a suspicion I would. I assumed I was registered in a beginner's class, and that was comforting. But I was overcome with anxieties: from not knowing where to park my car, to what time to get there, to the exact location of the building, to whether there would be a place to change my clothes, and finally to whether I would be wearing the 'right' clothes. Anxiety, anxiety, anxiety.

I nervously set out for the class, determined to see if yoga was something to which I would be drawn. I tried to look cool, because I really wanted to be cool. I have always wanted to *be cool*. I watched people come in who knew just what they were doing. This made me even more agitated than I already was, and that was *plenty agitated*. Other people set up their yoga mats. They got out their blocks, their straps and their blankets. I didn't have a clue what these things were for, and I didn't know whom I might ask. I was feeling dumb, dumb, and dumber. Thankfully, someone noticed my agitation and came to my rescue. She pointed me in the right direction, whatever 'right direction' meant. By this time, I was as vulnerable as I'd imagined I might feel. I knew *nothing*, and this information was clearly written all over me. Others could see my vulnerability.

Well, I did my best to follow the crowd, to look cool. I took my mat and did what the other people were doing. I placed it on the floor. That seemed like a fitting enough start! There were about twenty people in the room with me. My anxiety level soared as I watched some of them lift effortlessly into headstands. *What was I doing here?* In that moment, to further my distress, I discovered I was not in a beginner's course at all, but an 'all levels' yoga class. I knew then that I was about to undergo a major exercise in humility. I swallowed my terror, and followed along.

The class began with a wonderful meditation. I was relaxing just a bit until the teacher began to give us instructions to move into yoga postures. I was lost. Not a map in sight. I couldn't tell my right foot from my left. My body was twisted into such a strange position that I couldn't even see the instructor to know whether I was doing what I was supposed to be doing. Still, I forged fearfully ahead.

After a few minutes, the teacher looked over at me and asked, 'Ellie, are those tights you have on?'

'Yes,' I said. I was too embarrassed to say more.

'Can you take them off?'

How humiliating, I said to myself, *You didn't wear the right clothes after all, and now everyone knows it. Everyone in this room knows you have no idea what you are doing. Everyone knows there is nothing cool about you.*

'Well,' the instructor explained—with great compassion, I might add, gratefully—'your tights have feet, and you could slip.' So I walked through twenty 'all levels' yoga students over to a room where I could remove the tights-with-feet and strip down to ones that had no feet. I was mortified, utterly humiliated.

The morning continued like that. A gracious assistant instructor helped with my stretches, such as they were. She smiled at me in a wonderfully reassuring way. She affirmed me, encouraged me, and told me I was 'doing great.' But all morning, I stayed in beginner's mind. I didn't have the skills to be anywhere else. And I knew how important it was for me to be there. I thought of Jesus' teachings. He didn't say:

> *Blessed are those who are the most skilled.*
> *Blessed are those who can stand on their heads.*
> *Blessed are those who wear the right outfits.*
> *Blessed are those who are cool.*

He said:

> *Blessed are those who mourn.*
> *Blessed are those who are pure in heart.*
> *Blessed are the peacemakers.*

I simply allowed myself to participate fully in beginner's mind. Zen mind. The Buddhists like to say that this is a high state of being, the place where the old no longer works for us, and the new has yet to take hold. I entered into a state of vulnerability that must surely be a direct path to increased understanding, empathy and compassion for others who, like me, stand outside the circle of those who belong or who know what to do. This class was an exercise for me in abandoning my will, an exercise in recognizing my own ego needs to look good in front of others, an exercise in catching myself in an attempt to pretend I knew what I was doing when I did not, and I am truly grateful for it. The class was a stretch for me in a spiritual as well as a physical sense.

I am a minister. Much of the time, I get to be the leader, the one who knows. In a yoga class, I am the beginner all over again. It's good to remember the importance of *beginner's mind,* and all it has to teach us about ourselves. I think I will go back. I believe I will keep trying. I will, over time, even improve my yoga practice. What matters is not how skilled I am at yoga postures, but that I was willing to explore my own growing edge and to discover that, once I shook off my mortification, I loved being there. Awkward as it was. Embarrassed as I was, I stretched outside the familiar range of my comfort zone, and survived the humility of it to become bigger and more courageous than I thought I was."

Zen mind. Beginner's mind.

We'd all like a spiritual path that provides us with answers. Most of us would rather be reassured than be expanded, but that's not the trail the spiritual path most often follows. It usually sends us right into the path of the unknown, into unfamiliar territory, and requires that we stretch through our discomfort to find a more expanded sense of self. The Mystery we call God is not looking to comfort us or to collude with us in the little games our egos like to play. It is always seeking to *develop* us, until we have become all we are designed to be. That is the spiritual task, that is the goal, and that is truly the gift.

℘

- When you are clinging to an idea of yourself, whatever the idea might be, what part of you is clinging and what is it clinging to?

- In what ways have you been presented with an unexpected challenge to become a more courageous person or to grow into a more expansive version of yourself? How would you rate yourself on having met this challenge? Is there anything you would do differently today?

- When in life have you found yourself to be on an unfamiliar path, no road map or compass, when all you really wanted was the safety and comfort of the familiar? As you reflect on those experiences or events, ask yourself how they have served your spiritual growth. What did those experiences come to teach you?

Fear as teacher

It is in each of us that
the peace of the world is cast . . .
in the frontiers of our hearts.
From there, it must spread out
to the limits of the universe.

—*Cardinal Leo Jozef Suenens*

I've decided that my niece Jillian, just turned seven, is here to teach others about living joyfully in these all-too-human bodies we inhabit. Jillian loves the experience of embodiment and finds an astonishing number of things her body can do that my body has never considered. When she was barely walking, at about eleven months old, Jilli would suddenly jump straight up into the air and land, hard, bottom first. While the rest of us watched, convinced she would hurt herself, Jillian would giggle and do it all again. My sister Beth rolled her eyes heavenward and murmured a prayer for this child who wanted to experience *everything* a body can do.

My mother, always a worrier, was certain Jillian would not survive her infancy and that Beth was not a watchful and worried enough mother. She tried explaining this to Beth, who tried explaining in return that Jilli was a highly spirited child who took the world on her own terms and didn't accept direction or intervention easily. For a time, they were at an impasse about the need to control Jillian. The standoff was no more in evidence than around the issue of Beth's pond.

My sister and her family live on a lovely little piece of land in New Hampshire. There is a pond behind their house that always terrified my mother. The pond is not big, but my mother was afraid that one of her grandchildren—Jillian, the likely candidate—would accidentally fall into the pond and drown. Operating under the notion that more worry was always better than less, she lobbied all of her other children (and any grandchildren in proximity at the time) to urge Beth to build a fence around the pond. Given Jillian's bold nature, none of us saw the sense in this. We thought the best approach to this particular child was to teach her to swim. That idea did not ease my mother's fear in the slightest. She remained frantic over the pond.

So the pond became something to avoid. Something to fear. Something Not To Discuss In The Presence Of My Mother. Once started, that conversation could lead to places we didn't want to go. We adopted the strategy of all dysfunctional families: Pretend the lovely little pond didn't exist. *Don't talk. Don't trust.* And the fear held and expressed by my mother went underground.

My mother died many months ago, and many things have changed. We all miss her, of course, because she had a great heart and love for us, as we did for her. Yet there are some things that none of us miss.

The worry with which she enveloped us—even smothered us—

is one. *Call me when you get home so I know you got there safely.*
Be careful. Take no risks. Life is full of unexpected dangers.
Those were her guiding principles, and we subtly assimilated
them. When she died, those fearful admonitions were lifted. I
noticed my own immense relief when I boarded a plane for the
first time after her death without having to call to reassure her
on both ends of the flight that I had taken off or arrived safely.

A huge wave of release poured through my body, and I thought:
I'm free at last to fly, free to soar. A metaphor for re-claiming
my own adventuresome nature, which I always felt the need to
temper while she was alive because any daughter's or son's
attempt at adventure was guaranteed to thrust her into fearfulness.
Weeks after my mother's death, my brother confessed that one
of his first guilty thoughts had been: *The reign of terror is over.*
Loved as she was, my mother held an entire family firmly in
the grip of her fears.

The following winter, months after her beloved grandmother died,
Jillian was invited to a skating party at an indoor skating rink.
Jilli had never skated, one of the few physical activities still
unexplored. Beth went along to help her learn some of the
fundamentals of balance and maneuverability. No need. Jilli was
soon skating quite well. Beth surprised herself by finding that
she too enjoyed skating, so, later that week, she and Jilli went
to an outdoor rink near their home and skated some more. They
were having a great time developing their prowess on skates. Beth
decided it was time to check out their little pond.

She swept an area of the pond clean of snow, and John, Jilli's
father, cut a hole in the ice to determine if it was thick enough
for skating. Once they had determined the ice was safe, Jillian
laced up her skates and, to borrow Beth's description of this
event, "flew like a feather across the pond."

Jilli had been released from fear, and also Beth, and later John, to fly like a feather across the pond. A child born to love living in the body and to learn the outer limits of the body's capabilities, Jillian was free to discover the range of her own ability without being derailed by her grandmother's fear and limitations. My mother never intended fear to limit her life, or ours, with such force. She was a great-hearted woman who had learned through experience that catastrophes happen when you are least expecting them. Since she was determined not to be caught unprepared, she would run out ahead, anticipating any danger. She meant well, though her fearfulness caused considerable, if unintentional, harm.

Fear has the power to keep us from embracing life to its full. There are countless times in my life where fear stands between me and a next significant leap of faith or courage, when it stands between me and meaningful connection with another person, when it stands between me and my ability to name a truth. When I am afraid, I am more apt to stiffen into life, which adds to the chances that I will fall or be hurt. If I soften into my fears with the innocence of a child, I am less likely to fall. This is a paradox most of us don't consider when we're stiffening, but it's the first thing that should come to mind: *Soften, soften in the presence of fear.*

No doubt of it: fear incapacitates. And we live in a world that offers no shortage of good reasons to be afraid. We do need to make our choices *mindfully, consciously, intentionally*. We need to be informed of events that may threaten us, may loom on the horizon of our lives, without being bound as prisoners of worry and anxiety. None of us enjoys walking with fear as a constant companion. That only leads us to narrow our sights and close the parameters in our lives. In the presence of fear, especially threats over which we have no control, perhaps we're being challenged to find a balance between *consciousness* and *courage*.

Ellie was reading *Freeing the Soul from Fear* by Robert Sardello when she found this statement: "The presence of terror in the world is like a great process of compression. Living in the midst of images of [terror] eats away the most ordinary forms of human connection, producing numbness and isolation.

"For example, we're told to be on guard, to be aware of anyone leaving behind an unattended bag or parcel. A twinge or more of worry enters anyone who travels on a train, plane, bus or subway. The news announces every new terrorist alert. We've been told to expect further incidents of international terrorism, with the United States the prime target. I know of families who are afraid to travel on the same plane.

". . . Becoming free of fear does not mean getting rid of it but rather developing an inner capacity to stay with it, which gradually produces a transformation, not only within us but also within the world. Of course, it seems that the best solution is to find a direct way to eliminate terrorism. We always want to do away with what we do not like. But it would be a mistake to assume that eliminating the proximate cause would bring an end of fear altogether. Getting rid of terrorism, for example, without changing the undercurrent of hatred associated with it, can only mean exchanging it for some other form of fearful situation. When we assume that a fear or threat can be removed without inner change accompanying it, we do not see the phenomenon for what it is.

"Instead of asking how to eliminate this atrocious thing, our question might better be: what is fear doing in the world at this time? What purpose does it serve? What is fear doing in me at this time? How can we see its characteristics clearly so that it no longer dominates us?"

Several years ago, when the people of the world were celebrating the approaching New Year and arrival of the new millennium, my son was living in Washington, DC. There were whispers of domestic terrorism during those celebrations, and my son was living in the most likely at-risk place in the United States. Mindful of my own experience with an over-wrought and anxious mother, I tried to communicate the risk of being on the Washington Mall for the huge New Year's Eve celebration.

The most difficult aspect of this for me was that I did not want to participate in fearfulness. I knew from my own firsthand, up-close experience how corrosive that was. Nor did I want to participate in the *denial* of fear. I wanted to inform my son of the *possibilities* and encourage him to make a wise decision. He didn't like hearing this. He wanted specific details, which I couldn't give him. I told him as much as I knew or at least suspected. I listened as his own fear emerged. He talked honestly about how difficult it would be to explain to his friends that—based on his mother's reports of a vague threat of terrorism—they should stay out of the city and avoid the year 2000 extravaganza. We quarreled.

I told him that I couldn't live with myself if I denied there was good reason to be afraid, only to have him—or any other mother's child—hurt or killed because I hadn't been brave enough to admit: *Sadly, the world is changing, and it's time to make your choices carefully. There isn't enough latitude for you to be careless.* In the end, he and his friends made other plans without the need to quibble about my worries.

At the time of our conversation, I was reading a biography of Dietrich Bonhoeffer—the German pastor who actively resisted Hitler's actions in Europe and who was captured, imprisoned and killed for his attempts to rid Germany of Hitler—and learning how painful a process it was for him to determine where he would stand, when he would speak, and how he would protect the people he loved from the growing Nazi threat.

The author told how the Bonhoeffer family would gather each

night, read the news accounts reported in the papers, and try to assess (from the few details the government made available to them) the dangers for German people who opposed Hitler's rise to power. The peril was far more grave than young Dietrich knew at the time, though he would later discover that as he tried to bring world attention to bear on the plight of the Germans, particularly Jewish Germans, under the Nazi regime. Dietrich Bonhoeffer ultimately died for his courageous efforts to tell the truth of the rising abuse of power under Hitler. But he offered the citizens of the world an example of courage in the presence of reasons to fear: *Gather information carefully, deliberate upon it in council with trusted others, and chose a course of action that represents an act of informed conscience.*

The Buddhists call this *living mindfully.* Do we believe for a moment that Dietrich Bonhoeffer, choosing a difficult path to pursue, was not filled with fear?

I look to others for examples of action in the presence of fear, so that my spirit is neither overwhelmed nor silenced. I look to Dietrich Bonhoeffer, who died in a brave attempt to bring truth to light. And I look to Jillian, on new skates, flying like a feather across a pond that had been off limits because fear intruded upon the fullness of life. For my part, I pray that I won't collude with fear-mongering and that I won't be complicit with silence.

The only thing I can say for certain is that my fears quiet only as I examine myself for what I know in my heart to be true, when I risk speaking and living that truth, and when I allow others to arrive at their own conclusions or to make their own choices. Fear can become a teacher, opening awareness, when we turn to face it rather than hide or flee from it. Fear is not meant to be avoided, but embraced, welcomed into the continuum of human experience, and learned from. *Soften, soften.*

Joan Chittister says: "The world is in the state it's in because there are things *in me* that need changing." How I meet my fears is one of them. Can I bear my fear with compassion for myself, and still not allow it to control my actions? Can I remain faithful to what is true, no matter how fearful I might be? If I begin to change the things *in me* that need changing, won't everything taking place around me seem just a little gentler, a little kinder, a little more safe, a little more forgiving in circumstances that are not ever in my control?

If I can make small but courageous shifts in my inner world—practicing discernment, letting go of fears that constrain me needlessly, daring to fly like a feather on the pond there's the hope, at least, that my efforts will contribute toward making it possible for the human family to move into the millennium feeling less afraid. Reducing the fear, one decision at a time.

All I can ever do is my one small part . . . but I can take my risks with the same sense of wonder and hope with which Jillian bounces into the air and down again, or puts on her skates and flies, like a feather.

§

- How much power do you give *fear* to control your actions and decisions? How is fear at work in your life at this time? Does your fearfulness help or hinder you? Be very specific about how it positively or negatively impacts the quality of your life.

- Where might the Mystery be at work, at least in you, during this fear-filled time in the world?

- Where do you turn for solace when you are afraid? Are there particular spiritual practices that help to comfort you? Any that help you to move through the experience of fear to what lies beyond it?

- If you were to retract the amount of power you allow fear to have in your life, what risks would you take that you're not presently giving yourself permission to take? How would this make you more of the person you're here to be?

- What would it mean if you decided not to avoid fear but to embrace what it has to teach you and to integrate those lessons into the fabric of your life?

Thousand petal lotus

I look upon the mystery of you,
and in what I see residing there,
I discover all that is holy.
I surrender to what I see.
What else is there to do?

—Meredith Jordan

It was the summer solstice, when light fell longer on our corner of the earth than did dark. There was peace at work in the Balkans. Refugees had begun to emerge from hiding places in mountain sanctuaries and from the devastation of the refugee camps to start the daunting task of rebuilding their communities and homes. Rosa Parks, at last, had been awarded the Congressional Medal of Freedom. Small mercies in a troubled world.

I woke one morning, pushing up from the murky depths of sleep, with a vivid image of the Buddhist thousand petal lotus bursting into bloom and unfolding, petal by petal, at the center of my forehead. I had just spent a long day and night in vigil with my grieving daughter and had finally fallen asleep for a few hours, not enough, when the image abruptly awakened me. Until that morning, I had only a passing relationship with Buddhism. The image of the lotus meant little to me.

Suddenly, inexplicably, I had received a very personal image of the lotus. An understanding of what the Buddhist image means that came not from the head, but from the heart. In the fragile hush of that early morning, so easily and abruptly changed the minute the world startles awake, I wrote:

As I was lifting out of dreamtime this morning, groggy from a long night comforting a broken-hearted child, I had an image of the Buddhist thousand petal lotus. It burst out of my forehead as if that was its residing place. In a flash of inspiration, I completely understood that the Creator-Birther-Mystery that is God unfolds each one of us a single petal at a time, through a thousand layers of attachment, clinging to illusions, false constructs or wrong beliefs, negative self-talk, fears and human brokenness, and whatever else keeps us from the truth of who we really are . . . until we finally and inevitably fall toward the center of our own longing to be whole.

We have the choice to cooperate with that process by setting the ego out of the way and allowing the unfolding to proceed. Or we can actively resist the process, in which case we make it necessary for us to be broken open. And it is the breaking open that is often so filled with anguish.

Once we have touched the center of that longing, however, nothing can stop us from starting out on the journey to become whole. The God in us has awakened and wants nothing more than our attainment of the knowledge that we were created to be . . . as beautiful as the lotus, opened into a thousand petals and free of everything that binds us into a too-small self. The

Creator wants us to understand our own divine nature and will pursue us as ardently toward that end as we ourselves seek experience of the Sacred.

This understanding of how the Mystery unfolds us into our true nature is depicted in the Michelangelo painting where the finger of God extends its downward reach as far as possible to meet the human finger reaching upward toward God. In the fraction of an inch between the touch of fingertips we see the profound desire, the *longing*, between the human spirit and the *holy other* to know one another.

Some believe God wants to know us so intimately that God will do everything necessary to assure that connection. That concept presumes that God is a being, located outside of us, wanting to be let in. My personal experience is of God as *expanding consciousness*, with its locus inside us and inside everything that is alive, wanting to burst out, burst open, and expand. God is not a person. Not outside or inside, but in all places simultaneously, infusing all things with *awareness*.

God is the thousand petal lotus, unfolding the multiple layers of self-obfuscation that finally allow us to burst into being . . . and God is also the natural impulse of the flower to unfold. God is the active principle that initiates the *unfolding*, and God is the receptive principle of *being unfolded*. This process of the lotus petals opening takes place because it is the true nature of a lotus to bloom, just as it is the true nature of every human being to become what each of us is designed to be.

According to a friend who has lived for long periods of time in South America, there is a word used by the people of Brazil to describe a *yearning, longing kind of love*. Brazilians who live far from their native land use it to describe the heart's ache for its homeland. The word is *saudades*. This is an appropriate word to reflect the yearning-longing we contain for the blossoming of our own true nature, this petal by petal unfolding of True Self, in all of its complexity and magnificence.

The word *saudades* matches my understanding of the thousand petal lotus: a yearning ache in the soul to faithfully, courageously, often haltingly and hesitantly, reveal our essential nature. As our slumbering nature awakens, aroused by any number of ordinary or unusual events, something in the spirit of us begins to ache desperately to touch, to know, what has awakened us. To know the One that is, in most Western traditions, called *God*.

Many who are well indoctrinated by religious traditions envision God as external to us—a *being*, usually paternal, though sometimes maternal—and search for God *out there*. Since the mystery of God permeates every particle and cell of life, it's not hard to locate signs of *the holy other* in the glorious colors of a sunset, in the infinite variety and wonder of creation, in the coincidences or synchronicities that appear out of nowhere as holy surprises. God can be found in everything that is whirling, spinning, churning, birthing and dying in our fascinating and mysteriously contracting-expanding universe. The fundamental flaw in this is that we are only looking to find God outside ourselves.

If we stop the search at this point—which many people do—we miss the point of it all. God is also *within* each of us. *There is no place that God is not.* I learned this at the most fragile of times and in the most personal of experiences.

I was very ill, bleeding profusely, unable to rebound from a medical crisis that placed my doctors at the far reaches of their skills to help me. I was twenty-six years old, and it was less than a month after the birth of my first child. I had been hospitalized for two weeks with no relief from the hemorrhaging. I had been transfused repeatedly, endured numerous diagnostic tests, and had come to the point where I was emptied of any resilience. I was a professional in the medical field who believed in the power of allopathic medicine to heal. But it was not healing me. I'd become a medical conundrum.

One day, sitting in my hospital bed, frightened and alone, I closed my eyes and began to meditate upon the question: *Who really heals?* I had not lost faith in allopathic medicine, but I'd reached a conclusion that its capacity to heal was *limited.* In my difficult situation, even the best of medical attention wasn't working. I knew I needed to find another way to heal my body, but I had no idea what that might be. *Who really heals?* I turned that question upside down and inside out, looking at it from every perspective, reaching no answers. Having exhausted the limits of my knowledge, I fell asleep for several hours.

I have stories to tell that many people find difficult to believe, though all of them are true. This is one of those stories. I now know that, pondering my question with such profound yearning to be helped, I had invoked a response from . . . something that remains mysterious to this day, even as I write this story thirty years later.

When I woke from my exhausted sleep, my body simply healed itself. For over an hour of remarkable events, none of which I consciously controlled, my body underwent a dramatic transformation. The massive uterine tumor causing me to bleed until I had become so seriously ill . . . spontaneously aborted. I went into a form of labor—familiar to me since I had given birth five weeks before this event—until the tumor had been released from my body. I experienced what the doctors called a miracle.

Who healed me? What mysterious impulse was stirred from its latency when I finally sought an answer to the question: *Who really heals?* I had to give up all the training I received and the beliefs I had been taught to accept as true. I had been forced to acknowledge that there was nothing left to hold onto but a question. The question wasn't much, but it was as honest as I had ever been. *I truly did not know who or what could help or heal me.*

Neither did my physicians. What was asked of me was something I didn't even know existed at the time: *a surrender to the God within.* That surrender arrived on the heels of my desperation. I was seriously ill. To be well again, I had to immerse myself in the dark river of uncertainty or *not knowing.* The Buddhist spiritual teachings consider the condition of *not knowing* to be a high state of spiritual consciousness: the place where our prior beliefs or behaviors no longer work for us and new beliefs have not yet formed to take the place of the old. With nothing familiar to fall back on, there is an *opportunity* in the void to discover what's trying to unfold or be revealed in us.

Try to imagine the trapeze artist, hanging suspended for a few death-defying seconds between the trapeze bar she has just let go of and the bar that is waiting, on the other side of the void, to catch her. That is the place where the thousand petal lotus begins to awaken in us, to carry us to a next level of consciousness. Not many of us can tolerate swinging, vulnerable, in the uncertainty of those suspenseful moments.

I had no concept of this at the time. Looking back with the perspective of age, I can see how young and utterly vulnerable I was. Then, I knew only that I had to let go of everything that had ever informed me or sustained me in some degree of certainty about life. I had to be willing to drop to a place where I had nothing left for me to grasp, to cling to, to hold me safe and sure. I had nothing but the sense I was in free-fall . . . and the impulse, rooted in terror, to cry out: *Who really heals?*

This one moment changed all the others that were to follow Michael Dwinell, an Episcopal priest and spiritual director, frequently asks those he engages in the hard thinking required of us on the spiritual path: *What is God up to in this event?* I knew none of this as it happened, but, in that astonishing experience, my life was abruptly lifted from one trajectory and placed on another. I asked a haunting question that—once the question had been asked—I couldn't retract. That question opened a door to the Mystery. Some inexplicable intervention or force healed my exhausted and broken body. *I had to learn what that was.*

This eventful medical crisis was the catalyst for my beginning a spiritual search and a personal transformation toward a life of greater meaning and purpose. The most significant discovery in this process of change was that I had been living inside a too-small version of myself. There was a bigger life, a bigger world view, waiting for me on the far side of the void I had to cross.

It was time for the thousand petal lotus to open. Petal after petal of a new self unfolded in me. I began to teach others how to advocate for themselves inside the health care system. I helped initiate changes in the delivery of health care services. I challenged health care practices I had internalized on the way to becoming a highly skilled but compliant professional caregiver. I saw potential for prevailing models of health care *to change* in response to the needs of sick people and advocated for those changes. With prompting, doctors realized the significance of making health care decisions in collaboration or partnership with their patients. Patients did better when they felt empowered to participate in their own health care. I learned health care providers were more effective when we asked questions and listened to our patients' stories than when we held out answers.

I grew to understand each person has a vast well of healing wisdom inside him or her that, with encouragement, can be tapped for his or her own well-being. This is old news now, but, in 1973, as I was changing through the events of my own health crisis—as I was unfolding, petal by petal, to a much-expanded world of possibilities—this was an exciting discovery. My own health crisis positioned me squarely on the cutting edge of these changes.

As I began to live with the growing evidence of an unfolding, emerging *mystery*, my search repeatedly turned me *inward*, where the Mystery revealed itself as my source, my companion, my path, and finally, my destination. This process took years to accomplish and led to decisions that would break my heart, though they needed to be made. Time after time, I was stripped of anything that had ever promised me comfort and security. Myths, masks, roles fell away. I felt as if I was dying; no, I was *certain* I was dying. And, in fact, I was: a spiritual death rather than a physical one. My ego, the small self who had made such lovely plans for a safe and predictable life, had to release the bar of her trapeze and reach—*reach!*—for whatever would catch me on the other side.

What both propelled, and caught, me was the original and holy impulse in me to unfold, to become all parts of the spirit-being who volunteered or was sent to inhabit this life. This is the thousand petal lotus found within each of us. It's another image or name for God. Not the God of the heavens, not the Divine Puppeteer manipulating one string and then another to control the outcome of our lives, but the *life force* in all that lives and breathes, bursts into blossom, dies back, and blooms again.

Meister Eckhart, the 13th century Dominican preacher-mystic who wrote so movingly of the God-Force unfolding within us, once penned these thoughts:

Now consider this: God is in everything, but
God is nowhere as much as in the soul.
There,
where time never enters,
where no image shines in,
in the innermost and deepest aspect of the soul
God creates the whole cosmos.

Our lives, our bodies, are verdant fields of potentiality where the Mystery plays and where the Mystery incarnates. We are implanted with the holy seed. We are the fertile soil in which the seed germinates, throws down its thread-like roots, throws up the first sweetly-scented shoots of green, grows tall and strong, produces its buds, and then opens, at last, into bloom.

Each one of us is a thousand petal lotus, emerging one petal at a time into our true nature.

Just imagine how different the world might be if we lived as if we believed that about ourselves. If—when we looked at another—we saw the thousand petal lotus bursting into bloom from the center of that person's being. If we held out our hearts in reverent acknowledgment of the Mystery who stands before us in the form of that person.

How different our world might be.

ℭ

- Are you where you are asked by Spirit, or by the Mystery, to be? Are you on your heart's path?

- Are you aligned with the tasks your soul has agreed to undertake? Are you willing to follow the little scraps of paper that fall on your path when the Mystery intervenes in your life, even if it means you are directed to pursue a path you did not expect to follow? How has the Mystery bloomed or emerged within you to place you on this path? What events led you here?

• Write a letter to yourself about your life path. Write *as if* you know where you are coming from and where you are going. Are there are holy surprises? What are you learning about your deep longing?

• In what ways does your walking this path, consciously and intentionally, contribute to a greater good?

Anna

A human comes to life as a child:
excited, curious, trusting;
aided by her own will
and commitment from her family,
she retains these qualities her entire life.

—Grandmother Kitty

Sukie Curtis is a friend of mine, who also happens to be an Episcopal priest at Saint Bart's Church in Yarmouth, Maine. She is the life partner of David Heald, also a priest, and the mother of Anna, seven at the time of this event, and Becca, who was ten. Sukie's family lives in a house so cramped that, as Sukie tells the story, "A person can be in one room and have a perfectly audible conversation with a family member in any other room." This particular day, Anna was in the bathroom and Sukie was in her bedroom, writing in her journal. Sukie heard Anna let out a big, tremulous sigh. Then she heard her say: "Oh! I'll never be able to do it!"

Sukie called out: "Never be able to do what, Anna?"

Anna, with more than a few heartfelt sighs, possibly a little over dramatized, as a seven-year-old can do so effectively, replied: "I'll never be able to change the world!"

Sukie called Anna into the bedroom and asked what it was about the world she'd like to change. Anna thought about that question for a while and then answered: "Well, I could start by saving the animals' habitats." Her mother explained that Anna could— if she wanted—grow up to be a naturalist, a scientist, or an animal behaviorist, any of which would make a positive difference in the lives of earth's creatures. As they were having this conversation, Sukie was noting Anna's comments in her journal so Anna could return to the memory of a time when it was important to her to make a change toward a better world. She wasn't sure why it seemed important to record the conversation; she was acting more on intuition than reasoning. But, as Anna opened her heart and talked freely about her hopes and dreams, her mother faithfully recorded them.

Not long after that conversation, as she was repeating Anna's longing to me, Sukie was struck with a memory of her own. There had been a time when she was in college, and she too had been filled with an energy and eagerness to make a positive difference in the world. She had all the innocence of youth with none of the disappointment-in-life that can develop as we discover how deeply entrenched human beliefs and dysfunctional behaviors really are.

During this time in her own life, Sukie was at a family gathering where she heard her mother reporting to an aunt: "That Sukie! You know, she just wants to change the world. She has so much to learn!" She remembered her heart crumbling as she heard her mother dismiss her big dreams as unattainable. How little it takes for someone, even someone well-meaning, to dismiss our dreams, or steal them from us. Perhaps we should all hold this in the front of our awareness: *it is never our right, or responsibility, to determine how big or how valuable another person's life is intended to be.* If we take authority onto ourselves to decide this for someone else, especially a child of our hearts, we risk inflicting injury to that individual's spirit that may take years for them to heal. Everyone has the right to determine for herself or for himself how big or small those dreams must be.

This world needs all the big dreamers we can foster. We need all the positive change we can possibly create. We live in challenging times, when the natural human tendency is to be fearful, to contract, and to prepare for the worst. It could be our collective failure to listen to the big dreamers in our midst, and to the wisdom of our children, that brings us to this precipice at all.

It takes so little, just a few minutes, to affirm the dreams of a child. Those affirmations help to validate a child's dreams and to keep them alive in her spirit until she is old enough, and experienced enough at life, to recognize her own divine blueprint . . . and to know how and when she might be called on to make her particular difference. How much better to tell our children the long-ago story of the Native American child whose mother, instructing him in the way to become wise, promised that the Creator would drop little slips of paper—his instructions—upon his path.

How much better it would be to borrow this profound truth from the Welsh poet David Whyte: that our task is to encourage, teach, nurture our children toward "*the one life that waits beyond all the others.*" Anna, like her mother before her, is looking for hers.

In each child born of the human family, regardless of age or any other defining characteristic of life, there's an inner compass.

This compass directs us to the one life that waits for us to claim it. And it will "wait for us beyond all others," as long as we teach ourselves, and teach our children, to recognize and call upon that internal locus or point of reference. It is the equivalent of the road map of the inner life.

Once we locate this compass, oftentimes after digging for years through layer after layer of lies and distortions, we are on the road home to our true selves. And when we are on the road home, we have become living embodiments of the Sacred Mystery. We become who we've each been created to be: one small but essential participant in a great mystery that is still revealing itself to and through us.

Anna's inner compass is pointing directly toward her future. Her mother is alert and wise enough to know this and to take copious notes. When Anna grows up and is ready to piece together the "little slips of paper" that will guide her in the direction of her original blueprint, those notes will be waiting for her.

𝄞

- Name the people who have encouraged you to follow your true nature and to become the person you were uniquely designed to be. What did they see, and support or encourage, in you?

- With whom have you carried this on? Who are the ones you have encouraged to become all they are meant to be? How have you done this?

- In what ways do you believe that God is present and alive in encounters like these? Stretch yourself beyond the usual thinking that God is the one at work behind the scenes. Try to imagine that God is present in the activity of the encounter rather than the force that creates it. Can you comprehend the possibility that the Mystery is *encountering*

its own divinity when the mother listens for the truth in the
heart of her child?

- Take time to remember yourself at the age of seven, longing
  to *become*, not a something, but *your true self.* Consider this
  thoughtfully. What is "the one life that waits for you beyond
  all the others?"

No holding back

When you look in the eyes of another,
any other, and you see your own soul
looking back at you, then you will know
you have reached another level of consciousness.

—Brian Weiss

As you know from many of my stories, children have been among my most important spiritual teachers. I've told you about the haunting voice of a child calling out to me in the middle of the night. Hours later, that child was standing in my driveway, looking at me through the eyes of anguish. The fear, loneliness, and deep longing to be loved that I saw in that child's face will stay with me, perhaps forever. That boy's story is alive in each of us. I remember myself at about the same age, a time when my family was not a safe or a loving place to be, much less to be a child. That child's face was my face too.

Since then, two more children have appeared to serve as teachers. Shelby and Jillian are both seven years old. They live in different parts of the Northeast and almost surely will never meet each other, although if they did, I am certain each of them would find a kindred spirit in the other. They are both bright, beautiful children with great hearts and lively imaginations. The world has not reached so far into their spirits that it has tampered with the natural wisdom flowing in each of them. I hope it never will.

Shelby is the sister of McKenzie and Colby, the daughter of Honey and Dave, the granddaughter of Bob and Ann. I was the lucky witness to a precious scene between Shelby and her Grandpa, late one night just before Shelby, then five, was to start school for the first time. Her Grandpa was stretched out on the living room floor, with Shelby resting on top of him so that her whole body stretched against his, her head resting on his soft belly. Her arms hung loose at her sides. She was the picture of innocence and trust.

"Tell me a story, Grandpa," she insisted, and her grandfather wound his way, quite adeptly, through *Ferdinand the Bull*, *Snow White and the Seven Dwarfs*, and *Cinderella*. Shelby's eyes grew weighty with sleep and she started to drop off, but, just as she hit that delicate margin between waking and sleeping, she would snap back for more of Grandpa's stories. Midway through one of them, her Grandpa paused momentarily, catching his breath, trying to remember the way the story played out. Shelby released a long, sleepy, utterly contented sigh. "I love my Grandpa," she said to no one in particular.

Jillian is my niece, the daughter of my sister Beth and her husband John. Matthew is her older brother. You may remember the story of Jillian and her new Christmas doll, Katie Rebecca. Katie Rebecca is not a doll but Jillian's "little sister" and her best friend. In the months since I wrote of Jilli's relationship with Katie Rebecca—emphasis on *real person*—she has been besieged by other children who insist on making it clear to Jilli that Katie Rebecca is, really and truly, *just a doll.*

So far, Jilli has refused to surrender her experience. Katie Rebecca is alive to Jilli, as my mother's dolls were alive to her, as my dolls were once alive to me, my sister's were alive to her, my daughter's were alive to her. It's a time-honored tradition among the females in our family (as well as some of the now-grown boys) that dolls are alive . . . thus, real people. Their feelings are easily injured if other people don't know this about them. This is something everyone in the world is just supposed to know. I understand Jillian's frustration when other children don't comprehend such a simple fact of life.

But many children didn't seem to know this, and it was wearing on Jilli. She had heard enough from her friends about Katie Rebecca's status as a doll. One day, she sat her mother down and patiently began to explain what she had been thinking: if other children didn't understand Katie Rebecca was real, and only she could see that this was true, maybe it would be better if she gave Katie Rebecca away to someone else. Maybe it would not be so difficult for Katie Rebecca to belong to a little girl who thought of her only as a doll.

Beth listened to Jillian in a state of quiet anguish. When she told me about this later, she was still aching for her daughter. "What's happening to our children," she asked me, "if they have forgotten the power of imagination? Isn't that what they're supposed to be doing at five? Aren't they supposed to still believe in magic?"

I had no answer for my sister. We all value Jillian's unique and delicious belief in the world of wonder and awe, and my sister wants to do everything she can to preserve it for as long as possible. She explained to Jillian that she had been gifted with a lovely ability to see beyond the small world that most people see—to see with the eyes of her imagination—and that was something to celebrate rather than regret. Jillian listened carefully and agreed with her mother. Fortunately for Katie Rebecca, she will stay where she is.

Shelby and Jillian know how to love without reservation. They love Grandpa and Katie Rebecca *and life* with no holding back. There is a purity, an innocence, in their ability to love that ought to be instructing us all: the adults who forget to love like this, to live like this, to see the wonder and awe that is all about us, to marvel in the magic of a bedtime story or a special doll who has come alive. Children like Jillian and Shelby approach life straight from the heart. They become a profound mirror to us about our jaded, compromised, and world-weary approaches to life. When we have forgotten to look for the Mystery in its myriad of manifestations, children like Jillian and Shelby show us what we neglect to see and remind us to look at life from hearts that don't hold back.

Burrowed deep inside you and me, there is still a spirit of trust and love, an ability to live straight from the heart, a sense of awe and magic that, at one time, infused our first encounters with the world. We may have buried it deep in a subterranean self, but we have not lost it. It isn't *losable*. It's a significant part of the divine blueprint upon which each of us is fashioned and therefore, it's impossible to lose. And yet many of us spend days, months, and even years we can never regain . . . *holding back* our full vitality, our full truth, our true heart's longing.

How we approach life is—at every moment, for every one of us—a choice. We can approach it open to life's wonders and mysteries and surprises, not all of which we will like but all of which we are certain to learn from, or we can approach life armored and holding back our love and trust. I recently met with a friend whose husband died unexpectedly just before Thanksgiving, after a too short but very great affair of the heart with his wife. She is trying to comprehend the enormity of her loss, and how the Mystery is at work in her husband's early death. When she approached her minister for answers to her questions, his responses struck her as stale, shallow, hollow. She could tell from the emptiness of his answers that he had never allowed himself to meet death on its own holy ground, or to dance with death in the dark of the night. He had never grappled, or come to terms, with his own questions. She thought it possible that he'd never asked them.

As she sat with me, examining the questions again, she was mining for more than a formulaic response to what is surely not comprehensible. She asked, "What are people so afraid of that they can't say life, and God, is a mystery? That we have no answers to suffering. All we know is that we are given chances to meet life with an open, or a closed, heart. We choose which it will be." She didn't leave much for me to say. She had said it all herself. *We choose which it will be.*

All of us have to make this important decision. Will we meet life with an open heart . . . or closed? Will we meet life as a person who holds back, or as one who holds ourselves out to life? *Come and get me. I'm yours. Show me everything you've got for me.* As you make this decision for yourself—and life will give you ample opportunity to visit and re-visit this choice— think about Jillian and her doll, or Shelby and her Grandpa. The smallest of our teachers, untouched by the hardships and evils of the world, are able to love *extravagantly.*

Each one of us will some day have to account for the state of our hearts. Chose carefully. Listen to the wisdom of our children. *Hold nothing back.*

♌

- Name five people who come to mind as examples of extravagant love. These may be people you've known, or perhaps they are figures from some other time in human history. What have you learned from these people that shows you how to live, and love, with *no holding back?*

- Are you holding some part of you back: from yourself, from others, from life, from God? What have you gained from doing this? What would be the cost to you of encountering the Mystery with your heart wide open? And what would be the gift?

Sitting shiva

There is an energy, a life force,
a vitality in you that is unique and
will never be repeated in all of time.
If you do not use it, the world will not
have it, and it will be lost forever.

—Martha Graham

I have a new friend who might be an angel. I'm not exactly sure this is the right word to describe him, but I assure you I'm not using the term lightly. He is tall, graceful, elegant, and wears a heart on his sleeve that is deeply good and beautiful. Four years ago, he hovered close to death as the result of an allergic reaction to vaccines he'd been given in preparation for a photojournalism assignment in Africa. He was being sent there to photograph the "boy soldiers" conscripted into rebel armies, prisoners themselves in a violent civil war.

My friend never reached his destination. Instead, he spent four life-altering days in a coma in a London hospital, as his spirit floated on the ceiling, discussing the fate of his body with the invisible ones. *Would the young man on the bed live, or would he die?* When he finally woke from the coma—clearly alive— and returned to the life he had been living, he was not the same person. It seemed to him that someone else arrived to inhabit the body that was once his. I met him one year after this event tossed his old life into chaos and doubt; he was not finished with his need to make sense of what had happened to him.

While still hospitalized, he had a number of extraordinary encounters with other patients that helped them to heal from their illnesses or wounds. For a time after he awakened from the coma, it seemed certain the angelic worlds were speaking, acting, through him. He said things to others that he did not understand himself. His encounters with people took place at a level of truth he had never experienced. Something of a mysterious, puzzling, indescribable nature was at work in him.

He found he could no longer continue the photojournalism work he had been doing, at least the part of his work having to do with photographing violence. He couldn't hang out with the people he had called his friends because they had no patience with his changes. For a time, he had no work, no visible means of support. His relationship with a woman he thought he would marry came to an end; his suffering about that was prolonged. His life had, quite mysteriously, been claimed for a purpose that he still struggles to understand. There are days when it is all he can do to take the next step. Whatever happened to him in that comatose state—he is still seeking to understand it—he was touched by an encounter with Mystery that slipped, almost insidiously, into and across all parts of his life.

In indigenous cultures, this would be considered a shamanic initiation into the world of spirit. In Western culture, we have no name for this experience, no understanding of the power of mystery that pursued him to the point of no return. He was no longer living the life he had created, but a life that had been created for him . . . and he had few instructions for living it. He was, I think he would admit, floundering in unknown terrain.

He knew he could grow into that life only with the assistance of others who had been carried beyond the veil that separates the world of matter from the world of spirit . . . and returned, as he did, irrevocably and profoundly changed by the encounter. He was in need of kindred spirits to help in his struggle to understand what force had seized his life, and for what purpose.

I met him early in a summer when he sat next to me at a spiritual retreat. You know how it sometimes is: you look over at a new face in a group of strangers, and, surprisingly, you're looking at someone you have been waiting to know all your life. Or you see the face of someone who is oddly familiar, though it is almost sure you have never met. I knew him, and he knew me. We had a strong and immediate sense of *knowing each other*. It was that simple. Before we left the retreat center and returned to our separate lives, he had asked me to serve as a guide through the dense internal wilderness as his old life fell away and his new life struggled to be born.

I've had my own inexplicable plunges into worlds other than the one where we live and breathe and take our meaning. I have had difficulties integrating these experiences into the life I returned to inhabit. We talked about these experiences around the edges of the retreat, and even in the retreat itself. I agreed to companion him through some of his questions and changes, although as time goes on, I discover the gift in his invitation was really intended to be for me.

I don't hear from him often, but when I do, I hear straight from his heart. There's no artifice in him at all. There's no holding back of his questions, confusion, love, and appreciation of the people who stand patiently by as he traverses an unmapped territory. Everything that's happened to transform his life—in ways he has resisted and in ways he is struggling to accept—is completely and wonderfully *visible* on his face and in his heart. Whatever the reason, or for however long we are meant to benefit from the other's companionship, we've been given a rare opportunity to see the shining beauty in one another's souls, laid bare and vulnerable.

It is a rare gift to participate in the revelation of another's beautiful soul. We rarely come out of hiding to see and be seen. Most of us are too afraid to let our true light be seen and known by another. We turn away from that light in ourselves, and in each other, for the simple though profound reason that *we are sorely afraid of being diminished by those who haven't the eyes to see who we really are.* It's such a risk to peer out at the world, hoping against hope that someone will notice who we are, and afraid that no one will.

When I was young, I vividly remember my great longing for an encounter I couldn't even name. The closest I was able to come, and this took many years to articulate, was that I was searching for "my people." Many times, in moments of terrible spiritual loneliness, I called out to the Mystery: *Please, where are my people?* On the joyous occasions when I would catch a glimpse of a familiar shining spirit, my heart would leap in recognition. But all too often—I have done this repeatedly myself—that person would quickly retreat. The beautiful light I saw streaming from him or her would dim. As the biblical texts say to us, that individual shining soul would hide her light "under a bushel" . . . and my young girl's heart would break.

Once again—very recently—I witnessed this phenomenon. For a few brief days, the light shone in one beautiful soul, and then ... her hasty retreat. I was flooded with profound sadness at how difficult it is for me, for any of us, to allow our lights shine before others, and before God. I have watched the light flicker so many

times, in so many ways. Good people with magnificent gifts to
offer, would retreat into one form or another of unconsciousness:
into addictions that numbed or dumbed them, into behaviors that
overtly diminished or sabotaged their innate beauty and
goodness; into decisions to remain stuck when they had the
chance to grow. For me, there is no worse sorrow than being
forced to witness this diminishment, or dimming, of the inborn
light.

In unbearable sorrow at once again watching the approach-
avoidance tactic we all play with our souls, I wept with a friend
who has served as my spiritual director. He said to me: "Your
grief is an honorable one. The Creator, the Mystery, grieves with
us whenever any one of us shuts down our light. Tonight I want
you to go home, wrap your prayer shawl around you, and sit
shiva for all the beautiful souls you've loved who have abdicated
their beauty or divinity in favor of their ordinariness." Sitting
shiva is the lovely Jewish custom, following the death of a loved
one, in which family members spend the next week intentionally
honoring the life and the loss of that person.

When I count heads on this issue, I consider almost everyone I
have ever loved. I certainly count myself, as I recall times when
it was simply too painful to hold the light in situations where
others could not see I strongly believe the divine mandate of
every spiritual sojourner is *to turn into the light shining in each
of our souls, rather than away from it.* I suspect we allow the
light to pour from our hearts only when we have found "our
people" . . . rare and cherished individuals who recognize, affirm,
and value our authentic selves, and who show us theirs. As we
find one person—better, of course, a community of persons—
who welcome, affirm and celebrate us, we are liberated from the
long darkness of our hiding and loneliness.

So along comes a lovely man, perhaps an angel, who has no
hesitation in asking to be seen and known in both his beauty

and his confusion. He is willing to say: *Someone or something took my life and threw it all in the air. I no longer know who I am. I only know that I have talked with the Mystery. That I was sent back to this world for further service. None of that makes sense to me. I have no idea about what to do with this experience, but I know I need others in my life who see, who trust, and who believe in my light.*

There is a child-like innocence or naiveté in his asking. Certainly, there is a great gift in being given the chance to look carefully into his spirit and to respond affirmatively: *Yes, I see you. Yes, I recognize your beauty. Yes, I will tell you what I see until you can see it for yourself.* Who am I to turn away from the sacred opportunity to support another soul in his manifestation of light?

Through our exchanges, I am coming to know the gift is more for me than for him. I am slowly, quietly learning to see through the eyes of the Beloved. I'm learning that the unutterable grief I feel whenever a person I care about refuses, or denies, his or her light is only a small measure of the unutterable grief the Creator of Life experiences whenever any of us, including me, abdicates the truth of our inborn divinity. I am discovering I can see this inborn light more easily in others than I can see it in myself. I gratefully accept them as the mirrors of my forgetfulness in those times I cannot remember the life I'm meant to inhabit.

It's a stretch to consider the possibility that we are more afraid of this inborn divine nature than we are of our weaknesses or our character flaws . . . but it is more than likely true. What audacity to receive the gifts of the Mystery, placed inside us, and then deny them! Psychologist Abraham Maslow, identifying this human phenomena, called it "the Jonah Complex." Simply stated, out of fear that someone will see the true light shining, radiating, from us . . . we place that light far from sight.

I went home from my conversation with Michael that day, and I sat shiva. I lit candles throughout my house, shut out all the lights until I sat in total darkness, and wrapped my prayer shawl around me. Then I wept as my heart cracked open and rivers of grief poured from me. I wept for myself, but also for times I've watched dear-hearted people abandon themselves and retreat into unconsciousness. I wept for all of humanity. For the gifts we've been given by the Mystery and refuse to honor by embodying them. For the times our fear overpowers our love. For the courageous souls who have cast their light widely into the world when everyone around mocked or tortured them. For all the children who are newly arrived from the Source of All Light and wait to be welcomed by "their people."

I wept for a long time. When I was done, I folded my shawl, blew out the candles, thanked the spirits who accompanied me through the grief, and resumed my everyday life.

Soon, my friend will come again. We'll talk about what it's like to walk in this world and not be overtaken by it. We'll teach each other what we are learning about how ordinary people, living ordinary lives, can allow the Mystery to wash through them for a greater purpose, and still maintain two feet on the ground and keep the mortgage paid. In little circles of two and three people, we will help each other make room in our hearts for the light of God, which is using us as the medium through which that light may permeate the world. Though we may never understand why, we are called to be bearers of the light. We are here to hold the lamp high for one another so that all might find the way safely home.

I believe we're all searching, some of us certainly more consciously than others, for the people who will see in us both our beauty and our confusion. For those who will stand patiently by us, in love, while we emerge from our cramped hiding places into the full light we have been given to shine. All of us hover in different forms of "coma" while we decide whether we'll participate in our own lives or retreat from them, and all who love us.

This is no easy decision, and the Mystery that is God often takes extraordinary measures to call us into that destiny. My friend, who discovered the full range of God's *extraordinary measures*, would tell you this is true.

It is a moving experience to sit shiva for anyone—including myself—who has given up or withdrawn into ordinariness. It is even more moving to open our hearts and greet the light another person dares, *dares,* to show us. It is the most moving experience of all to uncover our own true light and allow it to illuminate the path for others. On the day that even one of us chooses not to shrink back from all we are created to be—a light to the world—the whole of Creation reverberates with joy.

Step by tentative step, one person at a time, we begin to understand what my friend came to know as he approached death and then returned to life: our lives are not totally our own. Our lives belong to the Mystery. Simply in being here, each of us has a purpose to fulfill. We are asked, never told, to embody the gifts that are given to us. We are asked to know that no one else in all of time is incarnated for our particular purpose or to hold the lamp of our particular shining light.

When I stumble into forgetfulness, as I often do, what helps me recover my balance are the words of Martha Graham: "There is an energy, a life force, a vitality in you that is unique, and will never be repeated in all of time. If you do not use it, the world will not have it . . . and it will be lost forever."

This is a significant charge, and I receive it seriously, humbly, joyfully. No matter how dark the day, no matter how confused my spirit, no matter how much I wish to retreat, when I remember these words, I can pick myself up and go on. When I remember that my life is not just about me, but also about *what must come through me for others*, I reach for as much light as I am able to allow through me at the time. And I go about the only work that counts: *being a lamp unto the world.*

It is an imperfect process, and I am an imperfect person. There are many days or weeks when I fail miserably at this effort. But I try, every day. And you try too. Together, we hold a little more light here, and a little more light there . . . and the world seems less dark.

Years ago, I had a dream in which I was standing on a city street at the base of a great mountain. One at a time, people came from their homes, holding their lanterns, to climb the mountain. In small groups at first, then in the hundreds, finally in the hundreds of millions, the people came bearing lanterns. Soon the mountainside was ablaze with lights held high. Hundreds of millions of lanterns, illuminating the dark night: a sight to awaken the spirit of awe in even the hardest of hearts. This is the mandate given to the people of earth. It is a deeply personal spiritual mandate, and, just as important, a collective one.

If we light one lamp at a time, and hold it high for all to see, we encourage others to bring their lamps out of the secret places where they have been hidden for too long. One day, we can hope, this beautiful dream will become a common reality. First, one person holds the lantern high. And in time, millions of others will lift their lamps for all in the world to see.

$$\mathcal{J}$$

- Have you ever had an experience that took you totally out of your ordinary self and showed you the full radiance of your divine nature? Perhaps it lasted seconds, maybe days. For what purpose do you believe this experience was offered to you?

- What are the means you use to abandon or abdicate the gifts that are secreted inside you? How do you hide those gifts from the world? If you consider that these gifts "will never be repeated in all of time," how does this change your decision, conscious or unconscious, to abdicate the gifts you have been given?

- Imagine that you, using instead of abandoning your divine gifts, could change the course of just one other person's life. Imagine that each of us, using our gifts, has that potential. Imagine the intricate web of interconnected threads that weaves our individual lives into a vast tapestry of wholeness. Do you see the possibility that your hidden gifts could make a significant difference in the greater whole?

Say yes

Whatever you become, my child,
may it be rooted in grace.
Whatever your path through life,
may it offer you steepness and rough places,
so that you do not become complacent.
Nothing is owed to you,
but everything is available to you.

—Nancy Wood

There comes a point where we must say *yes* or *no* to the active presence of Mystery in our lives. The spiritual principle we know as *free will* gives us considerable room, as well as time and opportunity, to figure out if we truly desire to grow closer in relationship to the Sacred or to make a graceful retreat. Ram Dass, a professor at Harvard before he became a dedicated seeker, is fond of saying: "There's a difference between wanting God, and wanting to want God."

At some point on the spiritual journey, each of us has to

determine which relationship we're looking to have. The Mystery, on the other hand, is always longing for us. We are ardently courted and pursued by a presence or a consciousness—sometimes referred to as the God of Many Names—that seeks experiences of *intimate connection and deep relationship* with us. It is through these experiences of *holy connection* that we expand, that which we call God expands, and the entire universe expands in the direction of its true nature. But, in the end, the choice for intimacy with God is ours alone to make. In the quiet corners of our hearts, sometimes in joy or perhaps out of desperation, we either allow the Mystery to enter or we turn away. We open the door when the knock is heard, or we simply neglect to answer the knock.

I suspect we are given many opportunities to rise out of our unconsciousness (or our spiritual malaise) to answer the call at the door. If we miss one chance, we are given another, and another, and still another. The call becomes more insistent, more urgent . . . but at some point, unanswered, the angel at the door simply stops knocking and waits for us to realize the guest we ignore is the holy one who resides at the center of our own soul.

This is the story of a winter's night in March of 1999. It had been an ordinary day except for a Lenten meditation service scheduled at church that night. For reasons that were equal parts choice and fate, I hadn't gone to church in weeks. But this day I felt an inner insistence that I go back. The winter had been fierce, one of those that drives me into a comfortable hibernation. I wasn't looking forward to the prospect of going outside into the raw, dark, biting cold of an early March evening.

I had also scheduled a telephone appointment with a client in crisis for later that evening. I was afraid that I would forget to call him if I went to church. Torn with uncertainty and anxiety over what to do, I left notes in a hundred places around the house to remind me to do both.

I entered the sanctuary of the church later that evening with every muscle tightened to guard my body from the draining cold. I hurt everywhere. As I stepped through the door, cold and tired, I caught my breath at the beauty of the sanctuary lit by hundreds of candles, placed randomly to illumine the way. The strains of symphonic music filled the air. Ellie was the only person there. She has such a talent for creating beautiful sacred space. This raw and bitter night, I felt warmly embraced by her gifts of *spiritual hospitality*. I hugged her, but neither of us spoke. We sat in the silence of the sanctuary, holding the energy of a prayer-filled space as a few other brave people arrived.

Peter entered the room. He and Ellie co-pastored this old New England Congregational church. It was his evening to lead the Lenten service. I noticed his attention ricochet around the sanctuary in the few moments it took for him to be caught up in the felt experience of sacred space. Then he too dropped down into the strong presence of *silence*. Everything was still. I drew breath and released the worries of a long day. The few people gathered sat in silence for a long time. Then Peter's gentle voice began to lead us into meditation. His words guided us to find ourselves in a house—real or imagined—that had special meaning for us.

I returned to a house I had visited in a dream the previous week. In that recent dream, I was traveling with many others when we reached a wide river that could only be crossed if one knew how to activate an unusual, retractable bridge that connected one side of the river to the other. I was the only person who knew where to find the secret switch to start the mechanism that would retract the bridge. I quickly swung the bridge into place for many people to cross. When we finally arrived at our destination—a huge mansion on the top of a hill—I was startled to realize I had come too soon. After I made the journey, it was not yet time for me to be there. Regretfully, I left my traveling companions and turned around for the trip back into my familiar world.

Peter's meditation took me immediately back to the mansion on the hill. His words directed me to enter the imaginary house by the front door, but that was not my way. I was amused at my own contrariness. I briefly considered entering the front door, but instead went to the right side of the building and found a window that could be opened easily. I rolled and tucked my body to tumble through an open window into the grand ballroom. This room was empty of everything but shards of bright sparkling color refracting from thousands of miniature crystals hanging from the ceiling chandeliers. In this room of refracted light, I danced my prayers of praise to the Creator.

Peter's words guided us on to another room, a room he called "the room of confession." I found my way to a tiny, warm, comfortable library where I offered my private prayers of confession. In the meditation, my everyday worries were rapidly slipping away. Grateful for time to personally reflect, I thought how important it was for me to sacralize my everyday life. This was something I lost far too quickly in the daily demands of a busy schedule.

Peter's next instructions led us to "the room of our beloveds." I was now in a children's' nursery, with an altar at the center of the room. One at a time, I lifted my children, my ailing mother, my dearest friends, many of my struggling clients, and placed them on the altar. I was overwhelmed with appreciation and love for each person. I noticed the uniqueness of each individual as I lifted him or her onto the small altar and prayed for that one's well-being. I felt this prayer emerging from deep within my heart. "Oh Mother of Life," my heart called out, "These are my beloveds. Please take them into your care. Fill them with your light. They are your children, and each one is so beautiful." By this time, the ordinary world had fallen away. I'd entered a deeply *internal* sacred space.

Peter's final words guided us to a "room of discipleship." This room was large, lovely, totally empty but for me. Here, I said

the same words I use in my personal prayers: "Oh, Mysterious
One, here I am. I belong only to you. Use me to the highest good
of all sentient beings. Let my life make a difference to those in
need." As I prayed this everyday prayer, I became aware of a
pulsing sensation located in the sanctuary, external to me, above
me, not far from where I was sitting.

I felt a sense of throbbing like an enormous heartbeat, no sound,
but a whooshing pulsation I could palpably feel. This energy was
alive; I felt it as clearly as I would sense the presence of a person
approaching me. It was huge: perhaps twelve to fifteen feet high
and six feet in diameter, and descending into the room where I
sat meditating. I'm a person who *senses* or *knows* rather than
sees or *hears*. I *knew* this was an enormous column of living
light, pulsing in gentle waves of energy. My skin tingled slightly,
as it does when I smell a storm in the air or lightening is about
to strike.

I knew immediately what descended. In the first seconds I was
aware of its presence, I almost laughed to think: "Well, well,
here comes an angel." I realized Peter would be more comfortable
with the term "the living Christ." One thought quickly followed
the next, in succession, until I decided that the words I used didn't
matter to this presence. It didn't need to be named. It simply
was what it was. It's our human need to name such a presence,
even though our words are often limited and limiting. They don't
begin to speak of its grandeur.

The pillar moved through the sanctuary, approaching slowly, until
it came to settle gently above me, then to descend upon me.
Nothing was actually spoken but I heard or sensed the words,
"Be not afraid. I come before you always. Come, follow me." I
understood how easy it must have been for the fisherman to lower
their nets, pull their boats to shore, and leave their lives with no
backward glance to follow the carpenter from Nazareth. I was
completely, deliriously, helpless to refuse its approach.

The pillar descended until it completely surrounded me, and then began to pour its contents into me. I was a cup, filled to overflowing. I was a dry riverbed, and the rains fell on me and swelled the banks of my being. My resistance rose up, momentarily ferocious. I wasn't sure that I could tolerate the pleasure of this experience. I considered pushing it away. I was aware I could do that, and the pillar of light would simply rise again and drift away. No offense taken. I hesitated, then decided to accept the light. *I said yes*. Knowing full well that this choice would change my life, I said "Yes!"

The Light poured into my heart, swelling me with a love more profound than anything I've ever known. Wave after wave of love poured into my heart and spilled out into the sanctuary. I was filled with a passion for God. The Mystery overflowed my pores, streaming out onto the floor and into every crevice of the room. I was completely, totally, overtaken by this presence. Having said yes, there was no stopping this. Wave after wave, the presence flooded me with an ecstasy making me want to cry out or explode in sounds or "tongues." I was afraid. My spiritual life has always been a very private relationship with the Mystery of Mysteries. I was frightened I might call attention to myself or to what was happening.

At some point, I asked the question, "Who shall I tell them you are?" And the answer I heard in return was brief, *"You may tell them I am a Pillar of Light."*

The part of me that remained an observer of this mysterious visitation calmed me. I commanded myself not to cry out or to alarm others. After several minutes, I felt a soft explosion through my heart, like an orgasm that claimed my whole being, and then stopped.

I was literally vibrating, thrumming, with the energy that had infused me. I thought of Theresa of Avila, the 15th century

Christian mystic, and understood what she meant as she wrote about her experiences of "infused recollection." I thought of Father Thomas Keating, abbot of a modern contemplative order, who speaks of the "mystical union" with God. I felt a cord connecting me, through a long lineage, to the mystics throughout the ages. I was an ordinary person experiencing an extraordinary, mystical episode.

I was engaged in a living encounter with the One Light many people call "God." The experience was the whole point of it all. The alpha and the omega of the journey. The reason for the journey itself, and the journey's destination. The experience of this Presence transformed me.

I completely understood the words: "I am that I am." There was no name. There was no bearded old man, sitting in judgment over the heavens. There was just Is-ness. A tsunami of presence and consciousness. I recalled Job, despairing on the ash heap, wanting things to be different until the moment God revealed a holy face to him. Overwhelmed by the face, or appearance, of the Living Mystery, Job stammered: *Forgive my little mind. Now I understand what you are. In the mystery of your presence, I am transformed.*

I left the sanctuary that night without speaking to anyone. I had experienced something *extra-ordinary,* something outside the ordinary reality that we assume is all life has to offer. It called for me to stay silent, and for time to help me absorb and assimilate the experience. If we don't stop to honor to the Mystery at the very moment it's presented to us, we lose something of its inexplicable worth.

Months later, after struggling to come to terms with this experience, I shared the story with my spiritual director. He referred to this as a process of *ensoulment.* In these mysterious experiences of grace, he suggested, we come to the awareness that *God Simply Is*. There is no person, no gender, no form, not even a name to God. Just a pulsing, vibrating *Is-ness*, permeating every cell of *me-ness* or *you-ness* without obscuring or obliterating a single dimension of our uniqueness.

The *Is-ness* pursues every one of us until we remember who we are. Its very nature is to infuse us with recollection-energy-aliveness-love until we finally remember. This is just one way the Mystery follows us until we turn toward it, agreeing to be in ever-deepening relationship with it. There are many other ways. Michael said he has wondered if Jesus' last words might have been translated: *Father, forgive them, for they have forgotten who they are.*

A long time later, when I finally wrote about this experience—which I had been reluctant to do for fear words would trivialize it—I remembered something about myself that is significant. *I only learn what is true by experiencing it with my body.* The words of religious texts are like a foreign language to me, devoid of meaning, until I experience what the words talk about directly in my physical body. *Words assume truth and meaning only when I have had direct, embodied experience that those words can be trusted.* As I experience sacred reality through the medium of my body, I finally understand that *it is*.

This was true when I was young and very ill, almost dying, and cried out for healing. *Who really heals?* I asked. And I was shown, through my body, the mysterious power of God to heal what my physicians could not. My life was changed forever, directed to an entirely new path, by that experience. It was true when I had such severe atrial fibrillation one night long ago that I left my body, drawn near to a warm glowing light and the presence of a powerful love. I wanted to stay with that glowing presence forever, but my children were young and needed a mother. With that thought, I turned back toward life.

In that experience, my body taught me not to be afraid of death. I was changed in that moment, just as I was changed by the visitation in the sanctuary. I was transformed by *saying yes* to the Mystery when I could have said *no*. As are we all. This is not something that is unique to me: it is available to any of us who say *yes*.

Perhaps God only learns what is true, as I do, by direct, embodied experience. Being without form—that is, having no body of God's own—the Mystery chooses to embody in and through us. Chooses to take on its lessons about love and hatred, tolerance and intolerance, justice and injustice, cruelty and kindness, through us. Perhaps God experiences everything of the human experiment through our experiences of embodiment of life. Perhaps God is transformed along with us whenever one of us allows the veil to part, and remembers. Perhaps life is a co-creative encounter between God and human. In this encounter, we are both made new. Through our experiences of life incarnate, change comes: not only to the individual, but also to the heart of humankind, and also to the heart of God.

To believe this, to even suspect it may be so, requires that we adopt a mandate to live as if the God in each of us—the Mystery in all of life—matters. Every lesson, every small or significant event, and every person we encounter on the path is the Mystery in a process of *becoming*. God isn't finished with the light-years-long work of exploring the potential for its own developing Godliness . . . just as our efforts to become fully, wholly, authentically en-spirited human beings take most of a lifetime, if not more.

We are invited to see what's there to be seen, to know what's there to be known, and to let our illusions fall away gracefully . . . because they only separate us from what is true. We are also called to seek and to serve the highest truth. Everything less is a failure to remember.

I am dreaming that I am in my grandmother's attic. In the dream, there are two doors. One is a typical door, with a hook and eye latch, leading from the house into the attic space. But the other door is quite unusual. It leads directly from the attic out into the heavens, and it is closed with many intricate kinds of locks. I want this door to open so that light and air might pour into this musty attic. I struggle for a long time to unlock each of the intricate bolts and locks keeping the door shut. When I finally unlock the last lock of the second door, something amazing happens: a great power blows the door from its hinges, rapidly tosses the door end over end through the air, and sets the door on fire. It lands at my feet, still actively burning, its edges so badly curled or damaged that it's impossible to put the door back in place.

I can see directly out into the galaxy. I am looking at a black sky and millions of stars light years away. I am looking directly at the Mystery, and it is beautiful. As I look down at the door burning at my feet, I realize that this is the door between the worlds, and it wanted to be opened with as much urgency and power as I wanted to open it.

That dream was real, coming a long time after the experience in the sanctuary, but it serves as a metaphor for those of us on a spiritual journey. The knock comes, no doubt of it. The holy visitor will arrive at the door one day. When that opportunity comes to us, will we unlock the bolts that keep the door shut and allow the divine guest to enter our lives?

Will I, will you, say *yes*? Or will we settle for less than a full encounter with the reality of Sacred Mystery? Do we genuinely *want God,* or will we persuade ourselves that *wanting to want God* is enough?

❡

- What do you believe Ram Dass means when he states that

there is a difference between "wanting God, and wanting *to* want God?"

- Think of a time when the Mystery that is God might have attempted to show you something of its true nature, and you were afraid enough of the encounter to consider pushing it away. In the end, what did you decide? What was the cost, and what was the gift in your decision?

- Do you really want to experience God enough that you are willing to accept the changes that might accompany that encounter? Or do you want someone else (a minister, a priest, a rabbi, an imam) to act as an intermediary for you? What about wanting your own personal encounter with the One We Call God?

- Write a letter to yourself about your spiritual journey. What are your goals for the highest unfolding of your own soul? How can others assist you in this intention? What companions will you take with you as you move fully into this intention? What spiritual practices or teachings show the way for you to follow?

- Finally, write a statement that you consider a covenant with your soul, a promise you make that you will uphold for the rest of your life. Make it as detailed or as simple as you need it to be for now. You can always return to this covenant and revise or update it. Read this to yourself periodically and note the ways in which the covenant begins to come alive in you.

The shadow knows

I have a little shadow
that goes in and out with me
and what can be the use of it
is more than I can see . . .

—*Robert Louis Stevenson*

We all have a little shadow that goes "in and out" with us. It's a puzzling part of our humanity. Few of us understand it, and fewer still even know it exists. Almost none of us know how to manage it. Yet the shadow parts the curtain between conscious and unconscious selves, and shows its presence, again and again. We see *shadow* emerging through aberrant behaviors we engage in but don't always understand, through something we say but may not mean, through things about ourselves we try to disguise, whether or not we're successful at the masquerade.

To be on an intentional spiritual journey—that is, to consciously seek a closer relationship with the Mystery—means that, sooner rather than later, we will almost certainly come face to face with hidden aspects of our true nature. Remember: *the purpose of our efforts to deepen intimacy with the Sacred is so we might blossom in awareness or consciousness, become fully embodied partner-participants in the expanding of consciousness through all of creation, and reclaim and fulfill our own whole, and holy, nature.* For us to be whole, we must search for parts of ourselves we have lost, abandoned, neglected, or discarded over the course of our lives. These are the parts of us that make up what psychologists call *the shadow*.

Several years ago, Ellie and I—wisely or foolishly, we've never determined—decided to offer a group called "Embracing the Shadow." We envisioned this as an opportunity for ourselves, as well as group members, to explore the innermost regions of our unexamined lives, to learn what had been relegated to the realm of the unconscious, hidden from awareness, and to mine the gifts we would unearth from what we called the "catacombs of the spirit." At the time, neither of us realized how much of our own shadow material would be evoked just by our decision to call the group together.

Later, a friend familiar with shadow work told us that we had "signed a contract with the shadow" at the instant of our decision, and that we wouldn't be let off the hook until the shadow was finished with us. In retrospect, this observation probably saved our friendship. The moment we started to plan the group, we had an argument—the first in six years of friendship and work partnership—in which the not-so-nice things we'd never said to each other were finally spoken. We did this in an overarching spirit of kindness and compassion, but the truths we spoke to one another weren't easy to say or hear. These were the truly hard things that each of us had been too polite or lacking in emotional courage to acknowledge.

Ellie thought I was relying too heavily on our work to fill the emptiness in my life. I thought she was using the constant chaos in her life to hide from something. Both of us zeroed in on a reality neither of us wanted to admit to ourselves, much less to the other. The conversation was painful, and we had to take it slow enough that we didn't hurt each other as we flushed out hidden parts of the story that lived, without previous awareness or acknowledgment, in both our friendship and collegial relationship. I thought only I could see the emptiness in my life; she believed she alone knew she was running from something in hers. Both of us were wrong. What we tried to hide was right in front of us, all along. This was one part of my shadow, and one part of hers, visible to those with the eyes to see.

As we put out the call to begin the group, we unwittingly invited the shadow to take residence in the relational space that was our friendship. We started something in motion that had a life of its own, a force we couldn't have stopped even if we had known how to stop it. More than that, we had given it permission to go to work in our lives. We stepped onto a path that was going to take us into truth . . . whether we were prepared for truth or not. Innocents that we were, we understood none of this.

But we were fortunate to have a colleague to guide us through many of the rough waters that began to churn so furiously when we entered shadow's world. He gave us some principles for understanding when we stood in the presence of shadow material, our own or the other's, and how to navigate our way through this decidedly uncharted terrain, using it to grow as conscious persons. Becoming more conscious was, of course, the reason we dared to dip a toe into the dark, murky waters of the shadowy unconscious in the first place. It was certainly not a destination either one of us would have chosen for a retreat or a relaxing vacation.

Why did we undertake a descent to the catacombs at all? Why not leave to the shadow, or to the unconscious, those parts of ourselves we've already made the decision not to explore?

Certainly, on the surface of things, it seems wise to leave the
shadow alone and unexplored. But the surface of things doesn't
tell the whole story. It doesn't account for the powerful impulse
in our spirits to continually move toward wholeness, healing,
authenticity, becoming real. We are all velveteen rabbits,
becoming worn and frayed at the same time we are becoming
more of who we are truly intended to be. Sooner or later, one
way or another, shadow *beckons us* to descend into the one place
where our missing parts are tucked away.

We go when shadow beckons because we reach a point in the
ever-changing spiritual journey where it becomes necessary to
go. A point where we are overdue to turn our attention inward
to see what lives, unexamined, hidden, in us. A point where the
unconscious material begins to leak out of us in ways that sneak
up on us or on others: in sarcastic or unkind remarks; in behaviors
we regret but cannot explain; in the deficits of our parenting or
partnering; in parts of ourselves that sabotage our best intentions
for a project or for a relationship; in longings of the spirit that
have been unattended until they begin to scream for our
attention. In the end, we go toward the shadow because *we are
commissioned to go.*

In God's own ever-changing journey, we serve as companions
or partners in the forward movement of consciousness. At a
certain, unpredictable moment in the life of a spiritual seeker,
the call will come: *Go inside. Descend into the catacombs of
your being. Down, down, down. Drop to the center of your own
earth, and discover who—or what—lives there. Bring it to
awareness. Awaken it. Resurrect it. This is a significant part of
your essential nature.* To be whole, as we're created to be, we
must return these lost parts to consciousness.

The shadow knows things about us that our conscious selves
don't know. It holds parts of our personal and collective stories
from which we have turned our faces. It would be so simple if

all we had to do was secret those stories away, but the shadow will not allow us to do that. It holds all that material, subdued for a time—sometimes a very long time—but one day it emerges and demands its due, which is nothing less than restoration to the full truth of our lives. Some people, a rare few, manage to sleepwalk through their lives without ever being handed the bill for a lack of consciousness in their decisions and actions.

Spiritual seekers are not left off the shadow's hook. For us, there comes a time of reckoning with all the dimensions of self, a time of unearthing anything we've hidden from awareness (our own and others'), a time of integrating the hidden parts of ourselves into a whole, honest woman or man of integrity.

The Great Mystery underlying this process is one of co-creation. The work we do for ourselves extends far beyond us and reverberates to the rest of the world, though we may never know this. Ultimately and intimately, it even ripples out to change God. God awakens more as we awaken. God expands to become more whole each time one of us returns a lost dimension of self to our consciousness. In staccato rhythm, fits and starts, humanity evolves in the direction of spiritual maturing. This is how we "grow ourselves up" spiritually, in time leaving the concept of being a "child of God" for the spiritual integrity of the "adult of God." We do this because it becomes evident, somewhere along the rocky road to God-consciousness or enlightenment, that we must.

We live in a world made chaotic with troubles. Fear and hatred have long had their way with us. We lose our hearts to petty resentments a hundred times a day. We waste our lives on activities that matter very little (though we tell ourselves differently) when our efforts, spent elsewhere, could change something wrong for the better. Succumbing to a sense of pervasive powerlessness, we remain entrenched in inertia while

our world leaders take actions that bring the human family to
the precipice. If we topple over that edge, we face a long fall
toward destruction of our earth and of each other. We are closer
to the edge of that precipice than we have ever been.

It doesn't work to sit back and do nothing. Yet what is there to
do? It's in recycling that question that we walk around and around
in a labyrinth of our own construction, never really reaching the
center. Yet if we approach in the manner that a labyrinth is meant
to be approached—with sacred intention and the desire to listen
as we walk one mindful step at a time—we'll hear whispers of
a mysterious and ancient call: *Come. Keep coming. Dive into
me. Deeper still.*

By the time we reach the center of the labyrinth, we will have
sharpened our senses and slowed enough to recognize the holy
impulse that throbs in us: the impulse toward life, toward love,
toward authenticity, and toward reverence of a Great Mystery
that awakens the yearning in us to become our best selves.

We cannot become authentic individuals living out our divine
blueprints without taking a plunge into the depths of our own
darkness: the parts of us that lurk in the shadows, present but
unacknowledged and unclaimed. These parts are like orphans
with no one to care for them. Left to fend for themselves in the
shadows, they use any means they can to survive. If we adopt
them into our care and compassion, they will thrive, adding their
gifts to fill out the blueprint of our lives.

Attending to what lives in the shadow does not have to be a
dramatic process. Shadow-tending can be a quiet, meticulous
effort to "clean up our acts" so that we function in a relationship,
family, or community as a responsible member. Author Christina
Baldwin uses the metaphor of shadow-tending as a process of
"psychic housecleaning." She plays with the notion that those
who are awake to the presence of their own shadow material—

the unspoken, often unconscious, elements alive in them—live like members of a household where each person conscientiously picks up after herself.

If we all make the effort to tend to shadow, the homes (families, communities, organizations) in which we live rarely seem cluttered or dirty, yet no one person in the "household" is designated as the person to clean up after the others. Everyone takes responsibility. Everyone helps to keep relationships uncluttered or uncontaminated by behaviors that cause others harm. Everyone takes part in creating an environment that supports and encourages everyone else who lives or works in that environment. There's no psychological or spiritual mess left for someone else to clean up.

This isn't easy. It is easier to linger in a state of unconsciousness, but not better. The problems we confront in today's world make the option to remain unconscious less and less appealing. Someone has to do something, or we might, in our sleepwalking state, cause irreparable harm to the people we love, or to the world in which we live. Individuals taking small measures in our everyday lives, inevitably, as quantum physicists tell us, generate actions that can be felt across the globe. Why don't we give it a try? Anything is an improvement over the shaky ground on which we teeter now.

To begin, we have to give each other shadow lessons. What is the shadow? How do we create it? And what in heaven's name do we do about it?

Swiss psychiatrists Carl Jung and Marie Louise von Franz originally developed the theory of *shadow*. In recent years, poet-author Robert Bly popularized the term and made it accessible and understandable to the lay person. He's neatly woven the ties between *shadow* as a psychological construct and *shadow* as a theological construct. Bly postulates that every child is born with a "360-degree" radius of radiant light. This is our divine nature, our first nature, a thumbprint of the Mystery left at the core of our being. A child radiates pure light, undiluted brilliance, in all directions at, and from, the moment of birth.

This means you. It means me. It means the person who lives next door to you, the teenager down the block, and even the driver who's riding your bumper on the way to work in the morning. No one is left out when the imprint of God is placed upon his or her soul. The 360-degree radiance is a birthright gift to all of creation.

Each of the three-hundred-and-sixty points of radiant light represents an elemental gift in the nature of that child. Each birthright gift is intended to be celebrated, to be encouraged into full expression, and to be shared generously, even extravagantly, through our lives. It is the mandate of every human being to live out of this original radiance. This is a message that needs to be told many times, in a multiplicity of ways, to every child . . . because too many forces in a child's life conspire to counteract that message. Regrettably, few of us sustain the fullness of the inborn light once we enter the realities of the family, the community, the society and the world into which we have come.

Soon after arrival, most children begin to recognize that the people into whose love and care they have been placed are unable to welcome or to accept (at least some) parts of that child's inborn nature. Some of us are born girls in families or cultures that assign boys a greater value. Some of us are sensitive and reactive to troubled family circumstances. Some of us cry or worry or laugh more than the ones around us can tolerate. Some of us are loud when a parent wants quiet, some of us are messy when a parent wants order, and some of us are artistic when a parent really wants an athlete or a scholar.

Whatever the issue, we're not *valued* for some part of our original nature. Almost all of us receive these devaluing messages some of the time. Some people receive little else. When that happens, that original radiance flickers, falters, and finally, fades from sight. *Each time, one point of light flickers from the spirit of a child, a little bit of God vanishes from the world.* That information must be held in the sacred trust of every parent, every grandparent, every teacher or caregiver of children. It is information to give us pause whenever we withhold our love from a partner, a friend, or anyone else who unsettles us because they're different . . . or because they are not who we want them to be.

Fortunately for us, the human spirit is resilient. Under siege, we rarely annihilate that radiance: we send it into exile, deep in the recesses of the unconscious/shadow, placed in what Bly has called "the long bag we drag behind us." As time passes and lives move on, we forget such a part of us exists, *but it does not forget us.* It waits. And waits. And waits until such time as something happens to rock our world and we realize the time has come to turn inward and begin the search for the abandoned parts of the self. At this moment, knowingly or not, we start the descent into the personal underworld, where the "long bag" and its contents reside.

The impetus to turn our attention inward may come after a major life upheaval, where strategies that always worked in our favor before, no longer work . . . and we're forced to alter our lives. The impetus may come in the form of an illness or depression that requires a whole new outlook on life. It may come on the tailwinds of divorce, death, or loss of another kind. It comes in dreams that tell us, if we're tuned to that frequency, the moment is at hand to begin the descent.

And down we go. Most of us are afraid of what we'll find. Long since having learned to deny these parts of ourselves, we imagine them as something monstrous or terrifying. This is where the notion of *shadow lessons* can be very helpful. If we understand that the contents of that secret container are parts of our original light, our divine blueprint, not to be feared but—like the prodigal—to be welcomed home, then we will have a positive frame of reference to do this work. More positive still, if we understand that we are restoring ourselves to wholeness, to our original holiness, the place from which we best embody the Source of our creation. The shadow includes parts of us that contain our most deeply held secrets. It also includes the parts of us that contain our most valued gifts.

It's still difficult work, this process of rooting around in the shadows to find we-know-not-who-or-what. At first, it's much like being lost in a cemetery on a stormy night, afraid that the unknown ghosts of the past will rise up to haunt us. Long discarded parts of the children we once were reappear to surprise us. Old incidents we have mercifully forgotten come round again to gnash their teeth at us. Some of the work is delightful, reclaiming gifts we can put to immediate use. Some of the work is messy and ugly, as we own up to things we have said and done, and wish we hadn't. There is nothing tidy about the shadow. Yet every person has his shadow. Every relationship, every culture, every race, religion, and nation. We see evidence of this splattered all over the wars we stage and wage, the transgressions we commit against others, and those others commit against us.

What we do not claim in ourselves, we force out onto others as *projection*. We sit back in smug judgment of those onto whom we have projected our gifts or our liabilities. We love them, or we hate them. Maybe we just ignore them. What we fail to do is to see ourselves in them: mirrors for the soul. We fail to admit that shadow material is present in all of us, most of the time, and this will be true until we have done our psychic housecleaning.

The shadow, in all its untidiness, is blessedly true and real. Little by little, we learn how to stand before the mirror of shadow, and admit the full truth of ourselves into our hearts. This takes spiritual maturity. We often flinch, but we grow slowly into a strength of spiritual character as we learn to be, in the words of theologians, "God-bearers." We grow to bear the fullness of human experience, the fullness of life in all its joy-pain, the fullness of unpredictability and of mystery, *with God*. We step to the plate to become partners in the forward movement of both human and God consciousness.

My friends: not the easiest of tasks.

David Richo, author of the book *Shadow Dance*, asks: "How much consciousness can we stand? We can never know all of our shadow, only a piece at a time, only what we are ready for, and we will never be ready for all of it. The shadow can never be totally tamed or befriended . . . We must become psychological spelunkers, which is often an unappealing prospect. Our visible persona, the image we present to the world, feels threatened by the possible exposure of its dark underpinnings. The underworld is, of course, our inner world."

It is indisputably the place where the Mystery is most alive in us.

Richo continues: "Know that we are never alone on this venture. Assisting forces are collaborating all the time. Even now, many saints and bodhisattvas are gathering to help. They are attracted to the hearts of those who want to wake up and learn to love fully. They are the guardian angels who accompany us over the bridge we notice is unstable and even perilous, but nonetheless know we have to cross."

In the work of shadow-tending, we become all of one piece, as close as we can possibly put the pieces back together, Humpty Dumpty style. Even if the cracks are mended badly, the original light still shines through. It may even be at the badly mended or still-broken places where the light shines through most clearly.

This light is the original radiance, coming alive in us once more. Ours, but not ours, it emanates from the light of Creation, the Mystery, the Source of all living light. We are simply a vessel to hold that light for a time. We are here, and gone too soon. In the time we are given, however long or short, it's our primary spiritual task to illumine all three hundred and sixty degrees of light that's designated to shine through us.

Each of us, it is said, is here to be a light unto the world. Reclaiming the light from all its hiding places, letting that light shine before the world . . . this is high, holy work. Ellie and I learned a great deal about the powerful force of her shadow and mine as we signed the contract to explore it. Much of what we learned was unpleasant, but all of it was authentic. Each of us had to claim for herself: jealousy, envy, bitterness, desire, longing, delight, playfulness, joy. Just as Jesus examined himself through his strenuous days and nights in the desert, facing his inner demons, we examined ours. The long bags were plenty full. And the participants in our group found their own demons stalking them. While we were spiritually spelunking (and the spelunking doesn't come to an end the way the course did), we laughed as often as we cried.

We emerged from the expedition grimy and sweaty. After all, we'd become miners after hidden gold, and the work is messy by nature. But we also emerged fuller, richer, more self-aware, and able to laugh at our foibles. The journey was—and still is— worthwhile. We embark on it not just for ourselves but also for all of humanity. I would do it again in a heartbeat. It is such a relief to be more fully me. No more of my energy wasted in pretending to be more, or less, than who I am.

Such a burden lifted when the soul is finally liberated, authenticated, and welcomed home.

⚓

- What parts of your true nature have you sent into hiding? For what purpose?

- Start with this simple exercise. Who are the people onto whom you have projected positive parts of your own unlived life? What is it about them you admire? Are you ready to begin to re-claim and to develop those qualities in yourself?

- Give the same kind of consideration to those people onto whom you have projected negative parts of your own unlived life. Who are they? What is it about them that causes you to judge them? What is it about this person that holds a negative mirror for you? What qualities in the person you blame, judge or shame are also true of you?

- John O'Donohue writes in *Anam Cara* that, "we are sent into the world to live to the full everything that awakens within us, and everything that comes toward us. Real divinity has a passionate instinct for creativity and the fully inhabited life. The greatest sin of all is the unlived life."

How are you participating in an "unlived life?" How do you envision yourself, your personal and work relationships, your participation in the community and world around you, *benefiting* if you made the choice to fully inhabit your own 360 degrees of radiant light?

Lost radiance

There is only one life
you can call your own
and a thousand others
you can call by any name you want.

—David Whyte

So I am responsible, am I, for re-claiming the lost 360-degree radiance with which I was born? With which the Sacred has imprinted me? Now there is a sobering thought.

I am looking for parts of me that were lost, stolen, or surrendered in the years of attempts to please others or to become the girl-woman someone else was convinced I should become. No one so much as hinted that the real task was to become myself! I didn't know this until I was approaching mid-life and stumbled upon poet May Sarton, a high-spirited woman then in her fragile eighties but still firing off messages from an elder of the human clan to those who followed behind her. An imperative message: *Don't lose sight, as I did, of what you are here to do. In the sunset of life, I discovered my real purpose was to embody this one authentic life.* I imagine no one ever left you these instructions either. How many of us are wandering, confused, in this unmapped territory?

I remember once talking with a seven-year-old girl, the daughter of friends who'd entrusted her to me because she was showing clear signs of childhood depression. She was a child who was different, who didn't quite "fit in." Her classmates teased her mercilessly. Her parents worried that she'd begun to believe the teasing, ridiculing, and bullying messages from her peers were indications something was wrong with her. She was beginning to feel ashamed of herself. Her mother and father wisely hoped to interrupt the cycle of hurt or self-diminishment before shame burrowed into her bright spirit deeply enough to cause damage that might not be mend-able. So they brought her to talk with me.

What could I say to a beautiful seven year-old child whose only "mistake" lay in being born biracial in a community that was almost exclusively white? I was present at this baby's birth. I had seen her minutes after she arrived in this world. I saw the first sweet parting of her lips when she reached for her mother's breast. I knew how precious this child was. It was daunting to try to find the words that would give her back a sense of her value and worth.

We went to the playground near my office. We slid down the slide, crawled through the tunnel-tubes, hung from the overhead bars, and swung, side by side. Nothing much was said: we just played together. Walking back to my office, we decided to sit for a few minutes on a bench overlooking a little field. I was searching, reaching into my experience with children to find the right words to comfort this child's broken heart. Still grasping for answers to an unanswerable question, I finally said: "Meghan, did you know every child is born with something inside that makes them special, and that no one else, in all the world, will ever have just like she or he does?"

Her head snapped around to catch my eyes. She was listening. That was a good beginning. I continued: "Did you know that some people believe everyone is supposed to be like everyone else . . . but that's not true. Everybody's made to be a little different from everyone else. No two people are exactly alike. I think that's amazing, don't you?"

Her button brown eyes were fastened on mine, unmoving. She nodded. I was striking a cord with her. I kept on talking: "Like the way some kids are good runners, and some are good talkers, and some are good at dancing or singing." I didn't need to go further. She interrupted me, urgently asking: "And some kids are good readers, right?"

She had found her own strength.

"Yes," I told her. "Some kids are very good readers. Everyone has something special in them, and everyone has a job to find out what that is."

She was silent, teary, thoughtful for a long time. Minutes passed without words. Finally, she let out a long, heavy-hearted sigh and said, almost in a whisper: "I wonder why no one ever told me that?"

Like Meghan, I wonder why no one ever told us that it's not our job to work so hard to become what everyone else wants of us. Our only task is to become the unique person we were designed to become. What a price we pay for not learning this!

Recently, Ellie and I led a retreat for a local group of interfaith church women on the topic of *claiming one's true vocation*. We explained at the start of the retreat that we generally don't spend a lot of time reflecting on the topic of what we *do* with our lives. That is, our *activities*. In the retreat, we would focus on who each of us is uniquely created to *be*. Predictably, this is a new idea when we first present it, whether we present it to children or to adults.

It often catches women by complete surprise, since women have long been socialized to develop a sense of worth through the singular lens of what they do for others. It takes effort and time to peel away those layers of socialization. Time to plant the notion that *who we are* is well worth discovering and cultivating so that we can participate, whole-heartedly and intentionally, in shaping and inhabiting our unique lives.

At these retreats, it's common to hear considerable self-deprecation, as women struggle for a glimpse of the qualities in them that are worth developing. One woman made a concerted attempt to convince us that she truly was worthless. Another— a teacher who thought teaching was the most noteworthy aspect of her life—sought me out during a time of private reflection and began to ask me about dreams. Rather than answer her questions, I listened to her story, which is that she has always been a vivid and prolific dreamer. Often, her dreams prophesy something that happens soon after the dream. Did I think this was in any way connected to what we were talking about in the retreat?

I explained that, in tribal communities or indigenous cultures, it's considered an honor for a person to dream like this. That individual is believed to dream, not only for the purpose of personal awareness, but also for the emerging awareness of the entire community. By unfavorable contrast, Western culture isn't one in which we take dreams seriously . . . and therefore, we don't harvest the bits of wisdom contained in them. I asked her to think about the question: *What if being a teacher is what you do with your life, but being a dreamer is who you really are?*

As I asked this, her eyes flew open in delight. Her whole face became animated and luminous.

Spiritual directors call this an *ahah!* moment, the precise second where something deep within the spirit of a person recognizes a truth . . . and that truth erupts in an explosion of gnosis, or knowing. I watched this lovely woman spontaneously combust and catch fire with purpose. Like the little girl sitting with me on the bench one summer day, she discovered one lost strand of her own uniqueness. She remembered or awakened a precious aspect of her lost radiance. What she does with that is now in her hands.

She could do what many people do, and simply leave it dormant, undeveloped, throughout the remainder of her life . . . or she could take the risk to learn more about the potential of dreams to lead us, individually and collectively, toward greater consciousness. The choice is hers to make. At the very least, she now knows she has a choice.

Life is a circle, of course, and these stories bring me round again to my own neglected parts. I believe the helping work we do with others is ineffective if we aren't also tending the home fires as meticulously as we ask others to do. It is my willingness to act on these principles in my own spiritual life that makes me a believable guide for people in search of someone to companion them along the way. For someone to help them decipher the road map. For someone to help them remove the obstacles they are sure to encounter on the rocky road toward a life centered in Spirit and Mystery.

I had been facilitating a retreat on the *shadow* with a group of people who wanted to go deeper into the practice of circle leadership, and I'd given them a project. Each person chose a brightly colored bag from the center of the circle, and they were to reflect on what they had tucked away in that (metaphoric) bag long ago. The project provided an opportunity for them to search their own depths for lost or stolen parts of their essential nature that might have been shamed, blamed or judged into hiding.

My intention was to sit back while they went to work. I would assist if assistance was necessary, but I wanted them to start the task of "psychological spelunking" and see what they found along the way. I picked up a magazine, one of many out of which they were cutting and pasting images that sparked recognition in them, and began to idly flip through it. Wham. Right then, right there. In the sudden convergence of opportunity and synchronicity, I held a magazine in my hands that contained cross-cultural interviews with individuals known as "life guides."

I was staring at the photograph of someone who had been a spiritual guide or hero in my early life. He was a Native American elder who spent more than sixty years studying the world's religions, ceremonies, and dogmas in order to derive "the simple truths that bind us all together." His name was Stalking Wolf, but to me and many others who read Tom Brown's fascinating tales of a boyhood spent learning to track the many creatures of the eastern pine barrens, he was simply called, *Grandfather*. I had devoured every one of Tom Brown's books with a voracious appetite and passed them on to my son, who did the same.

My eyes fell on the image of Stalking Wolf's face. *Ahah!* In that old Indian face I saw mirrored my own persistent desire to look beyond the separate religious traditions to identify "the simple truths that bind us all together." I had last seen that determination in my own face when I was fifteen years old and defiantly told the group leader of a confirmation class at my church that it made no sense for there to be only one "true path" to God. *How could all the other religious traditions be wrong? What if they weren't wrong? Wasn't there a possibility all religious paths ultimately lead to God?* That girl fled into the bag the day the confirmation leader suggested, in full view and earshot of my peers in the class, that my thinking was heretical. But she came alive in me again when I looked into the face of an old Indian and saw my own curious, questioning nature reflected back to me.

Shaken, I flipped another few pages of the magazine. In the next photograph, I found myself staring at the compassionate face of animal behaviorist Jane Goodall who lightly touched her fingertips to the lips of a caged chimpanzee. There was such love on her face, such respect for the life of this beautiful creature, and such understanding that we are meant to share this earth with one another. I was profoundly touched. In her face was another beam of my own lost radiance. What was it that stopped me from living out my passion for Creation, the way Jane Goodall has done?

What stops any of us? A thousand high anxieties and paltry excuses, none of them worth much in the overview, but, accumulating over time, enough to diminish the light that resides in me.

I squander myself on activities too small—ultimately unnecessary—to mention. I remember the ancient Chinese poem by Lao Tzu about a woodcarver commanded to create the perfect bell stand for the Prince of Lu. His failure to accomplish this meant his certain death. Under that kind of pressure, how could the woodcarver remain true to himself and to his original blueprint? Yet he did, and the perfect bell stand emerged from his efforts. In the poem, the woodcarver—when questioned by the Prince—explained his accomplishment: *I did not expend myself on trifles.*

Well, I expend my life on trifles. Little things, big dramas, distractions that lure me away from who I'm here to be. And, while I am actively squandering this life, what do I think I'm waiting for? One particular moment when the clouds will part and a resonant voice will call my name? When do I think that time will come? That moment is already here, and my overwhelming fear is that I won't recognize it, won't seize it, won't use it well. It seems safer and more comforting to ignore the parts of me not yet actualized or emboldened. To leave the template unfulfilled. To allow the radiance to grow dim, dimmer, and then dark. I call this *spiritual lethargy*. Michael, my spiritual director, calls this "dumbing down."

Sometimes, it is more comfortable to dumb down than to stretch into full radiance. I don't kid myself that I am the only one who has made this choice. I have many companions in "dumbing down" school.

No one else can do the arduous work of re-discovering the lost radiance for me, or for any of us. We are each responsible for the right direction and use of our lives. We are each born with an inner map to guide us toward our own true north. We have all the tools. We just need to look inside for them. What more do we need for us to put foot to the path?

For me, it's courage. The courage to live into parts of myself I have neglected or forgotten. The courage to seek those lost degrees of radiance and light them anew. The courage to tell the truth of my life, and then to live it without hesitation. The courage to become everything assigned to my blueprint.

This isn't always a task to be welcomed. Sometimes it's just plain hard. I received an e-mail forwarded recently from a friend who clearly believed that I shared her thoughts on a certain matter. As I read the letter, I shuddered at the intolerance it perpetrated. She's a well-meaning person of good heart and great intelligence. There was no *intention* on her part to foster intolerance, and yet, there it was. With it came the request that I send the e-mail along to everyone in my computer address book.

I wrestled with this. I wanted to accommodate her. I wanted her to think well of me. I wanted nothing to harm our friendship. But I couldn't take part in distributing this particularly alarming message. I knew she would ask if I had sent it along, so I had no wiggle room, no way off the hook. I had to say what I thought, and I had to do it in a manner that neither blamed nor shamed her for her choice to participate. I struggled for words, and eventually, I found just the right ones. I said what I thought was true without any implication that her choice was wrong. She had her own path to walk, and I had mine. Her blueprint called her to one action, mine called me to another. Life demands this of us more often than we'd like to admit.

We must dare to be courageous in the attempt to become who we are here to be. Eventually, this gets easier and more familiar. After enough practice at it, it becomes impossible to return to behaviors that appease others but devalue ourselves. All of this takes time, commitment, effort. We need every one of the angels and bodhisattvas David Richo promises will come to our aid. We will hear our voices tremble, we'll want to flee, and we'll wish we had never started on the spiritual path. The re-claiming of the true self requires most of the courage we can summon. But summon it, we must . . . if we truly want to encounter the Mystery that is God.

I pray that we might summon that courage and learn to embody the light born in each of us. I pray for us to find the courage to turn away the expectations others place on us, to move bravely into the lives we are born to inhabit. We live in a time of world-wide darkness, and not one light can be wasted, lest we succumb to the forces of unconsciousness.

All of this, I pray for each member of the human family, and nothing less: 360 degrees of radiance. This is our divine birthright.

ℐ

- On what occasions have you backed away from the truth of your experiences, your opinions, or your feelings because you were afraid you might be shamed or judged for them? How did this serve you at the time? Does it serve you still?

- Stop to consider one place in your life where it's safe to show others the light you carry in the world. What one degree of your own radiance could you open up? What one step could you take now to let your light shine?

- Practice this in small ways at first. Notice the results without making them wrong or right. Notice how one step opens into another, and then another, in the same way one simple move with the game of solitaire can suddenly open up a "win."

- What, in the words of poet David Whyte, is "the one life you can call your own?" Picture that life for yourself as vividly as possible. Infuse it with all of your senses. Make it real . . . and it will become real as you reawaken your own lost radiance.

Esperanza

Be true. This is the essence of the
spiritual life. The note of the spirit
is sounded on the higher planes, and
the knocks you receive in everyday life
are to test you, whether you can ring true.
To ring true, you must always sound the
note of God, or good, which is within you.

—White Eagle

I hadn't slept well one night. The escalating anxieties in the difficult weeks after the September 11th terrorist attacks on the World Trade Center and the Pentagon had collected in my spirit and drained it of its usual resilience. That night, I wept for the state of the world and for the state of our burdened hearts. I did not dream. That too was indicative of the psychological aftermath of the violence that was suddenly, dramatically, inserted at the center of our lives on that grim day in America. I watched friends and loved ones struggling to absorb more difficult news each day: terrorist alerts from the Pentagon, anthrax letters and the deaths of innocent people, the need for increased airport security, a passenger on a plane with bomb materials in his shoe.

I was struggling myself. I had been in a major metropolitan airport for over six hours on a recent trip, sufficient time to notice people as they walked through one concourse to another. I was struck by the visual impact of thousands of people moving along in surges, as planes arrived and emptied. Many of them wore black. I couldn't help noticing that we looked like a people in mourning: an enormous black tidal wave of broken-hearted people. Six hours is a long time to watch somber faces and to notice heavy hearts. I heard little laughter and saw few people smile. The grief and fear I witnessed in them were the visual reminders that we were all struggling.

The morning after my restless, anxiety-ridden night, I was sitting at my window, watching the sun rise gradually over the bright colors of the fall treetops in the woods around my house. I love the beauty of that early morning hour, when the autumn sun lifts over the horizon and sets trees afire with the first light of a new day. I was sitting in the morning silence—my tiny Zen house is a quiet place to be—when I noticed Cali, the neighbor's calico cat, sitting on the rail of their back deck.

Cali found the first rays of sun streaming through the trees and lay down in a patch of it, content enough, and warm. No matter the nip of frost in the air that morning. From where she rested, all was well with the world. I continued to watch her, to use this as a meditation in *being present*. I had suffered through the long night: fears waxing and waning, some past and some future. But here was Cali, greeting the day: *simply present.*

Cali had no fear of the next act of terror. Her heart had not been struck dumb or numb with worry. She was just *there*, and she was just *now*. As I watched her, I thought of Eckhart Tolle, the spiritual teacher who speaks of the power of *presence* and the power of simply remaining in the *now*. Tolle has said cats are among the greatest of his spiritual teachers.

I took deep breath after breath, exhaling my anxiety and opening myself to learn the morning's lesson from Cali, the cat teacher: stretch in the sun, watch the birds, take full pleasure from the moment that is right in front of us. This moment is all we have, and—although we know this well, most of us having lived long enough to learn that this is true—more of us than not charge through our lives, throwing our thoughts far into the future, or keeping them caught in the grip of the past. This was not true of Cali.

My daughter had called the day before this incident. She's a social worker whose work is to treat troubled and anxious preschool-age children, of whom there are many right now. She was telling me that children are experiencing nightmares and night terrors in greater numbers than ever before, and appropriately so. The times in which we live are worrisome, and children are small *emotional barometers* who sense and show the strain under which we're all functioning. After relating the stories of her children to me, my daughter said, "Mom, I'm scared too. I feel very susceptible to the fears of other people. I can't keep the fear out, and I can't seem to pray. What do I do?"

We talked about our fears openly and honestly: fears for ourselves, for our micro-family spread across thousands of miles, and for the human family itself. The conversation calmed us both and helped us to gather ourselves for another day in which we would each bear witness to frightened people of all ages.

It is an insidious enemy, this sneak attack of anxiety in our midst, and for those of us who witness this anxiety—hour after hour, day after day—the psychological and spiritual toll can seem beyond measure.

A week before this conversation with my daughter, a dear friend who's a skilled translator of the teachings and culture of indigenous people to those of us indoctrinated into the ways of Western values, wrote me from her home in Colorado, asking: "How are you holding?"

I answered with the story of my conversation with Sarah and then asked her the same question. She answered with these words: "I'm reminded to continue grooming my thoughts so that each individual I meet is seen as a person, rather than a symbol, and no person becomes the target of my anxieties and anger. I'm clearing my intention so that I am capable of waging peace. I pray. My heart breaks open so that I may live without division and without illusion. It is not easy. I'm out of practice. I am constantly distracted by personal problems. I am entrenched in habits that drag on my energy, mask it, or numb me.

"But here's how I'm holding. I turn my face to the sun, the stars, the season. I put my hands in the ground to turn the earth. I admire the strength and beauty of the plants. I listen to the wind for the voices of the ancestors. I give thanks for the meals that fill my belly, hot cleansing showers, even my soft pillow. Sometimes I well up with tears."

Sometimes I well up with tears.

This was true for me, as well. I discovered that I could easily well up with tears for no apparent reason except we are living in times such as we've never known before, and I am aware of my ill-preparedness for living in them. I'm frightened, and so are the people I love most, who are all very far away right now.

The terror is circling in on us, preparing to steal—if we allow it—our hopes, our hearts, our love, our life force, our *presence*. We must not allow this.

In the days following the first attacks of terror, Clarissa Pinkola Estes, a widely known psychologist and storyteller, circulated an e-mail letter that advised people of the subtle dangers of sustained trauma on the human psyche. In it, she said: "The primary objective of a terrorist is to make fear contagious, to steal our dreams and hopes, our esperanza."

Esperanza is a fat, juicy word. I love the way it rolls around in my mouth before it forms sound in the air. *Esperanza* means *hope*. Where do we find hope in the midst of an impossibility-turned-reality that's too big for our imaginations to grasp and our hearts to bear? We know the journey ahead will be a long one. One scare will follow another. Resolution is not within our grasp or even our sight. We are required to be spiritual warriors, to hold the sacred center when others stumble or falter. I know I'm not always up to the task. Where, then, is our hope? It will be difficult to survive this massive assault on our spirits if we don't have the means to nurture and sustain *hope*.

Several days after I pulled myself back from the dangerous edges of my sleeplessness and catastrophic thinking, I participated with 400 people in a gathering of shamans from all over the world at a spiritual retreat center. Shamans are the wisdom-keepers: the spiritual elders, teachers and healers among the indigenous peoples of the earth. There were shamans at the gathering representing the people of four continents, women and men, eight in all. With a hint of humor and a touch of pathos, they refer to those of us who have lived our lives in western culture as their "little brothers and sisters." To them, we're the newcomers who have not yet figured out how we are here to live on earth in harmony with all creation.

None of them spoke the same language. But the wisdom-bearers, trained in spiritual traditions thousands of years old, delivered the same message: *You are born for these times. You have everything you need to know already seeded within you . . . if you will stop the frantic pace of your lives, listen, and remember what you know.* I found comfort in this and have returned to it many times when I was frightened, tired, uncertain. Shortly after this gathering, I opened my computer one morning to find a message from the Hopi elders, written to the people of the world on September 11th:

To our fellow swimmers:

There is a river now flowing very fast.
It is so great and swift that there are those who will be afraid.
They will try to hold on to the shore.
They will feel they are being torn apart and will suffer greatly.

Know that the river has its destination.

The elders say we must let go of the shore,
push off into the middle of the stream,
keep our eyes open and our heads above the water.

And we say: see who is there with you and celebrate.
At this time in history, we are to take nothing personally,
let alone ourselves.
For the moment that we do, our journey of the
spirit comes to a halt.
The time of the lone wolf is over now.

Gather yourselves.
Banish the word "struggle" from your mind and mouth.
All that we do now must be done in a sacred
manner and in celebration.

We are the ones we have been waiting for.

Mitake Oyasin

Again, the elders speak. Their separate streams merge to
become one river pouring toward and through the heart of
humankind. *We must be the change we are seeking. We already
know how to do this. We are born for a time such as this.* Afraid
or not afraid, we are called.

Months before the attacks on New York City, people had dreams
forecasting such an event. I was with a friend who woke me
suddenly in the middle of one night. He was deep in the dream
world, shouting aloud in a language unknown to me, as well as
to his waking self. Suddenly, he called out with great urgency:
The time is now, now, now, NOW! And so it is.

Not long ago, I made a quick trip to the local corner store. As
I drove the short distance between my house and the store, I
glanced into the sky to see a brilliant sunset with an unusual
bright red plume shooting out of the clouds. Hildegard of Bingen,
that sage of the middle ages, might have called it "a feather on
the breath of God." As I entered the store, I urged the young,
nose-ringed girl at the counter to step outside for a look at this
phenomenon before it passed unnoticed. This prompted another
person, a boy of perhaps eighteen, to tell me about a sunset he'd
seen recently that stole his breath away. The girl was gone for
a long time. When she came back in to account for my purchases,
she smiled and said softly, "That was so cool! Thank you."

May our prayers encircle the innocents of all nations who are
suffering and afraid. And may we remember to nurture and sustain
esperanza, dear people. *Esperanza.* Turn your face to the skies,
the seasons, the sunrise and sunset. Give thanks for the small things
that make your life rich and fill your spirit. Small moments that
touch our hearts and lift our souls to rejoicing. Moments that
encourage us to look beyond our fears toward something beautiful,
mysterious, and unnamable. Moments of hope.

Hope will see us through.

𝄞

- How are you holding in these uncertain times? And who or what is holding you? From what sources do you draw and sustain *hope*?

- There is a group in which I participate where the members begin each session with a quieting breath. We close each session by going around the circle as one member after another speaks a word that, to her, encourages hope. The words are simple but authentic: *children, laughter, spring bulbs, birds, blue sky, sunrise, ocean, music.* Make a list of the words that symbolize hope for you, and keep the list in a place where you can refer to it often. Be sure to include something from the list in your life every day.

- Imagine each of the words you have listed refers to something or someone that is infused by God, and through which (or whom) the Mystery is sustaining you. What happens as you contemplate the myriad of ways that hope is alive in our midst?

- You might even make an altar in your home for objects that remind you, at a glance, to keep hope alive. In my house, I have small altars in many rooms. One is an cloth angel who sits with her arms around a turquoise pottery bowl filled with tiny shells from every beach I have ever visited. Another altar is a tall sculpture of a Hopi woman, around whose neck hangs my prayer beads. Be creative in your efforts to make altars of hope through your house. They will comfort you, but also others who visit your home.

Good neighbors

*People ought to think less about what they should do
and more about what they are.
For when people and their ways are good,
then their works shine brightly forth.*

—Meister Eckhart

This is a story of something lost and something found, and the snowstorm that precipitated both events. One February, the state of Maine was hit by a nasty winter storm: seven or so inches of heavy, wet snow on top of which fell freezing rain, which immediately froze to ice half an inch thick. We are a people used to digging out of nasty winter weather and getting on with our lives, but this storm stopped most of us in our tracks. But it did not stop a man who was partially paralyzed in a fall several years before. At the time of this storm, the man was homeless.

He lived at a local shelter or in his battered truck with his dog. Despite his own hardships, he gave what he could to others. In the bitter winters of the Northeast, he used his single possession, a snow blower, to help clear driveways, sidewalks, and parking lots in the neighborhood around the shelter. He did this asking nothing in return for his generosity.

During this particular storm, while the man was briefly inside a building to get warm, his snow blower was stolen. He was heartbroken and visibly shaken. This was the something *lost*. The something *found* was that a businessman, reading about the theft in a local newspaper the next day, bought the man a new snow blower so he could continue his efforts to be a good neighbor. The story captured our hearts, and lightened the burdens of a harsh, unforgiving winter.

There is a second, far more personal, part to the story of something lost and something found. That chapter unfolded in my own neighborhood after the same storm. Before moving to this neighborhood six years ago, I lived at the distant end of a long, dirt road. Though my neighbors weren't close enough to see, whenever bad weather blew through, we showed up to help each other get plowed or shoveled out. I simply assumed this was what neighbors do for one another. Then I moved into town, and into a small community of people I hoped I would come to know.

Here, I discovered a phenomenon that shocked me. When storms hit this neighborhood of forty houses, forty men would emerge from their homes with forty snow blowers. They'd clear their driveways without once looking up to speak with or to help one another. The first time I saw this happen, I was sure I was mistaken. *How could they not even talk with each other? Why weren't they helping each other to clear the snow?* But the same phenomenon happened with the next storm, and the next. I was baffled to see this occur with every front that brought us ice or snow. *These men did not look at one another as they worked!* They acted like the next house was fifty miles away rather than fifty yards across the drive.

I was a woman who lived alone and neither owned nor had strength enough to operate a snow blower. I'd stand outside in the cold, storm after storm, and shovel my own way clear. I placed numerous requests for help by the bank of mailboxes at the entrance to our little neighborhood, believing that the kids who lived nearby would want to earn a little money by shoveling. There was no response. I never saw children come out to shovel in the aftermath of a snowstorm. They were sliding down the long hill past my house the next day, or were outdoors building snowmen, but no one put a shovel in the hands of a child and said, "Let's go! We have work to do. Let's see if any of the neighbors need help."

This unfortunately dates me, but I recall rising before school on stormy winter mornings to help my dad shovel, or to shovel my mother out if my father was away on business. That was the kind of help families expected from, and gave to, each other. I was witnessing a change in cultural or family expectations; it caught me unprepared and surprised as I watched from the sweat and toil of shoveling my own driveway. Forty men clearing forty driveways, and not a friendly exchange or a helping hand among them.

Then came a storm that laced everything with a coat of ice so thick we could only punch our way through to the snow. Trees groaned audibly and eerily under the burden of the ice. Branches had bent under the weight, too heavy for the trees to hold in place. Many of them ripped from trunks and fell to the ground in a cacophony of creaking, popping and cracking before the final collision of ice-coated tree with ice-coated earth. The sound of trees crackling, tearing apart, and falling to the hard ground was heart-wrenching.

My house sits on a knoll, and the downhill driveway became a slick glaze of half-inch thick ice. It was impossible to get in or out of my house without the danger of falling and sliding straight down the slope into the street. Nor could I walk through the snow in my front yard. The yard had become a solid downhill stretch of gray, opaque, threatening ice. Even if I'd been able to drive my car over the ten-inch high ridge of solid snow-ice left at the bottom of the drive by the city plow, I could not have driven the car up the hill. There was no traction.

I was frozen in place for days. There was no warming trend in the forecast, and all the stores had been emptied of sand and salt supplies. Still, I had to go to work. Each day I would labor down the icy slope to my car in the road. Every footfall was treacherous. At night, I would labor back up the slippery hill, my hands groping for whatever small holds they could locate in the ice pack, until I reached the door and fell into my house, breathless and exhausted. At times, a neighbor would walk by as I struggled to get up or down the driveway and call out: *Tough driveway, huh?* No one offered to help.

The storm came through on a Tuesday, and by Sunday, I was out of food. I had to make a run to the grocery store. It took me four difficult trips up and down the drive to get the bags of food into the house. Once more, neighbors out walking passed me and laughed at my efforts, though there was nothing funny about the treacherous climb up the icy hill. *Having a hard time?* Not one of them offered to carry a bag.

That night, I hit bottom in my occasional despair about being a woman who owns, lives in and manages a home alone. I was angry at the lack of neighborliness in my community and desolate at the absence of compassion. I'd just read the story of the man who spent his days clearing his neighbors' driveways, asking for nothing, and wondered where the good neighbors were in my world. This was my something *lost*.

At the peak of my despair, Ellie called to see if I was joining them for a meeting that evening. I explained that I couldn't make

it up and down that hill one more time that day, especially at
night, when it was cold and a new glaze of ice would have
formed, making the daily trek even more treacherous. I'm quite
sure I cried. I gave up any pretense of courage in the presence
of adversity and collapsed into utter desolation.

Within fifteen minutes, Ellie and Peter were at the foot of my
driveway, chipping away at the ice, creating a narrow path and
enough traction for me to walk to and from my car. They worked
for several hours in the bitter cold, to create a six-inch-wide path
so I could walk from the house to my car and not be afraid of
falling with every step. It was comforting to receive their support
and help: my moment of something *found*.

The next morning, I woke to a fresh blanket of clean white snow
covering the ice: The goopy, wet snow that your feet can sink
into for a good grip. I was dressed and down on the street,
cleaning my car of the snow at the same time one of my
neighbors was cleaning his. As I shoveled and swept snow, I
pondered what it means to be a "good neighbor" and what we
lose if we neglect to be. For a few minutes, I nursed my
resentments . . . but then I remembered who I am and what I
teach to other people. *What if I stopped blaming others for not
being good neighbors and put the same amount of energy into
being a good neighbor myself?*

In that moment of epiphany, I released my frustration and decided
not to wait for my neighbors to figure out how to help each other.
We could learn together. I walked over one driveway and offered
to help Don clear his car. Then and there, I proposed a barter: if
he would use his snow-blower to clear the end of my drive after
the city plow came through, I would help him plan and plant his
gardens in the spring. He was delighted, and I no longer felt like
a victim of isolation. Another *something found.*

Spring came. As promised, I divided my iris and lilies, and

showed Don how to plant and care for them. I dug up a rose bush that hadn't favored the spot where I had planted it, and the two of us placed it in the sun by his deck, where we've both enjoyed watching it bloom profusely each summer since the treacherous storm. The seasons changed . . . and we have practiced being good neighbors.

One morning last winter, I woke up and wandered downstairs to see Don teaching his daughter how to sled on the little hill between our two houses, just the right size to be exciting for a little girl three-years-old. She was covered in powdery snow, head to foot, giggling as children do when they are having fun with their daddies, flying down a hill on a new red sled. I sat in the window—a cup of sweet, hot tea in my hands—watching the two of them fly over the hill, walk back up, and fly down another time. Lauren stood on her unsteady little legs, then fell and rolled around in the snow, before she made a next try to reach the top of the hill.

Months later, I watched from the same window as her baby brother took his first tentative steps on that same slope of lawn between our houses. Lucas teetered and fell, rolling down the slope like his sister, and came up giggling. These children delight me as they play. Sometimes, they delight me with fat tomatoes freshly plucked from their garden. Other times, Lauren tickles me by standing under my living room window and calling for me to come and "visit" with her. She pulls me away from my work and tricks me into attending to the things that are truly important: listening to a child, laughing over her stories and antics, stopping absolutely everything to enjoy a bowl of ice cream with her.

I found I do have neighbors, after all, but it took me making an effort *to become a good neighbor* before I found what I was looking for. It's an art, neighborliness. And, now that I have it, not one I ever want to lose.

But more than that, this was a lesson to me. I could have, as I've done on occasion, sat alone in my despair and waited for something good to come my way. I believe we live in a basically good world, among people whose hearts are fundamentally kind. Over time, when a need is apparent, someone steps to the plate. I had been waiting for someone to recognize my need. Wrong avenue of approach. When I finally chased away my despair and acted as if we were all good neighbors, I found a good neighbor living right beside me. I had to change before others did. I had to reach out in order for someone else to reach back, to free my heart from resentment before something else could enter. *I had to make the first move.*

As Gandhi once said: *We must be the change we wish to see in the world.*

And so it is. If I hold out my hand to steady you, there's a good chance you will hold yours out to me. As we make our way along the slippery slope of life, understanding that any one of us could fall through the cracks at any time, that hand holding ours makes all the difference.

I suspect that is God: in that moment where two hands meet and hold onto each other. Where one neighbor digs up a sluggish rosebush and plants it in another's yard to give them the promise and pleasure of watching flowers bud and bloom or the scent of roses on the morning breeze. Where two people work in a bitter cold, chipping away at a solid block of ice so a friend can make it to work without falling. When a little girl waits eagerly for "alone time" with the woman next door, and a chance to talk about her adventures over a bowl of chocolate ice cream.

God in small moments. God in our ordinary actions. God in each of us, at work chipping away the barriers we place between ourselves and others, when we forget that we are all one family. A homeless man, for whatever harsh blows life has dealt him, and I'm sure there are many, knows this. It took me more time, and a loosening of the bitter pill of resentment, before I learned it too.

℘

- What if . . . God is not a *being* who is taking action in the world, but the *action* itself? What if . . . God is the *action and interaction* occurring in the moment one of us helps a neighbor, plants flowers in someone's yard, plucks a ripe tomato from the garden for the person next door to enjoy with dinner? What if . . . God is in our falling down, and our getting up to try again? What if . . . God is the act of *reaching out* to another, and the act of *receiving*?

- What if God is always *happening*? What if God is a verb, as Rabbi David Cooper suggests, and not a noun? What does this challenge or change in your relationship with God?

Out of the emptiness

A woman's lesson is a practical one:
whenever there is dryness,
go and get the rain.

—Nancy Wood

Indigenous people have always used *story* as a primary medium through which to teach their children, and themselves, how to live in peaceful co-existence with each other and the world around them. They offer their stories in a magical way: sitting in circle around the fire late at night, accompanied by the soft beating of drums and blanketed by the vastness of the heavens, voices deep and resonant to imbue their stories with power to shape the lives of the people.

Jesus was another master storyteller. Gathering the people in circles around him, he would sit in courtyards, in simple mud homes, on hillsides, or beside the sea, and he would teach any woman, man or child who came to listen. We call stories that are passed to us through Christian tradition *parables*. Yet, many of us do not have a simple understanding that the parables were meant as *instructions* on how to live as children of the Great Mystery.

Some stories, like the teaching stories of indigenous people and the parables of Jesus, are given so they will be shared with others; so they will lend illumination to the dark corners of our lives; so that we not only learn from them, but others do as well; so the hardships of life become more understandable and easier to bear. This is one such story.

I'm a woman who has walked a different path. From the time I was a young woman to the present, my life has taken surprising turns and pointed me in directions I could not have foreseen and did not always welcome. Looking back through the humor and maturity of mid-life, I'm able to see clearly that the Mystery offered another script for me than the one I had in mind for myself. The only one of my original plans that has survived the events of my life is that I am a mother. All the other roles have dropped away, have been altered in significant ways, or have been stripped from me, painfully or poignantly, not without suffering. One process of stripping away has involved my desire for financial and material assurance.

I grew up in a family where there was none. For a number of reasons, my family perched on a financial teeter-totter. As the oldest child, I was aware of my family's financial unpredictability and my mother's terror about financial insecurity. Later, when it was my turn to make choices about a career and marriage, I made them—at least in small measure—with the hope of creating greater security and stability for my children than I had known. I certainly loved my husband dearly, but I arrived at marriage vigilant about the burden of worry economic hardships insinuate into a family. I was looking for a quiet life of financial predictability: bills paid, income enough for an occasional family vacation, a fund to educate our children. *That wasn't the life looking for me.*

Three times in the first four decades of my life, all my carefully gathered resources were swept totally away. Three times, I found myself standing at the threshold of a new life with no financial underpinning. The second time I stood at that threshold, I had one child in college and another about to enroll. I could not get a grip on a way to manage the enormity of the financial challenge ahead of me.

Through unexpected mercy, and by living very simply, I was able to rebuild my resources, help in the education of my children, and save several thousand dollars. The process took a very long time. I spent innumerable sleepless nights making it over one financial hurdle, and then another, until it seemed most of the hurdles had been cleared. My small savings account gave me a bit of comfort that we'd survive if my battered car finally gave up or the furnace self-destructed in the middle of a cold winter's night. I was breathing more easily than I had for six years.

About that time, I received disheartening news: my tax accountant had made a major reporting error for the previous year. I would owe in taxes and penalties the exact amount of money in my savings account. Not a dollar more, and not a penny less. Everything I had so carefully put aside was being stripped away *again*. It was painfully evident that I was not going to be allowed the financially predictable life I wanted to have. One could say *humorously* evident, though, at the time, I wasn't laughing.

I didn't take the blow well. For two days, I dropped into a very deep grief built out of too many years bouncing back after one loss, only to collide with another. I didn't feel victimized. I knew others in my position, most of them single mothers trying to stay afloat financially while raising their children. Nor did I take the blow personally. I didn't feel singled out for hardship. *This was simply a hard experience to undergo.* The grief felt clean and clear and straight-ahead.

I was faced with letting go of my lifelong desire for financial reassurance. It was dramatically clear that I wouldn't be indulged in my lingering illusion that something or someone *outside me* would provide what I'd longed for all my life: a sense that I was safely held in an unsafe world. Money wasn't the answer to this longing. It was also clear there was nothing to do but let it all go and lean into the Mystery for comfort.

Knowing this was far easier than doing it.

This collision of my plans with The Mystery came just before Easter that year. As I wrestled with an enormity of grief that life seemed so hard and unforgiving, I wrote these words: *We're entering Holy Week, and I'm on my way to Jerusalem. I'm not in the crowds, waving palms, celebrating the appearance of the Savior. There's no savior. I'm somber, quiet, and walking alone through the vast emptiness of an emotional desert.*

A friend reminded me yesterday that, during another Holy Week several years ago, I had asked her the question, "What part of you is willing to be surrendered or crucified in order for you to find new life?" I stand before that same question now.

Yes: I am on the road to Jerusalem. Nothing my ego planned for, or carried out, in my life has worked as I thought it would. I'm living, not the life I have chosen, but the life that was chosen for me. In a very strange way, in the center of grief and emptiness, I am discovering I've been given the life I wanted after all.

I'm learning where predictability, safety, security truly lie, and where they don't. In one more paradoxical intervention, the Mystery is teaching me what I haven't been able to learn at other times, in other ways. Am I willing to learn it now?

After two days of tearful conversations with trusted friends, I

arrived at an epiphany. *I stood at the place most people fear most.*
I had no money, no relief on the horizon, no partner to think
through the problem with me, or to help alleviate it. This was
as stark and alone as it gets. One of my friends said to someone
else at a juncture like this, "You're living my worst nightmare."
Well, it was also mine. Here I was, with no place to hide, nothing
to grasp for security, no one to turn to but me . . . and I'd already
exhausted my own resources.

At this realization, another part of me kicked into action. I
decided not to run from this place, but instead to enter it. I
decided to visit the emptiness in order to learn from it. It occurred
to me that whatever I learned from the emptiness, I could bring
back to help others learn. With that decision, I took a deep breath
and descended into the void.

I sat in silence for hours. I simply took one breath, released it,
and then drew another. On each intake of breath, I felt the
emptiness. It ran through me like a hollow tube, top to bottom.
I thought of the times I escaped from it by filling my life with
activity. I thought of my efforts to flee the emptiness by
pretending to be someone I was not. I thought of all the ways I
had bolted from the emptiness, using various forms of temporary
relief such as food, television, reading, or shopping.

I thought of times I'd been thrust into the emptiness before,
peered into its dark abyss for a few brave moments, and then
abandoned my courage. At no time had I believed it possible to
enter the emptiness in a sacred manner, humbled, to prostrate
myself before it. *To sit still for the emptiness to teach me what*
I obviously needed to learn.

It occurred to me that it was possible to visit this emptiness as
a tourist instead of a hostage. That I could look around with a
spiritual curiosity. That I could notice what I liked and what I
didn't like about being in a space where there was nothing and

no one to rescue me or make me whole. I realized that I could send postcards-from-the-edge of this abyss to friends and clients, using my personal suffering to benefit others. I could take the lessons I'd come to learn . . . and leave when I was ready to go.

I continued to breathe one breath of emptiness at a time, following the Buddhist mindfulness practice in which I allowed the emptiness to ebb and flow. Nothing to hold me. Nothing to anchor me on this earth. Allowing grief to pass through me without attaching to it. Feeling my fears without judging or criticizing them. Experiencing compassion for the difficulties I had endured. Just *noticing* the reality of a hard passage.

After some time, I became aware of a change in the emptiness. I was filling up, but with what? Nothing had changed. I was still poor. But there was a sense of comfort. A surprising sense that this was not so devastating as it seemed, that all would be well whether I had money in a savings account or not. All I was doing was taking a breath. Where was this comfort coming from?

More time passed. Another breath, and then one more. I began to experience a sense of deep peace and ease quietly running through me. I examined my life and learned that I was pleased with my choices, with the way I had lived, with who I have been for others. I watched as the faces of dear friends and family members came into awareness. My heart flooded with love for each of the precious individuals who walk this path through life with me, companions on the journey. The sun streamed into my living room and touched my skin with the delicious warmth of early spring. *Isn't this interesting?* I marveled. *I'm no longer feeling empty. I am not afraid.*

Nothing had changed except that I had entered the emptiness and made room for it to be *what it was* rather than flee from it or fill it with distractions and hollow reassurances.

I breathe in. I breathe out. Something is there in the breath. I begin to fill again. The emptiness eases. The next breath does not hurt as much as the last. There is room in my chest for the breath to expand me. There is more air filling me. There is comfort in the breath, and peace. There is presence with me inside the aloneness.

Could it be that this is grace? Could it be that I don't have to do anything but make room in me for grace and Mystery to enter? That God is as near as my next breath? That God resides in me as the breathing in and breathing out? Is this "ruach?"

With those questions, I experienced a groundswell of gratitude in the place that had so recently been filled with fear. I wrote: *This time there are no voices in the night. No revelatory dreams. No prophesies or visions. This is quiet. So subtle I could have— no, I would have—missed it if I'd chosen to lose myself in the drama and fear I was so busy generating.*

The spiritual tradition of my upbringing calls this the Christ, or God. I call it The One Whose Name Is Holy. The Quiet One. The Breath. I remember a friend standing at the edge of the cliffs near my home one day last week, looking respectfully toward the beautiful sky and magnificent ocean rolling in our direction, throwing her arms wide in embrace, and speaking these words in a hushed and reverent voice: "Ahhh . . . She Who Is."

He Who Is. She Who Is . . . is in my every breath. When I remember to breathe, I know *alone* is a relative term, and I am not.

As I lifted out of the emptiness that day, I was no longer the person who had entered it. I had changed in the emptiness. As I turned into it, breathed into it, lived into it, I made a deliberate descent into the void I had feared so strongly . . . and found a profound fullness of spirit waiting for me there. Every spiritual teacher from all of time and before time, has told those who seek a fulfilling life that it's not what we do, nor what we own of material wealth, that fulfills us. It's the *letting go* of everything that has outlived its time or usefulness—that which gives only an illusion of happiness—that offers the truest gifts of Spirit.

Diving into the emptiness, I made a difficult leap into greater spiritual maturity. Had I been in less pain, I wouldn't have taken the risk. Pain pushes us to go to places we would prefer to ignore. In the darkness of the void, something waited for me to claim it: a new understanding of *fulfillment*.

The Mystery waits for us everywhere: in the darkness and the light, in the expected and the unpredictable, in the known and the unknown, in the beauty and even in the ugliness, in the fullness of life and certainly in the emptiness. It waits for us to arrive, probably lost, seeking assurance, willing to learn, or ready to be transformed. It waits for us to take one breath in the direction of our own suffering, and, as we exhale, to release our fears. And then, to descend, dropping down, into the fullness of its amazing, inexplicable grace.

All we have to do is to stand still, stand still, rather than run from it . . . and breathe into, rather than away from, the gifts it holds out to us.

ʃ

- When have you experienced a total emptiness of spirit? Nothing left but the next breath. No one to help the situation but you. What was that experience like for you?

- How does it help you to be periodically emptied of your illusions or your own plans for things to unfold in a certain way? Why do you think this is a necessary part of the spiritual journey?

- Who or what was with you in the emptiness? What might the emptiness have come to teach you?

- Think for a moment about breathing in and breathing out, remembering that sometimes that this is the best we can do. What lies in the pause between the in-breath and the out-breath? What forces the turn from one to the other? What turns you back toward "saying yes" to life? Can you imagine that this is the Mystery of God *breathing you?*

- Based on your experiences of God, how would you describe *grace*? When has the Mystery held an experience of grace out to you?

Faith

*. . . people are established inalienably
in my memories only if their names
were entered in the scrolls of my
destiny from the beginning, so that
encountering them was at the same
time, a kind of recollection.*

—*Carl Gustav Jung*

I have been a practicing psychotherapist for almost twenty years.
Before that, a nurse, a health educator and advocate for people
coming into the health care system under unsettling and often
frightening circumstances. My professional work has been to
guide people through the unknown terrain of significant life
passages, from birth through death. This work carries the weight
of responsibility and the humility of privilege: it has been an
honor to witness such profound personal heroism. Along the way,
I've occasionally said or done something that was experienced
by another person as one of their "little scraps of paper"—a sign,
an instruction—on life's rocky road.

One recent morning in a place far from home, something happened that was so unlikely there is no explanation for it. There is no way this could have been random or coincidental. Surely this was one of those scraps of paper with instructions, possibly for me. For all too many reasons, this encounter wasn't even *possible*. Yet it happened just as I tell it.

I had been visiting a friend in Florida, twelve hundred miles from New England, where I live. It was the last of several lovely days together, and we were hurrying to reach an appointment when we made a spontaneous decision to duck into a fast food restaurant for breakfast. The place was crowded and noisy that morning, but we located a section of the restaurant that was quiet. We were alone there, chatting softly, when a young family came into our section and took a booth just to the left of us.

I glanced briefly at them as they entered and continued my conversation. Then something—just a hunch—made me look again. The woman looking directly at me, clearly as incredulous as I was, was Rebecca, my daughter's best high school friend. I hadn't seen her since six years earlier, on a beautiful summer day: the day of her marriage to Jamie. I was one of a small group of family and friends who gathered on the banks of a slow-moving river to bless the union of two courageous young people.

Rebecca had an unusual passage into adulthood. Like so many others of her age, she left home after graduation to attend college in another part of the country. She soon became involved with a man she met in this bright new potential of a life. And, while Becca's friends were settling into their dormitories and getting to know their roommates, she was getting pregnant. Many months passed before friends learned the hardships she was facing as a pregnant teen in a city far from home.

After Becca's daughter was born, she returned home to care for her with the help of her parents and friends. Everyone pitched in, and Becca began to get on with life as a young, bewildered single parent. Some of her friends, young people confused by Rebecca's radically altered plans, were unable to stick around for the hard work of supporting her in a new life. Becca, however, deftly regained her footing and established a routine, or as much routine as a new, inexperienced mother can develop. Then, one particularly difficult day, Becca was informed that—as a result of the short-lived relationship with her baby's father—she was now HIV-positive.

She barely had time or energy to think. She had a baby to raise. She took her medications with her morning vitamins and kept moving, placing one brave, determined foot in front of the other. The baby thrived in the warm and loving womb of Becca's family. Still, many of us who loved her were concerned that life for Becca would always be stressful, definitely fraught with more than her fair share of problems, largely lived without a mate. Enter Jamie.

I cannot remember any of the details. I don't even recall where he came from. I just remember Jamie becoming a regular presence in Becca's life, seeing strength and beauty in this remarkable young woman's sturdy character. Jamie loved her even with all the challenges that lay ahead of them. On their wedding day, they were filled with a wonderful joy. Jamie adopted Becca's then three-year-old daughter, and they immediately embarked on a mission to build more of a family. The last time I saw Rebecca, she was pregnant once again. This was the singularly courageous act of faith for which she would later name her second-born daughter.

Becca and Jamie left home and moved to another part of the country to begin a new life. From time to time, my daughter would report on their lives, but over several years the ties connecting my life to hers grew thin. That was, until the morning I looked up on a hunch and saw Rebecca's beautiful face.

She swooped down on me before I fully registered the remarkable coincidence that placed us at side-by-side booths in a restaurant I have never visited before. We were laughing and declaring our mutual astonishment to find each other under such circumstances. Rebecca told us that she and Jamie had recently experienced a setback in their lives and decided to search for a place to jumpstart their lives. She said she had multiple "signs" that pointed them in the direction of the city I was visiting. Stepping back, examining me to be sure I was real, she said, "And you're the best sign of all. I never imagined anything like this!"

Well, yes, imagine. The odds were long, but the Mystery sometimes dances with utter glee. God as the Ultimate Trickster. It's been known to happen.

Imagine what came next. Becca's young daughters, Cara and Faith, hovered at the edge of this cacophony of delight between their mother and me. Cara, a tall doe-eyed nine year-old with her mother's beauty and sweet disposition, hugged me warmly. But it was Faith, a child I had never met but whose birth I'd anxiously awaited, who took control of my heart. She was four years old, a miniature angel. This tiny girl slipped up beside me, wrapped her arms hard around my neck, and whispered, "I have missed you so much!" Faith remembered me. Yet we'd never seen each other before.

In my days as a nurse, I worked in a neonatal care unit where babies arrived immediately after birth and were observed for the first twelve hours of their lives. We considered this part of the nursery a favorite assignment because we were the first to welcome these spirit-babes into their just-incarnated bodies. We were the first people to look into their eyes, the first to see who was peering back at us through the eyes of the recently born. This experience was nothing short of magical.

Many times, all we'd see was a groggy newborn, coated with

amniotic fluid and vernix, wearing a dazed expression. You could read the questions in a baby's eyes: *What happened to me? How did I get here? Where am I?* But every once in a while, looking into the eyes of a newborn, we could see that a baby was *in there*, present with old, deep-seeing eyes and an almost ancient wisdom. They were not dazed or confused. They looked steadily back at us as if they had just arrived on assignment from another place in the universe. The nurses called these babies "old souls." We made up stories about them and believed—well, it was more that we just *knew*—they had come *remembering* what the other babies had forgotten when their tiny bodies slid into a bright, noisy and confusing world.

On rare occasions through my subsequent years as a pediatric nurse and childbirth educator, I would encounter a baby like this: an old soul, looking back at me with the eyes of the ancients. Or there would be a small child, usually no older than four or five, who would tell us stories of the places she had been and the people she had loved before coming here.

Years later, these *old soul* children came to my counseling office as teenagers or young adults. In fact, they still do, and I am always delighted to see one of them coming through the door. They sometimes describe themselves as "wanderers" searching for a place they refer to as "home" and looking for the people they call "my family." I have been at this work in one form or another for over thirty years, and I've met dozens of old souls in young bodies, struggling to make sense of their lives. They seem to retain a memory most of us have lost. Faith was one of those children: "*I have missed you so much!*"

My friend was as transfixed as I was. Faith was a beautiful child, radiating light in a brilliant orb around her. In one instant, hearing her words, I felt seen by her, known to her, connected with her in a bond of immeasurable love.

How do we explain these children? I can't. I only know they exist: these children who remember and wait, often longingly, until someone remembers them back. I know this because I was one of them. I searched most of my childhood to find what I called "my people." They were not my parents, though I certainly loved them. They weren't the friends I played with, happily enough. My people were somewhere else in the world, and it was my mission to find them. When we had finally found each other, I hoped they would also remember, as I thought I did, where we came from . . . and what we were sent here to do.

Time passed. I grew older and became more forgetful. Doubting my own truth, I began to think there were no "people" to be found. Like the children who came to see me, I felt *different*. Alone in a world that wasn't my own. Whenever I saw children or adults hurting one another, I wanted to weep. I was certain this was not in the plan for the human family. I had no one to talk to . . . and learned to keep this part of me silent. I walked out of church school when the teacher, who had us memorizing Bible passages, publicly humiliated a child fidgeting in his seat. At eleven, I went home, lifted my chin, and defiantly told my mother and father, "I'm not going back there. That man is a hypocrite!" It speaks well for my parents that they took me seriously and supported my decision.

Later in life, I found a few of my people, one at a time, and with great relief. They remembered many of the things I thought I remembered. With them, there was a powerful felt-experience of finding not just a friend, but also a friend from "home." These are people with whom I share an affinity and an understanding of the way we are meant to be with one another. Perhaps no more than a dozen of them in my entire life, most of them children or young adults. Faith is one of the twelve. All are close to my heart.

William Martin, Director of The Still Point, an educational and consulting center in California, has written a lovely book called *The Parent's Tao Te Ching*. Passage 21 is titled, "The Hidden Mystery of their Being."

> *Although you give your children names,*
> *their reality is nameless and mysterious.*
> *Their mystery is hidden,*
> *yet plain to see.*
> *It disappears when you stare at it.*
> *It hides when you seek it.*
> *To find it you must look into yourself.*
> *If you can discover the secret of your own life,*
> *you will glimpse the mystery of your children.*
>
> *Though this mystery cannot be described,*
> *it can be trusted.*
> *You can trust it in yourself.*
> *You can trust it in your children.*
> *How do I know this?*
> *I see it everywhere.*
> *Imagine yourself as a child.*
> *There was someone present there*
> *your parents never knew,*
> *a mystery they could not fathom.*
> *Look at your children closely.*
> *You will never know the mystery of their being.*
> *Can you love them still?*

He's writing about the Mystery inborn in each of us, but, for reasons we have yet to understand, more visible and palpable in these indescribable children. The other day, I was thinking about how I would write about them—mostly so you will notice them when they cross your path, as they surely will. Then I had an e-mail from a financial planner who's a friend and a "salt of the earth" kind of guy. He forwarded some information I needed to know and included with it a photograph of a beautiful newborn baby. Two days later, I phoned him to complete the business his e-mail began. When we were finished, I asked about the baby.

Which of his children did she belong to? What was her name?

He launched into a story that moved me to tears. This was Phoebe, and she was two weeks old. He told me he'd discovered that one of the best things he could do with his life was to hold his grandchild—her head cupped in one hand, her baby bottom in the other—and *rock her.* He told me that he sat that way for hours, sometimes singing to her, sometimes blowing a gentle breath on her skin, sometimes scratching her skin lightly. (My baby sister used to plead for this as she fell asleep at night. "Tickle me nicely, Sissy," she would beg.)

If he rocked and sang and blew and tickled Phoebe nicely . . . *long enough*, he said . . . sometimes she would release a long sigh of contented pleasure. His Phoebe encounters were important enough for him to close his business down for a day last week, for him to drive three hours to her home, and for him to spend the day holding her. He's learning how to be present to the hidden mystery of her being.

He asked me—this gentle man who loves golf and other guy things—why more men don't realize what a gift it is to sit for hours, holding an infant and looking deep into their baby spirits. "It isn't for her that I do this," he explained, making sure I understood the point of his story. "I do this for me. She is a reminder of what's important in life. I love Phoebe in a way I didn't feel when my own kids were born. Back then, fathers weren't encouraged to take part in the care of their babies. I think that's a big mistake!"

I have an interesting window on the world. Every year for more than twenty years, people with various forms of broken heartedness or whose spirits are weary, come though my door, sit in my office, and begin to tell me their stories. These are people of all ages, very young to very old. As I sit with them, I listen devoutly—or try to, most of the time—and hear what is heaviest on their hearts. From time to time, one of them will look at me, imploring me to understand what they're about to say, and ask, "Where are my people?"

I have come to the conclusion, based on listening to thousands of people tell me the truths they have buried deep in their hearts, that each generation born to the human family is more conscious than the last. That we are slowly growing in awareness. That each generation is made pregnant with, and gives birth to, the teachers of tomorrow. That our own children are the ones who lead us forward toward enlightenment, or full awakening into God-consciousness. The children born in this epoch of human history are far more advanced souls than the ones with whom I played as a child. More of them know who they are, and what they are here to do.

This is what I know from listening to them: that they are wise in the art of love; that they spread their love broad and wide and with no holding back; that they remember we are brothers and sisters under the skin; that they are baffled by wars we insist must be fought and troubled by divisiveness we insist on perpetuating; that they relate easily to the creatures who share the earth with us. I do not know the name by which they are called. I've heard others call them the Indigo Children, or the Crystal Children, and even the Spiritual Peacemakers. I don't know if they have a name for themselves. That doesn't seem to matter.

I write this lovingly to acknowledge Faith and all the children *from away*—as they quietly speak of themselves—who manage to keep the hidden mystery of their being *awake and alive* despite the strong forces conspiring to dumb down what they are born knowing. It should give us pause that our religious traditions frequently try the hardest to strip children of their own "first" or God-given nature. Of all they know when they come here. Of all they have come here to tell us. *Are we listening?*

While I believe every child is a miracle, the children who remember their origins and true nature are particular miracles. If you should be lucky enough to encounter one, give her, give him—in the words of the Quakers—your *devout attention*. Listen quietly to the mystery that lives within them. They have much to teach us about who we really are . . . and they will tell you if you sit with them long enough, quietly enough, looking and listening deeply enough, to hear.

ℭ

- Almost every one of us has, at one time or another, encountered a child who seems to be an *old soul*. Many of us quietly believe there are more of these *old soul* children coming to help the people of earth in our great time of need. These are children through whom the Mystery is able to pour extravagant love upon our tired spirits. Who are these children in your life?

- What is it about them that you recognize as *different*? What is it about them that makes you want to give them your devout attention?

- What do you think William Martin means when he writes: *If you can discover the secret of your own life, you will glimpse the mystery of your children?* What is that "hidden mystery" of which he writes?

- The joy of finding "our people" and the pain of losing them is a perpetual paradox. If this is a term you relate to, whom do you mean when you speak of "your people?" Name them. Many of us do not find "our people" in our families of origin. What transpires between you that has made your people members of your heart's family?

Dark days and nights of the soul

How ever great one's suffering is,
if it comes through God,
God suffers from it first.
And remember this:
all suffering comes to an end.

—*Meister Eckhart*

A number of years ago, following the prolonged and painful end of a long-term relationship, I found myself floundering, to quote from *The Never-Ending Story*, in the "bog of endless despair." The relationship left a wake of considerable heartache and destruction. My partner and I were among the walking wounded, a difficult enough truth to face, but this was compounded by undeniable signs that my son and daughter, innocent of complicity in the collapse of this relationship, also felt the loss in ways that impacted their young lives. I was burdened by a sense of accountability for the hurts we had inflicted on our family, our friends and our spiritual community.

Too many beloved people were reeling from our actions toward each other. Too many who had known us, loved us, trusted us, and counted upon us. We'd betrayed ourselves and betrayed others. A difficult truth to endure, and as dark a time as I had known. It would take more than two years for me to turn the corner on this grief.

In the months after my partner and I had separated, I had numerous dreams pointing the way to reconciliation. Neither of us wanted to resume the relationship as we had known it, but there was a persistent flicker of hope in me that we would each find forgiveness for the other. We tried, but one of us always rose up again in full wounded mode. The pain resumed, and we backed away from all contact. This was a deadly dance, nearly as consuming as it had been while we were together. But my dreams always indicated forgiveness was possible.

For this reason, I continued to hope we could eventually reach the point where it was more important to part in love than it was to prevail in the struggles that destroyed our ability to value the other-as-partner in the first place.

I had a long series of dreams in which we attempted to create healing and peace with one another. The dreams did not change the reality, however, and we both continued to push and pull in the struggle to say goodbye. In time, I came to the understanding that the reconciliation we were not able to realize in waking time, was actually unfolding through the medium of dreams. This gave me comfort and, finally, a quieting of the terrible pain. I allowed the dreams to guide me in the direction of the only reconciliation I could influence: the one within my own sorely broken heart. The healing occurred gradually, dream after dream, taking place over many months. The days and nights of my soul's despair lingered on, but it was loosening its grip.

By this time, my children had both left home for college, and I lived alone in a house at the edge of the woods. The house was isolated from neighbors, surrounded only by trees, salt marsh, and creatures who lived deep in the forest. I loved living in the middle of the natural world, so I had never put curtains on any of the windows. As I fell asleep at night, I looked up to see a thousand pinpoints of light thrown haphazardly across the nightscape of the heavens, landing in patterns that formed mythical forms and beings. Sirius the Dog Star, Orion the warrior, the seven-sister stars of the Pleiades, Cassiopeia.

One night, tired and lonely, I looked out on the round silver circle of a full moon. I was grateful for the light that filled my bedroom. In some mysterious way, moonlight connected me to the larger universe. I lay under the quilt for a long time, gazing at the moon, openly praying for help in my healing journey. *My heart is broken. I am so lonely. If you're listening to me, God, if you truly exist anywhere in this vast universe, help me to get out of bed tomorrow and begin another day. I don't have the strength to do it alone.* Truth spoken at last, and tears shed, I slept.

I was given a dream that night in which my partner and I met alone in a sacred place, where we asked for and offered forgiveness for the words and actions that hurt us both. In the middle of the night, I woke myself with the sound of my own sobbing. It was finished. There was nothing left to be said or to be acknowledged between us. We each confessed our transgressions and forgave the other. Spent with relief and gratitude, I wept long into the dark of the night. At last, I just lay there, resting from the arduous journey back to my self. I felt whole once more.

Then I heard sounds at the bedroom door. *I was not alone in the house.* A surge of panic. It was too dark to see. The moon had moved its position in the sky. There was no light streaming into the room. No light at all. Only darkness. And the sound of the bedroom door opening. I lay still, afraid of what was to come.

My eyes were open but I could see nothing. I sensed someone enter, move across the room, and come alongside my bed. The bed sagged with the measurable weight of this person, and the air moved as an arm lifted above my body. I was sure these were my last moments of life. Believing I was about to be murdered, I waited for the blow that would take my life. Though I tried not to breathe or make a sound, I could hear myself. My breath was ragged and raspy with fear.

What happened next is difficult to believe. I've told only a few close friends, although once I took a risk and spoke of this experience to a group of women in one of our spiritual direction programs. One woman suggested I might be psychotic. Her reaction was unsettling but didn't change the truth: I had an encounter with something holy and utterly mysterious.

The hand came down upon my body, but not with a weapon and surely not to kill me. The hand rested gently over my heart. I was instantly paralyzed by a potent stream of warmth-love that flowed directly from this hand into my body. Starting at my feet, my body began to fill with a sensation so delicious it seemed ecstatic and blissful. It filled my feet on into my legs, my torso and chest, through my neck and into my head. I'd have to guess at the time this took: perhaps one or two minutes. Abruptly, I felt so full of love, so full of bliss, that I had the thought: *I can't take in any more*. As that thought formed in my mind, the hand lifted from my body.

After a few moments of rest, the hand came down on my heart again, and the whole experience was repeated. The warmth-bliss started with my feet, running the length of my legs into my body, filling me completely. It seemed certain, so obvious, I would rupture from the *fullness* of this ecstatic love. I was completely loved by this being, and I was completely in love. Every cell of me vibrated with love, and I understood at last what it was like to be held by the presence of a love that is beyond my imagination. When there was no room left in me to absorb the feelings of ecstasy, the hand lifted again . . . and waited.

The third time, two hands came down on both sides of my head. What felt like fingers actually penetrated the bones of my cranium and began to move around inside my brain. The only way to describe this part of the experience is that it felt like the neural pathways in my brain were being re-wired. I was a telephone switchboard, one wire being pulled out and another being plugged in.

I was overcome with awe. *How could this be happening? Why was it happening? Who was this, touching my heart and healing me so profoundly?*

Finally, the hands rose from me one last time. The weight lifted from my bed, someone crossed the room in reverse from the entry, and the bedroom door was closed. I could move again: the paralysis was gone. Nothing else had changed. There was still no light from the moon, and total darkness in the room. All occurred in absolute silence.

Although I have often encountered the Mystery in my dreams, this was the most profoundly personal and directly mystical an encounter as I'd ever had. The evidence was the immediate change in me. I was healed of any residual emotional pain, and my heart felt like it had been transplanted into my body from a source closer to God than I. I throbbed with love. It flowed from me in all directions. Compassion took the place of resentment and anger. This healing-transformation-change occurred in a single night. More, during just a few minutes of a single night.

That was eight or more years ago. I continue to feel the power of that encounter in my daily life. My ability to care for others has greatly enlarged. I'm generous with my love because I am no longer afraid there won't be enough of me to go around. I used to be fearful that, if I opened my heart, others would take more than I had to give. Now I know that there is always enough love. If I empty out, I can easily replace the stores with prayer or meditation.

I'd suffered for two years, and suddenly—in a mysterious act of grace—the suffering was over. What did I learn from this encounter with the *holy other?*

That there is, in truth, a love greater than the human imagination can begin to understand. It's there for us to draw upon in our darkest days and nights of the soul. The *holy other* visits us, and fills us, so that we might know this love and pass it along to others. Love is meant to be in circulation. It's meant to be at work, touching people in the places where they have been broken, giving them courage and sustenance to go on with their lives after unbearable or devastating loss. And we have a part to play in the expansion and expression of that love.

If we hoard it, make it exclusively our own, love cannot do what it is intended to do: heal the world's suffering; eradicate the momentum of hatred and intolerance; open or expand the hearts of the human family; offer us a direct, personal encounter with the Mystery that many call God. We're given personal experiences of The Divine Heart so that we will grow in understanding of its true nature and pass on what we have learned.

When people ask me who or what it was that visited me in the deep darkness of my soul, I confess that I don't really know *who* it was. This was not the first time I'd been visited in the night. Another presence, perhaps the same one, came when I was twelve years old, suffering because of a rupture in the marriage between my parents. At the time of that visitation, I had burrowed into my fear and pushed the visitor away. Respecting my reluctance, the *holy other* sat on my bed for several minutes before leaving but made no attempt at direct contact. In the years between the first and the last encounters, all my direct experience of the Sacred occurred in dreams. There, I was visited often.

Could this have been an angel? Any one of the many great spiritual masters, including Jesus of Nazareth, Saint Catherine of Sienna, known for her great heart, or what we call the Holy Spirit? All are possibilities. But the truth is that I'll never know. My own thoughtful conclusion is that God exists more as the *energy* of great love than as the physical embodiment of it. I didn't see anyone that night because there was no one to see: *God is not a person.* I was visited by the Presence of Love, the source of all creation.

Embodiment of that love is the part that's been assigned to humans. We're put here on a mission to live out the full range of physical existence so that God might learn what it's all about. We are also here to incarnate the fullness of our divinity so that human beings might learn more about God through, among the many possibilities, our encounters with one another.

That's quite an assignment. Some of us accept it, and others turn away. Each of us is given the free will to choose this assignment, or not.

Because of my deliverance from suffering, I have chosen yes. For the rest of my life, I'm willing to serve the Great Heart that served me in my time of despair. That choice, however, comes at a cost: I surrender my personal will (or ego) in favor of the will of the *holy other.* Not my will, but thine. Anyone making this decision must agree to keep a portal open and available for the will of the *holy other* to work through him or her. I meditate. I pray. Often these hours seem to accomplish little but the slowing of my random, chaotic thoughts. Every once in a while, a still, small voice comes through: a faint whisper, a scrap of paper falls into my consciousness, or a dream illuminates another step. Then, I have my next instructions.

This is not a way of life many people can tolerate. It necessarily means an intellectual-spiritual state in which we always have our bags packed and are ready to travel. The uncertainty of it all can be too much for some. I understand this. It's often too much for me. I love my cozy little life and all its amenities. I'm not eager to become a spiritual vagabond. Still—and it's hard to explain this, especially as someone who generally doesn't defer to religious language—*having been touched by the hand of God,* I know that my spirit no longer belongs to me but to a greater and wiser plan. Surrender is the only option.

Since this encounter, and others that both preceded and followed it, I am convinced of the power of the *holy other* to heal us and to make us whole again. I want to participate in this effort. I want my life to be used in service to the mystery of reconciliatory Love. I have no quarrel with trading two years of suffering to come to this decision.

In one mysterious encounter, I learned beyond doubt that I—a woman living an imperfect life and in an imperfect body, afflicted by the ravages of grief and exhaustion—belong to the *holy other.* I am called to embody the *holy visitor:* right here, right now, in this broken life and this body. And in all probability, so are we all.

g

- On reading about this encounter, what is your reaction? At what times and in what ways have you felt the presence of God—or the holy other—descend on you? How have you been touched by the hand of God?

- Are there encounters with the Mystery you have held back for fear others would judge you or react in a negative way? What do you suppose some listening to this story are afraid to hear?

- In your "dark days and nights of the soul," what has sustained you? Write or tell a story about this experience. What do you know about the transforming presence of the *holy other?*

Troubles

God waits on human history
and suffers as she waits.

—*Meister Eckhart*

One recent August, His Holiness, the 14th Dalai Lama—a war exile from his own homeland of Tibet—spoke to 40,000 hushed and respectful people gathered in New York's Central Park and told them that "war is obsolete." He spoke those profound words to the people of a nation that has participated in every major war of the last hundred years. At the time, the President of the United States was actively campaigning to convince American citizens that the magnitude of suffering possible in future acts of terrorism made it imperative that we consider the use of nuclear weapons an option.

Since that time, we have crossed the thin line between the world as we knew it pre-September 11th and the world as we know it now. Wars have been waged in Afghanistan and Iraq, and we seem to be no farther ahead in bringing peace to those countries than before the wars began. We are still attempting to wage peace between reluctant Israeli leaders and resistant Palestinians. And North Korea awaits our attention, none too quietly. A Tibetan monk and the president of the world's most powerful nation offer two startlingly different visions for our common future. If they can't agree on what that future might be, *how are we—as earnest spiritual seekers—expected to make sense of the troubling times in which we live?*

Days before the Dalai Lama spoke to the masses assembled in Central Park, I returned from a trip to Northern Ireland. I'd planned this trip to meet my son, who was traveling in Europe on "the adventure of a lifetime." I was eager to participate in an experience that was maturing him in new and remarkable ways, but I also hungered for a great adventure of my own. This involved honoring an inner desire to plunge into the heart of what is commonly known in Northern Ireland as "the troubles."

I went to search for answers to my persistent questions about how a people who share blood, history and land could develop such strong hatred for one another. I wanted to explore the part played by religion in the war between Protestants and Catholics, and I desperately wanted some understanding of where, in the center of the suffering and wanton violence, *God is*. By the time I arrived in Dublin, I'd already embarked on a pilgrimage of my own.

My son and I passed safely through the military checkpoints that separate the Republic and the North of Ireland. We arrived in Belfast on the very day that former United States Secretary of State George Mitchell came to assist the deadlocked peace talks. Tension and hope were thick in the Irish air. Our first morning in Belfast, my son wanted to spend time with friends made on an earlier trip. I agreed to explore the city on my own. Our plan was to meet the next day to journey into the heart of Northern Ireland together.

I spent a lovely morning walking around the historic Queens University and the lavish Botanical Gardens that are at the center of the beautiful city of Belfast. The perennial gardens were in full bloom as far as the eye could see. Acres of rose bushes erupted with color, releasing delicate scents into the air. Some sweet, some spicy, some barely noticeable unless I lingered for the brisk summer breeze to blow the scent in my direction. The people of Belfast were warm, kind, funny, and generous to me as I meandered alone through an undiscovered city. It couldn't have been a more magical morning in Ireland.

That afternoon, I hired a driver to show me more of the city. When the driver asked me what I especially wanted to see of Belfast, I said, "I'd like to understand why this city is so divided and at war with itself." The driver had lived in Belfast all of his life, and he spared me nothing of the pain evident just under the surface of normalcy. Under his honest tutelage, I saw discrimination and dark brutality co-existing with Northern Ireland's succulent beauty. I saw the "peace wall," a stark emblem of hatred that winds through narrow, bleak streets and divides the city's Catholic neighborhoods from Protestant. He showed me ordinary sidewalks where men and women died in the bloody siege of hatred and terror, martyrs to the people of Northern Ireland, their names commemorated on walls throughout the city. I saw gaping holes ripped out of raw earth where tall buildings once stood. And I saw a solitary car in flames on the city streets.

The driver took me down a back street in an impoverished Catholic neighborhood and pointed toward a group of boys— who could have been my son or any of his friends—hanging out in a barren dirt back yard. Not a shaft of green grass anywhere. He told me the boys donned black face caps by night and transformed into paramilitary gang members. Most of them still had the pimpled, uncombed, unkempt, broody look of teenagers.

I turned to the other side of the street, so narrow that our car had to pass very slowly, and caught the eye of an angry looking Irish woman standing no more than three feet from the window of my taxi. She was sweeping the sidewalk and, though she seemed to be about my age, something made her appear twenty years older. Something hard and cold. Devoid of feeling. Penetrating. The woman's eyes bored her fury into mine, as she watched me drive through her life with the relative safety of an American tourist, curious about her world without having to experience it. Her angry, wizened face would return to haunt me.

After many hours, the driver returned me to my cozy inn, far from signs of *the troubles*. On the way, he turned onto a street my son and I walked together our first night in Belfast. I delighted in photographing the brightly painted doorways, the intricately wrought iron gates and miniature gardens that marked the quaint brick row houses. My son had told me this was a direct route to Queens University, the one he would take to reach the home of his friends. Just hours after he had turned down this street and walked into a city of people at war, the taxi driver warned me it was "the most dangerous road in all of Belfast. There's more paramilitary activity on this road than in any other part of the city. Don't you go walking about here, miss!"

His warning triggered an immediate, all-out fear for the safety of my son. And when Josh did not return to the inn that night, I was frightened beyond any fear I have ever known. I didn't know where he was, or who he was with, or how to reach him to confirm that he was safe. I had wild imaginings that, just as George Mitchell initiated the peace negotiations, the idea might strike a paramilitary group that holding an American hostage would give them an added leverage in the talks. In the terrible ache of a sleepless night, I imagined the worst possible outcome in the event I had to face it the next morning. Battling my fears, it seemed I could do nothing but wait until my son turned up at the time we had agreed to meet, and wonder: *Where is God in this anguish?*

I wept loudly. I prayed for him to be safe. In the dark hours of a merciless night, I grew angry with God. I yelled loudly, not caring if I woke other guests at the inn, "You can't have him! He's my son, and this is not his war!" And in the midst of my outrageous determination to keep a claim on my son's life, I was overcome with an odd kind of enveloping grace. This wasn't a peaceful kind of grace at all, but a disquieting, unsettling, troubling one. I stopped my angry tirade and simply paid attention. I was aware of a heavy blanket of silence.

In the silence of my own despair, I heard these words: *Woman, tell me what makes your son more precious than a son of Northern Ireland, a son of Kosovo, or a son of Guatemala, or Iraq? Don't you know that every mother's son is precious? The fear and dread you feel right now is the daily experience of mothers in nations at war. Throughout the centuries, across the borders that separate nations, all mothers suffer this same fear. Why should you be immune?*

For twenty-five years, this has been what every Catholic or Protestant mother in this city feels when her boy walks out the door to meet a friend. Are you willing to understand this is what war does to the hearts of the human family? Are you willing to tell people what you experienced on this night? I ask nothing less of you than this.

This was the reason I had traveled to Northern Ireland in the first place: to satisfy the nagging need to comprehend the effects of fear and hatred on the human spirit. Now that I'd found what I wanted to know, I wished for the cup of knowledge to pass from me. Pass from me, indeed. In one short moment of silence, my illusions were stripped and a new reality had taken their place. *There was nothing special about me or about my son that could protect us from the darkness in the human heart.*

This abrupt spiritual *comeuppance* forced me to encounter my own fear differently. Suddenly and strangely intimate with a circle of women whose lives were worlds apart from my own and whose names I would never know, I was confronted with the truths of war. I thought of women whose husbands and sons, brothers and fathers, have "disappeared" in the night, buried in mass graves, never to return. Women whose children died in their arms for lack of food or medicine. My thoughts kept returning to the haunting face and piercing eyes of the woman who swept her sidewalk as I passed by, curiously observing the life she couldn't escape.

How many sons, brothers, cousins, and friends had she mourned? How many of their names were painted on the walls I saw that day? For how many years had she dressed in black to show others her suffering? She was no longer a wizened, angry stranger but a woman who represented anguished mothers everywhere who lose their children to the effects of war. My trip was not an intellectual search for understanding now, but an emotional reality that touched my very marrow.

As I write this, I read of an Iraqi mother whose entire family was killed by American soldiers at a military checkpoint. The journalist described her flat, expressionless voice as she explained how violently her daughters, ages two and five, died sitting in her lap in the crowded SUV that was carrying thirteen members of her family to safety in Karbala. I think of the mothers and fathers of American military personnel who received the news today, or last week, or even thirty years ago, that their fathers, mothers or children died fighting to free the people of Iraq or Vietnam. I am not separate from their terror and grief. I know the ache in my bones that comes to a parent flooded with fear for the safety of a child.

In the dread of a long night in Ireland, I recognized my oneness with mothers and fathers of all nations who love their children and want a long, safe and healthy life for them. As my tirade subsided and grace fell around me and brought me to my senses, I remembered the Buddhist spiritual practice of tonglen.

This is a simple practice of mindful breathing. Some call it "peace breath," but I prefer to bow in the direction of the Buddhist tradition from which it originates. With each new breath I drew compassion into my heart, filling it. With each exhale of release, I sent compassion to myself: one frightened mother in a long lineage of frightened mothers and fathers. I repeated this until I could feel the anger drain from me, and a small measure of peace take its place. In the second stage of the practice, I took each intentional breath of compassion into my heart, and released it on the exhale to specific mothers and fathers I knew who were saying goodbye to their beloved children: some off to college, some to the military, some who were dying. In the third stage of the practice, I continued to breathe in compassion, then breathed it out to all of the mothers and fathers, worldwide, who lost a child through some natural or unnatural event. Finally, I imagined all of those people breathing in and breathing out, sending compassion to me: lying in a bed that was not mine, in a city that was far from my home, afraid for my child. One continuous loop of compassionate breath.

When I was finished with this practice, after perhaps thirty minutes, I was relaxed and comforted enough to sleep. After many anxious and angry hours raging at God, my heart was finally at rest.

It doesn't work for me to anthropomorphize God. God as Father or Mother is not the God of my experience. This is not the One who comes when I call for help.

The God who waits with me through my anguish, in the best way my struggling words can describe this Mystery, is a *consciousness*, or a *presence*, located within everything that exists in this vast and magnificent cosmos. A consciousness that is both eternal . . . and evolving. "Both/and" is its very nature. If this is true, and scientists as well as theologians are pointing directly at this truth, then everything animate—human beings, creatures of all kinds and sizes, great forests, oceans, mountains, vast galaxies—changes as God changes, or evolves as God evolves. It's within the particles and atoms of physical matter that God is most alive and active. The choice is not ours: we were created to *embody* god-ness.

And perhaps, since the entire cosmos seems interconnected as one enormous feedback loop of motion and activity, whenever human beings arrive at a new or changed state of awareness, the consciousness that is God—perhaps we might call it *God-happening*—changes simultaneously. We learn as God learns, God grows as we grow. Consider the possibility that we act as partner-companions with God, or co-participants in an infinite and ever-changing universe.

The consciousness that quickened in me that night, the presence rising out of the thick silence, brought me into a greater understanding of the human condition. It prompted me to surrender all illusions of separation, and it allowed me to experience a unity with all women simply because I participate in the great experiment of living.

God did not go lightly with me that night. In an act of terrible grace, I became every mother of every child in any nation at war. This was an *initiation* into a degree of anguish my own life hadn't taught me, and probably couldn't teach me, in any other way. I came alive that night, trembling with the awareness of my powerlessness to keep my child safe in an unsafe world.

My son arrived without incident the next morning. I was sitting at a dining table attempting to swallow past the lump in my throat when he walked confidently through the door. The sight of him brought tears to my eyes and overwhelming gratitude to my heart.

Two years would pass before I told him about the endless night I had wept and prayed and cried out in rage. I was sure he would think I overreacted . . . and perhaps I had. My best assessment is that I had simply found what I'd traveled to Northern Ireland to find, and discovering that, was changed forever.

As difficult as it is to imagine this, perhaps we need our *troubles* to keep us on a sharply honed growing edge. We don't seem to grow in awareness when things are going our way. Good times are generally not the hand pushing us toward enlightenment. It seems to be the time we log in the dark places that are more likely to crack us open, as I cracked open that night, and make way for God-Consciousness to rise up from the ground and source of our being.

There is always something to be learned in our troubles, if we give ourselves to that possibility. Whatever the lessons might be, they aren't our lessons alone, though they may have significant personal meaning: a meaning that both *comes from* and *returns to* God.

I find it useful, in comprehending my relationship with the Mystery, that—whatever I am willing to embody—I embody not only for my experience, expansion and understanding . . . but for God's expansion and understanding as well. This makes good spiritual sense to me. It helps me to bear that which, at times, seems to be unbearable. It gives me strength when *the troubles* threaten to overcome me.

If I'm unable to lift myself out of whatever frightens me, I remember that God and I are partners in this adventure we call life. That we are both experiencing-learning-expanding as we go. That we are mutual beneficiaries of a reciprocal process of expansion and maturation. I imagine I am helping God to bear what must often seem beyond even God's capacity to tolerate. That thought offers me courage in the face of fear, strength in the presence of certain collapse, and profound gratitude for the events and experiences we call "the troubles."

"The troubles"—as harsh and unforgiving as they often are— may actually bring us powerful lessons on the spiritual path. It's tempting to divert our attention from them. Most of us are experts at turning away from troubles, whatever they are, however it is they plague us. But we can't always run—and we can't always hide—from the God-Mystery that breaks through to us in the dark and brutal places of the human spirit. It's in that troubled mirror that we finally see the wizened face of God's humanity, and the wise, soft face of our divinity.

❡

- Reflect for a while on the quote from Meister Eckhart, written in the 12th century: *God waits on human history, and suffers as she waits.* What do you think Eckhart—a mystic, priest, teacher, philosopher—meant when he wrote this? And how does it apply to our present troubled times?

- Where do you believe God is found in "the troubles?" And why is God there? In your own life, have you been willing to meet God-as-Mystery in the dark and brutal places?

- What did you learn from that experience? How did that expand or spiritually mature you? How did it change your understanding of a mysterious God?

- For a few quiet minutes, try the practice of *tonglen*. Find a comfortable position for your body, let go of the cares of the day, and simply begin to breathe naturally. Once you are relaxed, become mindful of your breath. That is, notice your breath: Is each breath smooth, deep, relaxed . . . or is it ragged and shallow? Smooth out your breath by relaxing the muscles around your heart and lungs, allowing your shoulders to drop and the back of your neck to soften. Most of us are unaware of the tension we hold in those areas of our bodies.

Now, begin to breathe the quality of compassion directly into your heart, filling you. Deep, relaxing breath of compassion. When you exhale, imagine that you are sending that compassion to yourself. Whatever it is that troubles you, send yourself unlimited compassion. Breathing it in, breathing it out on the exhale, sending it to yourself. Imagine that you are bathed in the compassion you send.

When you have taken in enough compassion to quiet your troubles, think of someone you know—a friend or loved one, a person in your community, a world leader—who needs a gift of compassion at this time. Breathing in, fill your heart with compassion. Breathing out, direct compassion outward to that individual. Follow this with several more breaths, until you can visualize this person completely awash in compassion.

Next, still breathing in compassion with each breath, imagine that you are sending compassion to all people, everywhere, who are troubled and in need of kindness. Picture their faces, faces of all colors and cultures and religions and ages. Bathe them in compassion. Whatever their troubles, they can be helped by your gift of compassionate attention.

Finally, imagine that those people, wherever they are in the world, are turning to breathe compassion to you. See the one continuous breath of humankind, all sending, and all receiving, compassion.

Peace-breathing. Tonglen. We call it by many names, but it is a spiritual practice that unites rather than separates us, a practice to use whenever the "troubles" divide us or fill us with fear. Try it at different times, under different circumstances, to see what effect it has for you.

shed holy tears

Be courageous enough
to shed holy tears. Until
all the world is awake,
our holy tears will wash
over our troubled spirits
like a healing river
flowing homeward
to the heart of God.

—Meredith Jordan

I came of age under the dark shadow of the Vietnam War and developed an aversion for war that I carry with me to this day. This nation first went to war against Iraq just as my son reached his late teens. He and I spent many hours discussing war and its alternatives. A friend told me years later about a nephew who commanded a tank in the brief hours of the Gulf War. Long after he returned home, he remained distraught that men whose faces he never saw and names he would never learn *died* because of his orders to fire upon Iraqi tanks. It was precisely this

experience I hoped would never burden the consciences of my
son . . . or any other man.

Like many women, I don't understand war. I really don't want
to understand it, and I certainly don't want the ones I love to
ever have to experience it. I reluctantly acknowledge that, about
this matter, I have no control.

However, something happened when the movie *Pearl Harbor* was
released in the spring of 2001 that showed me another perspective
on this issue. A man I care about deeply had looked forward to
the release of this movie for months. When the movie opened,
he eagerly went to see it. He went alone, something that seemed
more impulsive at the time than intentional.

He later described to me how, without knowing what triggered
his tears, he cried through the movie in great heaving sobs of
grief. I listened to his genuine bewilderment about his weeping
and realized how few opportunities men have to release the grief
they carry for all they have to do in order to play their parts in
the collective script that humanity has written for them:

*Be brave, even if you are scared to death. Stay strong. Tough it
out alone. Never let others know how much pain you hold inside.
Prepare to give your life for a greater good, even if you've never
kissed a girl, fallen in love, or found the one true thing for which
you're willing to sacrifice your life.*

It's an astonishing burden we expect men to bear. And, for the
most part, men have carried these burdens in silence and alone.
Since I first heard his story, I have thought a lot about my friend's
tears . . . about the great waves of tears that pour forth from us
like a river and won't stop until they have run their course. I
call them *honorable* or *holy tears* because they're shed for more
than our own personal grief and sorrow. We shed them,
appropriately, in communal sorrow for the egregious sins we

perpetrate against one another and in communal high regard for the remarkable acts of courage we carry out. The man who wept at the movie said: "They picked up their buddies and carried them away from the gunfire to safety, even though each man already carried a seventy-five pound pack on his back!" Holy tears.

Not long ago, women cried holy tears at the names and stories of their ancestors who died at the stake, hung or burned, for being healers or midwives. Jewish families cried holy tears for the mothers, fathers, sisters, brothers, children, friends who walked to their deaths in the camps at Buchenwald or at Dachau. Lesbians and gay men cried holy tears at the deaths of one young gay man lashed to a fence post and left to die one freezing Wyoming night . . . or another, thrown into a bitter river in Maine like an old tire, left to drown because he could not swim.

It seems to me that it's also fitting for men to cry holy tears for the boys they know, or might never have known, who served their country in times of war and died before they could launch their own lives. Tears for the men who have tightly-held memories of friends who died beside them in foxholes, fighter planes or tanks. For men who witnessed horrors they never asked to see, much less execute. For men who've locked away the key to their secret hearts because, if they dared to open them, tears would pour forth and expose the pain that is buried there.

I come from a generation of women who taught our boys that it is all right to cry, that it is all right for them to be human and to hurt and to need comfort. *Real boys do cry*, we taught them, *and so do real men*. They have good reasons for their tears, as girls and women also have.

What do I see in the story of a solitary man watching a movie about war and weeping without ceasing for he-knew-not-what? I see a revelatory God: the Divine Being who lives in this man's spirit and longs to burst free of the constraints with which we have bound the hearts of our men. I see the Holy One in each of us—woman or man, old or young—who weeps in the presence of a pain that is greater than the heart can bear.

It doesn't matter if these tears are shed over soldiers dead in battle, over the bodies of sick or orphaned children, over the uprooting of trees, over African mothers and fathers dying of AIDS, over the millions of desperate people worldwide who are living in poverty or facing starvation.

What does matter, then? That we allow holy tears to pour through us. That we make a place for the God-in-us to weep when it is time for weeping. To weep for humanity is a holy, cleansing, transforming, honorable act. To weep *for God* is a holy, cleansing, transforming, honorable act.

If anything, hearing this man's response to the movie only strengthens my aversion to war. But it softens my heart toward the men and women who bravely go forth, pushing against their own terror, giving their lives for others to live. It's my fervent prayer that, one day, the absurdity of war will be evident to all who perpetrate and promote it. I pray that we will turn our swords into plowshares. The time for this has not yet come. I may not live to see it happen. But I'll continue to shed my tears for the wounded and fallen, and to honor the tears of all who weep with me for our transformation into the God-bearers we are intended to be.

℘

- Read this poem by Wesley McNair aloud, first to yourself and then to someone else. Talk honestly about what the poem says or means to you about God.

The Losses

It must be difficult for God
listening to our voices come up
through his floor of cloud to tell Him what's
been taken away. Lord, I've lost my dog,
my period, my hair, all my money.
What can He say, given we are so incomplete
we can't stop being surprised by our condition,
and He is completeness itself? Or is God
more like us, made in His image—
shaking His head because He can't
be expected to keep track of which
voice goes with what name and address.
He being just one God. Either way, we seem
to be left here to discover our losses, everything
from car keys to larger items we can't
search our pockets for, while those around us,
like the compassionate expert on overweight
holding the hand of a hugely obese
woman on TV, offer their best advice.
She is crying because she's just learned
it isn't really self-control she's lost,
but only her self-esteem, which she can gain back
with a few simple steps. It's not difficult
to picture her after the applause
and the last commercial returning to sadness
and a jumbo bag of chips. The hard thing
about loss is you've got to face it on your own.
Even though they give you music
to listen to and the dental assistant looks down
with her lovely smile, it's still your tooth
the dentist yanks out, leaving a soft
emptiness you'll ponder with your tongue
for days. Left to ourselves, we always go over
and over what's missing: tooth, dog, money,

self-control, and even losses as troubling
as the absence the widower can't stop
reaching for on the other side of the bed
a year later. Then one odd afternoon,
watching some ordinary happening like the way
light from the window holds a vase
on the table, or how the leaves
on his backyard tree change colors all at once
in a quick wind, he begins to feel a lightness,
as if all his loss has led to finding
just this. Only God knows where
the feeling came from. Or maybe God's
not some knower off on a cloud, but there
in the eye, which tears up now at the strangest
moments, over the smallest things.

• Think about that line: "maybe God's not some knower off on a cloud, but there in the eye, which tears up at the strangest moments, over the smallest things."

Remember a time when something moved you so deeply that you cried unexpected tears. Instead of brushing that off as an aberration, go back into that experience. Can you imagine God as the act of weeping as well as the tears, and you as the instrument of that act? How does this enhance or expand your experience of the Mystery we call God?

Untamed God

My barn having burned to the ground,
I can now see the moon.

—*Anonymous*

I am uncomfortable writing about the dark side of God-nature. *This isn't my issue to address*, I tell myself, *I stand firmly on the side of good, on the side of light, compassion, and love. How dare I consider that the nature of God embodies all things, even destruction and annihilation?*

I would like to stake my claim on the side of good and build my spiritual home there, except, to do that, I would sacrifice my faithfulness to the Mysterious God that has been revealed to me. I can't write or speak truthfully about a God of Mystery if I deny my encounter with a fierce God of destruction, an encounter that shook the fundamental bedrock of my theology. Michael, my colleague and spiritual director, gleefully declared that this encounter brought me into hand-to-hand combat and, thus, a full, authentic relationship with God. For me, there was no glee. I was dragged—kicking and screaming—into an expanded experience of the Mystery.

This unanticipated encounter with the Mystery occurred in a dream so vibrantly alive, crackling with truth, that I woke shaking, sweating, and exhausted from the fight for my soul:

I was a student at an unfamiliar seminary. Other friends were there with me. Every morning, my friends got up, dressed, gathered their books, and went off to class. I was always lagging behind, unable to organize myself to get to class on time. On many counts I was in my own way, falling all over myself, never accomplishing what I thought I was there to accomplish. While my friends went about their studies effortlessly, I was a failure at divinity school. This was a terrible feeling.

One day, I tried especially hard to get up early and to be ready for class. I flew out of my room, only to discover that everyone else had left earlier than usual. No matter how hard I tried, I was still late. Hopelessly frustrated, hoping to catch up, I raced down the hall, flew out the dormitory door, tripped . . . and fell over a railing to the ground two floors below. Certain I would break on impact with the ground beneath me, I prepared to die. All I could think of was that I had failed once again. As I watched the ground rush up to meet me, I was suddenly gripped by a force so powerful it rendered me helpless. My body flattened out in mid-fall, pointed like a missile, and was propelled through the air faster than the speed of light. I began zooming over oceans to a part of the world I'd never seen before.

As I neared Bosnia, besieged in the war between Serbs and Croatians, my body began to shoot fire-beams of light below, as if I was generating a meteor storm. While I soared over their heads like a fighter plane on mission, hundreds of laser-like beams blasted out of my body and rained down on the land and people below. These were not bombs meant to destroy, but blasts of light meant to illuminate a dark part of the world. When the fire-beams were finally spent, my body swiftly turned, zoomed back over the oceans, and landed with a hard thud below the dormitory balcony. Aware my body had been used by a power greater than anything I could imagine, I lay wasted on the ground, completely drained of energy and purpose.

When I could move again, I rose slowly, checked to see that all parts of my body were intact, and walked painfully back to the dormitory to rest. Now positive that I'd failed as a seminary student, I had no qualms about retreating to my room to sleep off the effects of this strange journey.

Inching along the hallway to my room, I used the wall to hold myself upright. It suddenly opened up under my hand and a round portal appeared, similar to a window, where I could look directly out onto the vastness of the galaxy. Then I was abruptly sucked through the portal, out into the galaxy beyond. Again controlled by a powerful force, I was thrust out into space, hurtling past stars, until I was plunked down in an exotic land. There I lay, catching my breath, trying to make sense of this bizarre series of events, spent of all vitality. When I had strength to lift my head and look around, I was seized with terror. A woman of enormous size and presence—eight feet tall, massive shoulders, brown skin, long, dark hair—glowered at me. Dressed in layers of intricate colors I had never seen, she stood, sword at her side and hands on her huge hips, ready to fight. Before I rose to my feet, she threw the first blow, and I was embroiled in battle.

I fought ferociously for my life: dancing, dodging, narrowly missing the swish and swing of her massive sword. I called on every ounce of strength in my exhausted body and fought back with a sword of my own, occasionally hitting my mark with unexpected accuracy. The fight went on well into dark, until neither of us could fight any more. Consumed with exhaustion, we stopped, heads hung low, swords dropped to the ground. The battle was over, but neither of us conceded defeat.

The next thing I knew, I was sucked back into the galactic vortex and thrown down in a heap in the dormitory hallway. I was now gasping for breath, unable to move. Aware that, unlike me, my friends were in class, doing what good seminary students were supposed to be doing. I consoled myself with the knowledge that this wasn't the first time I had experienced inexplicable mysteries that didn't "fit" with anything I thought I was supposed to be doing. This was one more thing to keep to myself, one more reason to understand that mine was not the ordinary path to God . . . that is, if any path to God can be called ordinary.

Believing the worst was over, I crawled twenty feet toward my room when I was overcome with a fear so powerful I couldn't move. Dreading what I might see, I raised my eyes slowly, and there she was—the ferocious woman—standing in the now familiar posture, a recognizable fire in her eye revealing the same determination to bring me to my knees. I was too tired to cry for help, or for mercy. I had nothing left: no action to take, no sound to cry out, no will to survive.

At that very moment, there rose up in me the deep desire to fight for my life, to engage with this terrifying presence, and to defeat her. I stood. I fought fiercely. And this time, I won. The huge woman disappeared in an explosion of light, and I was alone in the hall. Making my way to my room crawling on my belly, stunned and exhausted, I fell into bed, able to rest at last.

The dream ended here, but my questions about it had scarcely begun. Who was this powerful, ferocious woman, who wanted to humble me? Why me? *What was God up to in this experience?* I made an immediate appointment with Michael, the only pastoral counselor I knew who would take me on with the seriousness I believed this dream deserved. I was especially intrigued that it had followed my sanctuary encounter with the Pillar of Light by less than a week, suggesting there was an undeniable synchronicity to these two events.

Michael cackled: "Good! I was waiting to see if you'd allow yourself to know the other side of God's nature, or if you were going to stay only in the light. You were in a hand-to-hand combat with the dark side of God. This is the God of the Old Testament, the one who left Job sitting on the ash heap. What you encountered in the sanctuary was the vastness of God's compassion and love. With this experience, you now know firsthand the full range of God's true nature!"

I hated hearing Michael's words. I didn't want to agree. This wasn't the benevolent God of my Protestant upbringing. This was an untamed, unpredictable aspect of *something* very powerful and puzzling—a radical departure from anything I'd encountered, or been prepared to discover, in my developing and deepening relationship with the Mystery.

We talked about what it's like to develop relationship with a God that includes, in the words of Meister Eckhart, "all breadth, all length, all depth, all expansiveness." All light and all dark. All that is contained within God-nature. Nothing left out. Everything belongs.

Michael asked: "If it's this difficult for you to hold such a big understanding of God-nature, what do you think it must be like for God to hold all of this?"

I considered this for a long time, and answered that it must be as uncomfortable, as confusing, as humbling, as exhausting for God as for me, but to some exponential that I couldn't comprehend.

"Yes!" Michael said, "and once you understand that God-consciousness lives inside you and me and all of life in this way—

both the compassionate and the non-compassionate sides—that is the beginning of truly falling in love with the Mystery.

"Remember: it's all one. In each of us there's a God part that fights to keep us unconscious, to annihilate any chance of our awakening, just like in your dream. The dark nature of God wants us to remain asleep, unconscious, to stay small rather than to expand. And yet it is the natural order of life for all things to grow, to develop, to expand, and to change. This too is part of the nature of God. Part of the great mystery of life.

"We are asked to create a vessel in ourselves large enough to hold the expansion and destruction, the darkness and light, the consciousness and unconsciousness at work within the mysterious presence we call God. Many people aren't ready—or even able— to hold this awareness. We don't want to see the darkness, yet it's all around us. We're confronted every day with its existence: in the news, in the natural world, and in our own hearts if we're honest enough to examine ourselves.

"Here is what helps us over the threshold of such an awful realization: knowing that God becomes more conscious as we push our own edges toward more and more consciousness. This world can never change until we change. Like it or not, and mostly not, we have a personal responsibility to *become*. Perhaps it is that simple. And perhaps it is that difficult."

I listened harder than I had ever listened before. I admitted I didn't like experiencing the darker side of God-nature I'd encountered in my dream; I wanted my naiveté back. But I also realized that, having been broken through—not for the first time and surely not for the last—I couldn't possibly return to a state of *not-knowing*.

I left our conversation newly aware of an aspect of the Mystery for which Christianity, the tradition and community of my childhood, left me unprepared. It hadn't taught me to wage the fight of my life, though if I re-visited the story of Jesus facing his demons in the forty days and nights of his desert sojourn, I found deeper value in that story. Still, other than my colleague's understanding of the untamed God, I had nothing to assist me. Michael helped to stretch my thinking. Now I needed to plumb the depths of my own thoughts and feelings about such an experience. I wanted to understand who tried to annihilate me, and the purpose of this fierce battle for my soul.

I spent time thinking about Job, the nice fellow who tried to do everything right and still wound up on an ash heap, with nothing left to show for his godly life. I'd never liked Job's story; it was unsettling to think that Job—whose life was exemplary—could lose all that mattered to a fierce and mysterious God. If that could happen to Job, then it could also happen to me or someone I love, since we were all too imperfect. I was threatened by the quixotic God who thundered down upon Job, and disenchanted by the idea of an untamed, unpredictable aspect of God.

The questions persisted. *Must this be an either/or spiritual proposition?* I asked myself. *Couldn't God be both destructive and loving?* I remained at this spiritual impasse until I discovered that Carl Jung, a great scholar of the soul, had asked a similar question as a young man. While reading his book *Memories, Dreams and Reflections,* I learned Jung spent a great deal of his life wrestling with the possibility that the sacred contains both the terrible and the good. I was consoled that such a brilliant visionary thinker and devoted spiritual seeker asked himself the questions that also troubled me. Perhaps these questions belonged to all seekers, people of all faith traditions, who strive to understand the full, complex, authentic nature of the Mysterious One we call God.

I stayed on course in my search for understanding the deeper meaning of my dream. Elsewhere in my reading, I discovered

Kali—the wild, destructive, untamed Hindu goddess—who was simultaneously the destroyer and builder of life, consumer and healer, ferocious and nurturing, bestower and bandit. In Hindu tradition, Kali is the living fire, just as in the dream my body became the living fire shooting torches of light onto the pummeled, barren earth. Hindus have revered her for generations as the manifestation of both the dark and light parts of God-nature. Eastern mythology teaches Kali is a terrifying presence, much like the enormous woman of the dream. There's very little about the Kali-like nature of God that appeals to the Western spiritual seeker, but—like her or not—she serves an important purpose: *she carries the sword of truth to cut us free from illusions that interfere with our spiritual growth.* It's her purpose to liberate us of all that does not serve our awakening to what is real and true.

Just as God resides in us, so too does Kali. She's one of countless images in the human psyche that tell us something about the sacred. Her divine mission is to go to work on us whenever we most need to be freed from something we mistakenly cling to for comfort. The poet Mel Lyman gives voice to Kali in these verses:

> *I am going to burn down the world*
> *I am going to tear down everything that cannot stand*
> *alone I am going to turn ideals to shit*
>
> *I am going to shove hope up your ass*
> *I am going to reduce everything that stands to rubble*
> *And then I am going to burn the rubble*
>
> *And then I am going to scatter the ashes*
> *And then maybe SOMEONE will be able*
> *To see SOMETHING as it really is.*

WATCH OUT.

In the tale told through my dream, the Kali-like figure sought to free me of the desire to locate myself only on the side of light and love, of all that's good, and to embrace the shadow side of human nature and God-nature as well. In doing so, she reminded me that what seems to be bad, even terrible, can also be illuminating, stretching us in ways we wouldn't otherwise choose. My dream encounter, terrifying as it was, threw open my understanding of the power of the sacred Mystery, much as Job's incarceration on the ash heap awakened and expanded his understanding of God.

I met Kali a second time, outside of the dream world, after a spark ignited one hot August day, setting fire to the church I'd grown to love. I stood with hundreds of people helplessly watching our church collapse in on herself, her beautiful stained glass windows melting in the ferocious heat of the fire, first one wall folding in and then another, the bell tower toppling—all becoming ash and rubble. I stood in shock at the visible reminder of a Destroyer God. My innocence died that day, as it needed to do, and ferocious Kali stood at my side. Once again, with one swift blow of her mighty sword, she struck down my illusion that a building—no matter how beautiful—was home for my spirit. In the instant the last wall fell in pieces toward the scorched earth, I knew *I* was the home for my soul, that I always had been, and I would always be. I walked away from the destruction of the fire with that small measure of peace.

Having seen Kali's face, having darted from her sword, having managed to stay alive—first in body and then in spirit—I now consider her a mighty ally. Some would view the second meeting as annihilation of my ego so that only the part of me *born of spirit* survived the battle. All I know is that no visions of spiritual sugarplum fairies remained, no beliefs affording false comfort were left in me. In the ash and rubble, there was only the evidence of destruction. As the church fell, I stood as naked before the Mystery as Job was naked before God.

If our religious institutions are to survive—which may not be in our best interests—they must welcome the untamed, unpredictable dimensions of the Mystery we call God. They must open the doors to the Destroyer of Life as well as to the Life-Giver. When religious leaders abdicate this responsibility, they leave people unaware that there will be times when they will be called out to meet the Destroyer-God, and unprepared to battle for their lives. Until then, we need to prepare on our own for possible encounters with this fierce aspect of the Mystery.

Some people have already met this mysterious ally who appears more like an adversary. It rises up to challenge us with a diagnosis of cancer, a sudden loss or death, an unexpected reversal of fortune. It shows itself in the toppled towers of the World Trade Center, in the faces of starving or ailing children, and in the broken landscapes of remote villages destroyed by earthquakes and floods. Many people are encountering it now: in Afghanistan, Iraq, Israel or Palestine, Northern Ireland, here at home. Daniel Pearl encountered it in Pakistan, and lost his life in the encounter. Hundreds of people on vacation in Bali encountered it when a car packed with explosives ripped open the bar where they were relaxing, laughing, and dancing.

The untamed God is alive and present in this complicated universe of ours, and we must prepare to face the tumult of its decidedly difficult nature. Alongside the Holy One of Compassion, the Unpredictable Mystery resides within us, poised to emerge when we need the touch of a swift sword. Are we willing to entertain this expanded understanding of God? The evidence of its dark nature surrounds us in today's world. Will we retreat into spiritual naiveté and deny its existence, or can we bear to bring this difficult aspect of God to consciousness and hold it there?

This is a tough assignment. Many of us will reject it in favor of maintaining spiritual innocence. It seems to me, though, that the dark aspect of God-nature is revealed so that it can be brought to consciousness, fully experienced, and used to grow in us a greater understanding of the Mystery. If we're willing to include the dark nature of God-consciousness in our own, then God also has a chance to expand its own nature through us. But first we must radically alter our notion that God acts upon us, and consider also that we act upon God. That there is a feedback loop between God and Creation through which even God may grow.

God is an infinite and ever-changing flow of life; and we humans, in consciously experiencing this God-flow—sometimes as good and sometimes as bad—have the capacity to increase it. In other words, as we reflect upon our experiences and grow from them, we give that understanding back to God, which expands God as a result of our efforts. This, I believe, is what my colleague meant when he said that we each have a spiritual mandate, or responsibility, to *become*.

From this perspective, it would seem that the entire cosmos awaits our awakening consciousness. Waits for us to encounter, to recognize and reveal God's nature to ourselves, and to return our newly expanded awareness to God. The Mystery is standing by . . . waiting to awaken more of its own ever-growing consciousness as the family of earth learns to embrace and embody the many dimensions of God's untamed, wondrous, compassionate, complex and ferocious nature.

What an amazing mission we have before us.

♫

- Many of us have had encounters of some kind with the unpredictable side of God's nature. A time when something totally unexpected, something that doesn't fit our image of God, bears down upon our lives and takes over, leaving us helpless in its presence. Some people think of events like these as not-God, as something that stands outside the benevolence of the God we are taught to know or love, rather than as another dimension of true God-nature.

- Think of your encounters with the unpredictable nature of God. How have they informed or shaped your understanding of the Mystery we call God?

- When have you encountered the terrible, swift sword of Mystery, sweeping away illusions that no longer serve you? What made it possible for you to see this apparent adversary might actually be an ally?

- If you ignore the dark aspects of God-nature, what price do you pay in your relationship with the Sacred? How do you explain the signs that there is more to the Mystery than the qualities of love and compassion? What do you do as evidence grows that "bad things happen to good people?"

- What does it mean for you to consider that you have been given a charge "to become?" That you may possibly be called on as *co-participant with God* in the evolution of consciousness? Where would you describe yourself in the process of "becoming?"

when the bones ache

Waking up this morning, I smile.
Twenty four brand new hours are before me.
I vow to live each one fully,
To look at all beings
With the eyes of compassion.

—Thich Nhat Hanh

It had been a very hard week in which I was so sick that, at times, I could hardly think a thought or lift out of my chair. Yet I still needed to see clients. Sick or well, I had bills to pay. I was the only one in my life who carried these responsibilities. A heavy burden rested on my shoulders. It was no surprise to find myself ill . . . and consumed by anxiety.

There was a moment that week when I pulled into the office for a day of work that I thought I could barely manage. I was worn out from being sick and desperate for a long, restful sleep. It was at that moment I noticed the trash cans from our office building still at the curb. The students who lived in the apartment above our office had left for the day without putting them back into the garage. The wind was fierce that October day, and the big plastic cans rolled into the street, obstructing traffic. Though I was hardly able to put one foot in front of the other, I had to chase three trash barrels across four lanes of busy traffic in order to retrieve them. By the time I had unlocked the office doors, I was already breathing with great difficulty.

Adding insult to illness, the vacuum cleaner broke that same day, and there was no one else to clean the office or to get the machine repaired. This day, it weighed on my shoulders alone. It seemed that everything was waiting or dependent on me.

None of this was anyone's fault. It couldn't have been any other way. Ellie's mother-in-law died suddenly, and she'd left to be with Peter's family. The kids in the building had their own overly scheduled lives, and a morning when they forgot to retrieve the trash cans was more the norm than not. But I was . . . sick, exhausted, depleted, wallowing in self-pity and facing a stark reality that at no point in that entire week had anyone offered to make me a cup of tea. To get better, I had to make my own chicken soup. I even had to shop for the ingredients to make it. If I'd been able to find any humor in a week of unceasing demands, I might have looked at these events as comically absurd. Now, when I pass that building—no longer my office— I chuckle to see trash cans at the curb. But at the time, it wasn't funny: I was desperately lonely.

The one thing sustaining me during that week was the thought that, as soon as I had seen the last of my clients and locked the office door, I'd get in the car and drive west toward the peak foliage of fall. Fall is the most spectacular season in New England. I thought if I could see the beauty of mountains covered with fire-red and orange-glowing trees, I could easily replenish my spirits for the week ahead. I comforted myself with that promise.

The weekend arrived and departed without me driving anywhere. I lay awake both nights, too exhausted to sleep, drugged with despair, staring down the certainty that my life would never change. I was positive I'd always be the shoulders on which rested too much responsibility.

I had dinner with my friend Lauren that week, a wonderful conversation cut too short by my not feeling well, but enough of a deep, authentic time together to carry us both for a while. In that conversation, we agreed that—as single mothers, working and raising children—we had unmet needs for relief from the burdens of going it alone. Lauren told me she kept a hammock hanging in her living room, where she often rocked late at night, after her boys had gone to bed. It helped her to feel that she was somehow "held."

Both of us admitted the hardest part of the single person's journey seemed the lack of awareness in our partnered friends for what it's like to have no one with whom to share the complexities of life. All the decisions that fell to us alone. All the worries about the children. All the times that our houses made strange noises they ought not to be making, and there was no one to worry with or to wonder: *What do you think that was?* No "other" to put on boots, thump down into the cold, flooded basement in the middle of the night and start a faulty sump pump running again. Each of us feared the hardships were never going to end, and there wouldn't be enough of us to cover all the bases.

Lauren admitted her greatest wish. She simply wanted a friend to call and invite them—her and her beautiful boys—to dinner. *Come on over and let's make dinner together tonight.* Meal after meal, loneliness seeping into one's bones and taking up residence. I confessed that my greatest burden was that people always expected me to be there for them, to be *present and attentive* with resources from which they drew, whether I had them or not. The needs seemed to go on forever, no matter how depleted I was. I constantly pushed my relentless ache for companionship out of my peripheral vision while others complained to me about their relationships. She and I agreed that we each ached for people *just to be kind* to us. Just to appreciate us. Just to be glad we were here. Just to offer their love as a gift to our despair or depletion.

It takes so little for a heavy-hearted spirit to bounce back from the well of despair: *just a little kind-heartedness.*

On the occasions when someone was kind to me during that long relational drought, I often wept at the unexpected goodness. Once, during a snowstorm that dumped over thirty inches of snow in our area, Ellie and Peter showed up to shovel my back porch, where the snow had drifted to more than four feet high. I couldn't push open the door to get out of my house! I was so grateful I cried for days, thankful for friends who sensed-without-being-told that the enormity of this task was beyond my ability to manage alone.

It's wrong that we live this way. Sometimes, it's a stingy world. It is up to us to become a more generous people. It would be so simple for us to change. Building community, participating in community, is both a privilege and a responsibility given to us all.

The poet Nancy Wood writes: *Happiness comes from understanding our unity.* We are members of the same clan, sisters and brothers of the same family. We are born of the One, and we belong to the One. When one person's bones ache with loneliness, I feel it. When my bones ache, you recognize that I am struggling or hurting, and you respond. Over seven centuries ago, Meister Eckhart said: *The fullest work that God ever worked in any creature is compassion. You may call God love, you may call God goodness, but the best name for God is compassion.*

Compassion calls us out of complacency and moves us beyond ourselves into caring about one another's loneliness or pain, into action, and, finally, into service. Through acts of compassion, we ultimately sustain each other and enrich one another's lives. Compassion is not a quality we are born with; it's one we develop on the way to spiritual maturity. It is also a quality we must teach our children.

If we look for opportunities to make our hearts a home for compassion, we discover that there is no shortage of need. Mothers and kids who wait to be invited to someone else's home for dinner, just to have an evening of companionship. Porches or roofs that need to be shoveled. Elders who are unable to transport themselves to the doctor's, the grocery store, the movies. Trash cans that have to come in from the street. A shoulder to weep on, a friend to laugh with, a face that lights up at the sight of us.

The long drought in my life is over, although loneliness has imprinted me with lessons I never want to forget. How much we need the small comforts of each other. How precious we are to each other. How important that we gather community around us, inviting in others who share the belief that all we really ever have is one another . . . and that's all that matters.

$$\mathcal{J}$$

- Where and how is the Mystery at work in the times when your bones throb with loneliness or ache with despair?

- Consider Meister Eckhart's statement that *the best name for God is compassion.* How does that statement apply in your life?

- Make *compassion* your spiritual practice for a month. Whenever you spot an opportunity to show compassion to a person in need, do that. Stretch yourself beyond your normal "giving point," and give a little more, or a little longer than you normally would. Ask for compassion when you need it yourself. Notice how it feels to offer compassion. Notice how it feels to receive it. At the end of the month, what have you gained?

Memorizing each other

The only gift to leave to children is example.
The only road to show them is awareness.
The only blessing to give them is responsibility.
The only thing to ask in return is understanding.
The only memory to take with you is love.

—Nancy Wood

Three years ago, a dear friend of over twenty years died after fighting a debilitating cancer for four long, difficult months. This particular cancer had first appeared in her right eye twelve years earlier, diagnosed as an ocular melanoma, the result of playing too much in bright sunlight as a child. What a terrible irony of life.

She was blinded in the affected eye by prolonged and extensive radiation, but she had received a good prognosis for living a long and healthy life. It came as a horrible surprise to learn that the cancer had maliciously, silently metastasized to fourteen sites in her body until she had only months to live. At the time of this shocking disclosure, she was sixty years old, a retired therapist, an avid gardener, and the mother of two thoughtful, kind young men she had raised as a single parent.

She told me this news one day when we met for what we both had planned would be a pleasant cup of tea and our usual conversation about the meaning of life. I was far from prepared for what I was about to hear: "I haven't been feeling well. You know all that time I was in pain because of my back? The cancer has returned, and it's in several spots in my back . . . and many other places too. The doctors tell me I have four months to live." She sat very still, speaking quietly, as a tear spilled from her blind eye and trickled down her face.

What does a friend say to that? There are no words.

Audrey lived her last months as a warrior, as honestly and as elegantly as she could. As she lived her last days and as she died, she gifted me with insight into the nature of dying . . . and what we do well in this culture—or fail to do—as people are approaching death. I tell the story of her last months of life in the hope that it will inspire all of us be true to ourselves, outrageously true, as death arrives at the door. I also tell it to honor the unpredictability of God, that this good woman should die just as she'd come through her long tribulations and begun to enjoy the pleasures of life, and to acknowledge the nobility of her spirit in the midst of this holy, and wholly unwelcome, surprise.

Once she managed to come to terms with the startling news that her life was going to end far sooner than she planned, Audrey asked for what she called "living testimonials" from those who loved her. She meant she wanted letters, cards, poems, or objects that told how she had mattered in the lives of others, if she had made any difference with the way she spent her life, how well she had succeeded at loving others and being loved by them. "I'm not going to wait until I'm dead to find all of this out," she said.

And meant: *If there's anything left unsaid or unhealed between us, I want to know while I can still do something about it.*

Letters, cards, poems and gifts poured in. A former client of Audrey's handcrafted a stunning quilt that depicted all the major elements of her life. This quilt hung close to a chair where she sat to watch her gardens blossom and reflect upon her life in its final season; other letters and testimonials heaped into a small reed basket she kept at her side and carried, precious cargo, from room to room.

These messages gave her life meaning. They also gave her strength, courage and a full complement of love to burrow into when she needed it. She said the testimonials filled her heart with gratitude, precisely the attitude she was striving for in the face of death's steady advance. In the last hours of her life, barely lucid or able to speak, she opened her eyes—one blinded for twelve years, the other blinded by the metastasis of cancer to her brain—and found me beside her. "Oh, good," she said, "I want to ask you something. May I take your letter with me where I'm going?"

She meant: *I want to carry your love with me as I leave this world and go on to whatever I'll meet next.*

Audrey was courageous enough to tell the full emotional truth of her dying and to ask the same of her friends and family. The paradox was that this made it easier for her to live with the rapid advance of her death. "I'm afraid," she said repeatedly in those last months, "I don't how to die or what to expect of death. I don't know what it will be like, or how to get there. What do I do when it comes time?"

I described what little I knew about the stages of dying. I told her about my own years of experience as a nurse. During that time, I'd observed that most people die through cessation of their heartbeat or cessation of breath. We discussed whether it was possible to consciously slow the breath—and slow it again, then again—until the intervals between each breath became longer and longer, and one then released breath one last time . . . and drew breath no more. To us, that seemed both gentle and merciful.

And in the areas where my knowledge was limited, I would read to her. I read Christian teachings on the art of dying, of which there are few, and Buddhist teachings on the art of dying, of which there are many. We talked about what different religious traditions tell us death is like. This helped her to imagine the possibilities. She much preferred the knowledge of *possibility* to fear or avoidance of the unknown.

The time I spent searching the wisdom texts across different faith traditions led me to a disconcerting awareness that Christian tradition doesn't offer much guidance to a person moving toward death: no instructions or road map for the journey back to God. In the absence of good resources, we relied on the personal stories of dying other people were willing to share.

In our death-avoidant culture, we leave families to cope with death alone except at those times we share stories of facing death and moving through grief with one another. These real human stories bring us into *community* and *communion* with others, a remarkable experience of intimacy and love that supports a dying person in her last days. Stories sustained her, gave her comfort, and a sense that she could—and would—find the way to drop her weary body when the time came for her leavetaking from this earth.

There was a moment in Audrey's last day of life that serves as a final tribute to her wonderful spirit. I was singing softly to her as she drifted in and out of consciousness: "Go in beauty, peace be with you, till we meet again in the light."

She briefly roused, raised her hands to my face, and started to trace my features. Her delicate touch was insistent: she plucked at the fine hairs of my eyebrows and poked at my nose. Her long fingers followed the contours of my cheeks and jaw. I laughed and asked her what she was doing. She lightly traced my eyes and nose before she attempted an answer. By this time, cancer cells had spread to her brain, and words only came with effort. Finally she whispered in a voice so soft I might have missed it, had I not been drawn close by the pull of her hands against my face: *"I am memorizing you."*

Memorizing me so she had me firmly anchored in her heart as she crossed the threshold into death. Is there a better way to tell a beloved that he or she is dear to us? That is what a conscious, intentional process of dying affords us: the time and opportunity to tell the ones we love that they are dear to us. The time to finish our relationships well and to leave no unbroken threads in the tapestry of our lives. Time to watch our gardens flourish and flower one last season, to watch the sun rise again, and drop under the horizon, with awe for its mysterious beauty, emerging from and falling into the edge of the world.

Precious time to memorize the faces of our beloved friends. Contemplative time to reflect on our years and to appreciate all that we are given in our too-brief sojourns on this earth.

Audrey's dying was by no means a perfect process. It was as messy and imperfect as most endings are. There were moments when she became briefly delusional from strong doses of painkillers. Once she called me at five o'clock in the morning to say she had been kidnapped and was held hostage by her kind and loving husband. She screamed at me to rescue her immediately. While I struggled to respond appropriately, she raged at me for not taking her seriously. She would court death one day and rally to stage a last garden party for her friends two days later. None of us knew what to expect, including the one who was dying. She was on a physical-emotional-spiritual roller coaster, hurtling wildly toward death and trying to suck the last juices out of life before it was abruptly stolen from her.

All of us who loved her were carried along for the ride.

She lost weight. She grew skeletal. She often lost touch with reality. At any moment, she might be in France, re-living a last trip, lifting her arm to call for assistance: "Garçon! Garçon!" Or she would be crooning to a lover from a long-ago liaison, her voice soft, tender. Time no longer held any reference for her. In the waning hours of life, she lost a lifelong beauty and gained a mysterious translucency. Everything about her *shone* as she slowly groped her way out of life and into death.

She never lost her gratitude. She never lost her sense of humor. At the same time she was hovering between the worlds, she would abruptly return to give a last word of love or laughter to her sons, her husband, her mother, her friends. *I'm memorizing you. I want to take you with me where I'm going.*

Audrey's dying was a challenging time: a beautiful, exhausting, delightful, dreadful, crazy, and joyous process. It was life—the best and worst of it—telescoped into a few precious months.

She made her exit peacefully, late one night when the air was crisp and the gardens past their bloom. With her son Matt at her side, she left on one last gentle exhalation of breath, just as we discussed in those long afternoons alone together. I wouldn't have missed a moment of it.

Many months after her death, I opened a book she had given me years before, and I found a note in her handwriting. It was the last of her writing I would ever see.

It read: *To what am I called? To enjoy nature and through nature, the Creator. To be aware and more purposeful or mindful in my relationships. To develop aspects of myself relative to beauty and kindness. To not contribute to the oppression of others or the messing up of the planet. To develop in wisdom. To become a wise old woman. I expect that my real work is what I always thought was my professional goal: to make the world better for my passing.*

Audrey became that wise old woman sooner than she'd anticipated, and under a considerably more difficult tutelage. In walking so gracefully through her dying lessons, she taught us something about wisdom and a lot about love. We learn how to live and die from those who are courageous enough to use their living and their dying as models for the rest of us.

It's not easy to explore dying out in the open, where our fears and vulnerabilities are plain to others, but—in courageously stepping out to meet death as a spiritual warrior—Audrey offered up one final, splendid gift to the life she held so dear. She used her march toward death as a way to fully embody consciousness. And, just perhaps, God has become more conscious because she gave herself to that effort as she lived and, so magnificently, as she died.

$\mathfrak{g}$

- Think ahead, if you dare, to your own approaching death. Imagine that you have just been told, as Audrey was, that you have four months left to live. Don't shy away from the thought. Stay present and be as creative as possible. What would you want the last months of your life to include?

- Who are the people you want around you? What are the things you would say or do? There's nothing like death knocking at the door to make these matters clear.

- What does it mean to you "to memorize each other?" Where is the Tender Mystery present in such moments as these?

- Write your own answer to the question: *To what am I called?* Take plenty of time to consider how you might answer it.

- In what ways have you made the world a better place by passing through, or for your sojourn here? If you can't yet answer that question, how would you *like* to answer it someday?

- When you come to the moment of your approaching death, what do you want to take with you and what do you want to leave behind as your legacy?

Letting go

Your children are not your children.
They are the sons and the daughters
of Life's longing for itself.
They come through you
but not from you, and
though they are with you,
they belong not to you.

You may give them your love
but not your thoughts,
for they have their own thoughts.
You may house their bodies
but not their souls, for their souls
dwell in the house of tomorrow,
which you cannot visit,
not even in your dreams.

—Kahlil Gibran

Less than a week after my night of terror in Belfast—on a brisk, sunbright morning in Northern Ireland—my son and I sat silently on opposite sides of the road cutting through the mountain village of Cushendall, waiting for different buses to take us toward different adventures. Our joint leg of the journey was complete. We had traveled together for as long as a 23-year-old athlete could tolerate my slower pace. He was eager to be back on his own timetable, following his own agenda, heading for his own excitement.

He sat on the south side of the road, his brilliant red pack at his feet, ready to sling it once more onto his shoulders. He was returning to Belfast, where he would ferry to England and take a train to Amsterdam. I sat on the north side of the road, sitting on a wall beside a concrete hut meant to shelter travelers from the constant mists and sudden showers of a summer's day in Ireland. Near my feet was an oversized black bag.

After a week with my son's help, I now had to manage that large bag alone each time I got onto or off a bus in a new town, every time I walked from a bus stop to the tourist information bureau to find accommodations for the night, and every time I made my way on foot to a hotel or a bed-and-breakfast. For the next two weeks, I'd be on my own in Northern Ireland. Unlike my son, I was frightened and desperately trying not to show my fear to him.

Of course, he knew my fear without me ever saying so. It's that way when two people live together and love deeply for long years. We could be partners, or parents and their children, friends, and other family. The nuances of feeling written across each other's faces are intimately familiar, and there's little point in hiding from each other, although we try. If you can figure out why we do that, I hope you'll explain it to me. It makes no sense, I know; it's just the way most of us function when we are most vulnerable.

We had spent our last days together in Cushendall, which sits just at the tip of Northern Ireland, tucked into the glens that slash deeply through emerald green mountains plunging into the Irish Sea. There are two main streets in Cushendall, a few side streets, and nothing but steep mountain foothills to descend and climb again when we wanted to reach any part of the beach or town. The young and the native Irish skip lightly up and down the hills as though there is nothing to them, but I was neither young nor native to Ireland. I struggled to make friends with every hill I met.

The day before we parted, my son and I had walked to the beach. He wanted to follow a path that ran all the way around the bay and back again. I was exhausted by the time we finished the long descent to the beach. Knowing I still had to make the return climb, I stopped at a bench turning toward Scotland and soaked in the warm, moist air of an unusually beautiful July day. I saw that my exhaustion troubled him, although he went on ahead and completed his trek across the bay in search of whatever he might find on the other side. I searched too, but my search was directed inward: was I going to let the physical struggle, so much more than I anticipated, determine the limits of my adventure?

When Josh returned from his walk around the bay, while we were climbing back up the hill to the inn, he quietly told me that he thought I was in over my head. That I'd taken on more than I could manage if I wanted to complete my trip without help. Travel through the rural, isolated countryside of Northern Ireland without a car—by bus or on foot, our only options— proved to be considerably more difficult than either of us thought. He worried about leaving me to travel alone. Quietly but courageously, he called the question and asked me to consider going home.

I didn't sleep well that last night at the Cushendall Inn. His fears for me were as genuine as mine had been for him just a few nights earlier in Belfast. And I couldn't dispute his fears: he saw that I was not up to the difficulty of traveling on foot in mountain terrain.

The next morning, after wrestling with whether to abort this adventure, I chose to go on. I knew I would face difficult challenges, but I made a shaky commitment to face into them rather than to turn them away. That decision placed us across the road from one another that last morning. We were each heading into experiences that neither of us could imagine for the other . . . and neither of us would be available to help the other complete the unknown journey that lay ahead.

This is the fundamental metaphor for the relationship between parent and adult child. He had his life and his adventures to pursue, and I had mine. It was time to let go of the belief that there was anything we could do to make the other's travels lighter or easier. We had to go on alone. Each of us had to confront whatever hurdles lay before us without the other's presence or support. *Our joint leg of the journey was complete.*

So there we sat, no more than twenty feet from one another, waiting for the Antrim Coaster: one of us headed for Belfast with a brilliant red rucksack and the other toward Ballycastle with a heavy black bag. We smiled but said little to each other. I think now of the Emily Dickinson poem that says: *Tell the truth but tell it slant.* I couldn't look at him directly: I had to look *slant.* If I turned to see him head on, I was overcome with the sorrow of letting him go. Through my tears, I saw the small boy who was so delighted when I read him bedtime stories of the little hobbit Bilbo Baggins leaving his home in the Shire in search of adventure. Or when I sang him to sleep with the song about little Jackie Paper and his companion-in-travel over the high seas: the mighty, magic dragon Puff. By the time he was eight, he was choosing his own books to read; they always involved small creatures setting off on great adventures.

I always knew this child would have traveling feet. But now it was time to let him go. Time for him to let me go, too, into whatever difficulties I might encounter. This is another fundamental truth for all parents and their children: our paths will one day diverge and each of us will embark upon adventures that don't require—or even include—the other. I knew by his silence that this was no easier a process for him than it was for me. He too could only look at me *slant*. I don't know what he saw through the filter of his own memories of his mother, but I could see that it was too difficult for him to look at me head on.

There we sat, my boy and his mother, just a quick jump across a narrow road. I could have called a halt to his worries with the simple act of gathering my bag, crossing the road, and taking the bus south with him along the Antrim Coast, back into Belfast, where I'd find a train to return me to Dublin, and a plane to carry me in the direction of home. I did not make that jump. I sat where I was, on the cold concrete bench in the shelter, looking slant across the way at a young man I'd loved with all my heart from the moment they first placed him in my arms.

It was opportune that my bus arrived first. He watched me haul my bag to the side of the bus, open the heavy cargo door by myself, load the bag into the bin, board the bus, and figure out how to pay my fare in British sterling . . . without his assistance. He saw my first, small success. He did not see me weep as the bus pulled away and I left him sitting with his rucksack, waiting to be liberated from his fears about me.

All over the world, mothers and sons face life-defining moments where we have no choice but to let each other go—pray that it be in love—to discover the lives and challenges we are destined to live. Sitting by the road in Cushendall, Josh and I faced our defining moment. Did we love each other enough to loose the ties that bound our hearts and watch the other leave for another great adventure? Or would we tug on those ties and press our claim on the other's life and love? It was precisely what a moment like this is meant to be: life-altering, powerful, stripping us of *what had been* in order to make way for *what was to come.*

This is never easy. We live in a world similar to the one Bilbo Baggins encountered when he left the Shire and ventured into Middle Earth: a world filled with unexpected dangers. I sometimes wonder if it is like this at the beginning, when the Source of Creation breathes life into each of us and sends us on our way into the great human experiment. Is there weeping then? A loosening of the ties that bind us to the Source?

If I could create a world in which all children, all mothers and fathers, all people, were safe, I would do that in an instant, but I don't have that power. None of us does. And so we are left to struggle with the immense challenges of a world filled with high risk and, *simultaneously*, great adventure. We teach our loved ones the best skills we have at our command, and give the best advice we can offer. Then, at a moment hovering somewhere in time, there is nothing left but to let that loved one go: Josh into Belfast, Audrey into her death.

The Mystery that has made us must also let us go into whatever adventures we choose, or fail to choose, if we prefer a life of safety and predictability. We enter a world that is simultaneously filled with risk and with the potential of great adventure. Sometimes we're faced with hills too steep for our legs to carry us forward, and *we must go forward anyway.*

The experience of embodiment, or incarnation, is a great unknown. What will we discover as we unloose the ties that bind and move ahead to the next city, town, or step along our way? There's no way to predict. I have used the analogy of the trapeze artist, swinging from one trapeze to the other. There is a fraction of a second when we inevitably have to release the old bar in order to reach for the new one. We could swing indefinitely, hanging on, afraid to *reach forward* . . . or we can summon the outrageous courage to trust that there is a mysterious presence thrusting a new bar toward us, waiting to catch us when the time is right.

Again: the choice is ours, always in our hands. The Mystery may hold a hand at our backs and nudge just a bit, but never beyond the point of our free will. I could have turned back from my journey, or my son could have followed along with me. To do that, one of us would have had to sacrifice a truth, and it was not the right thing to ask of the other. Letting go was the one choice that allowed us both to pursue the map written on each of our souls. Letting go.

Letting go: the pause place at the bottom of the breath, when we have taken in the new and not yet let out the old. It's right there, in one fragile moment at the edge of time. We can hold on at that moment, or we can let go. The choice is always ours to make.

ℊ

- Maya Angelou is quoted as saying: *Life loves to be taken by the lapel and told, "I'm with you, kid. Let's go!"* To grab life by the lapel, we almost always have to let go of that which keeps us small and safe. What in your life would have to be released, in order for you to take life by the lapel and go for it?

- Choose one area of your life, and take a risk. Any risk. Just do one thing differently. See how other things change as a result.

- Where is God in moments like these? Is God the one releasing, or the one being released? Or is God the act of releasing, the pause at the bottom of the breath, the suspension in mid-air?

- When your day comes to pass through the eye of the needle, what do you imagine taking with you, and what do you picture yourself leaving behind?

Way will open

*It is easy, on looking back, when
you know how things have worked out,
to ask 'How could I doubt?' But it is
now, while the working out is in process,
that you have to give your confidence
to the Divine Wisdom guiding your life.*

—White Eagle

Many years ago now, I was trudging wearily through the valley
of the shadow of death. My world was dark, very dark, and there
was little light on the horizon. The specifics of this time are
irrelevant, but the lesson learned in them is not. At the time I
had a friend who was a lifelong Quaker. When I was suffering
from doubts that life would ever improve, I could count on her
to revert to a Quaker phrase she learned in childhood. *Way will
open*, she would gently remind me, *way will open.*

This is another way of telling ourselves to be patient, that this
shall pass as all trials do, that good things come again in their

season, that nothing lasts forever . . . even bad times. The passage from Ecclesiastes encourages us that there is a time for everything under heaven. Yet no words ever fell on me so gently as the Quaker words *way will open.*

Like the time my furnace gave up its good years of service in the middle of winter, and I had no money to replace it: Friends lent me the money until I could repay them. Like the time I was struggling to make my graduate school tuition payment: A friend came forward and paid for me. I had helped her through a trying personal time following the death of her mother, and this was an opportunity to reciprocate. Like the time I had no one to help following major surgery, and a healing practitioner I knew came to my house every day to make sure I had everything I needed. *Way will open.*

When my Quaker friend died several years ago, I took up the mantra myself. When I'm told of the heaviness that burdens other people, when I'm listening to heartaches or fears, when I am the container into which others pour their troubles, I think of her quiet, steady spirit surrounding me. In remembrance of her, I share the Quaker words of wisdom: *Remember, friend, way will open.*

☙

- What does it mean for you to give your confidence to the Divine Wisdom guiding your life?

- The next time you come up against an obstacle or a problem, make this your prayer. Keep it simple, and pray without ceasing: *way will open.* Repeat this again and again. Stay with it beyond the point where you are tempted to quit. What happens?

Primal Mystery

We ought to understand God equally in all things,
for God is equally in all things.

—*Meister Eckhart*

This was an early summer night so oppressive that I slept with my bedroom window open in order to feel air circulating around my body through the thick heat. Any other time, I would have avoided opening the window. I'm so sensitive to light that even moon or starlight streaming in is enough to wake me and keep me wakeful. But this night, there was no choice. The movement of air was more important than darkening the room.

Because the window was open, the outdoor noises were more audible than usual. The soft padding of Calico, the neighbor's cat, as she made her nightly rounds of my gardens, on the ever-vigilant prowl for mice or ground-feeding birds. The hoot of an owl. Wind tossing the tops of my tall pine trees to create a *swooshing* sound in the backdrop of my fitful, distressing bits of dreams.

I was startled at 2:30 by the short, violent struggle of one wild animal—a fisher or fox—killing another. There was a brief skirmish between predator and prey, a screeching cry of the doomed creature, and then silence. The skirmish was over. One creature had quickly, violently, taken the life of another. In the years since I moved to my house at the edge of the woods, I've heard such sounds on many occasions. I am sometimes able to tell the prey from the sound of its death cry.

Earlier in the week, the police of my small city distributed bright yellow notices to all of the mailboxes in my neighborhood: flyers alerting us to the presence of a fox in the woods around our homes. I could have told them about the fox. I often saw him in the middle of the night, his furtive-yet-distinctive dark form moving stealthily across the corner where my back yard and my neighbor's intersect. Always moving in shadow, the fox owned the night. He had as much right to be here—to survive, as he is created to survive, by hunting prey—as the people whose homes are built on his hunting grounds.

The danger was that the fox came close to our backyards, searching out smaller animals for food. For all anyone knew, the fox could be rabid. Concerned that people lived too close to the edge of the natural world without a healthy respect for our predator-neighbors, the police warned us not to approach the fox. They said nothing about what to do when we heard him take the life of another creature under the cover of night.

Each time I wake to a piercing primal death screech as the fox, a beautiful creature in its own right, takes its prey, I find myself noticing the presence of Mystery in that skirmish and in the ensuing moment of one creature's death for another's meal. God is there: in the hunter, in the hunted, and in the hunt itself.

I have always found it more pleasant to encounter God in the mist-draped beauty of my early morning gardens . . . or in the shimmering, changeling light of the evening sky as the sun drops from view, ending another day. But time, and a long process of spiritual maturing, have taught me to recognize God in the violence and ferocity of life, as well as in the beauty, even when the recognizing rattles or unsettles me.

It's not the least bit unusual for me to sit with one or more clients a week who battle with fear, illness or loss, and who ask the unanswerable question: "Why me? What have I done to deserve the burden that's been placed on me?" It's difficult to help them come to terms with the only answer possible: *You've done nothing wrong. Absolutely nothing. This is simply the nature of Creation. Suffering is one part of what we, as incarnated beings, are given to experience.*

We hold fast to a belief that God is always *present* in the goodness of human nature and in the extraordinary beauty of a sunrise or sunset . . . but we believe at times that God *has abandoned us* in the night when a person vomits from the toxic effects of chemotherapy, when we act badly toward one another, or when the predator seizes its prey in a chilling act of violence. Sometimes we convince ourselves that, in these difficulties, we've been forsaken by God, by the Mystery at the heart of life. Believing that, we would be wrong.

The truth is this: *There is no place where God is not.* God has never abdicated any part of life or any part of death. In everything that is now and ever will be, the compassionate, unpredictable, giving, taking, primal one we name God—more accurately, the Magnificent Mystery—is there: deeply encoded in the life of every living being.

It takes a considerable amount of grappling, reckoning, with the complexity of this before we recognize the truth of it. We have been so thoroughly steeped in the dualistic notion that God is only love or good that we've grown to believe, by inference, anything that is not loving or good must therefore be *not God*. In the process of splitting some parts of the creation mysteries from the rest, our "why" questions take root and flourish.

Once we make the difficult leap into awareness that the Mystery—God, the Sacred, the Holy of Holies, the Creator of All That Is—is present in absolutely everything, we shift our spiritual work from the need for answers to the effort of learning to bear the depth, breadth, and enormity of God with God. Once we surrender the psyche's need to make the Mystery *understandable*, a futility that allows us the *illusion* that we can control life, we become more willing to encounter the God of Mystery, which just is what it is: all of life, all of death, all of the light, and all of the void where there is only darkness.

Every experience in life is born of the Mystery, and returns to the Mystery. Born of God, it will revert to God at the end, when it is complete, or when life has run its course. *God is everything and has told us so from the beginning.*

I have always been drawn to the Native American practice of addressing God by the name *All That Is*. This term comes as close to a non-dualistic relationship with the Sacred as I believe it's possible to have. The God of Mystery is vast and unknowable. We can't begin to comprehend its vastness and complexity. Nor does it approximate the reality of the Unknowable Mystery to give it human face and form.

Most languaging or imaging of God still perpetuates a male God in supra-human form—the Old Man of the Heavens—even though most seekers who have given God any serious thought don't buy into this paradigm. So, if we can't *understand* God, and if we can't *theorize* God because our theories aren't enough to describe the reality of God, what can we do? We can teach ourselves *to see God everywhere,* present and at work in everything: in suffering as well as the joys of living, in darkness as well as light, in what is beautiful and in what is ugly, in the hunter and the hunted, in life and in death.

The fox wakes me from the dream that this is essentially a loving world and forces me to endure the harsh reality of the God of Mystery, heard in the chilling howl of a dying creature and in the ferocious snarl of its predator.

This is the enduring reality of God. As you go about the activities of your life, notice the Mystery in all its forms. Open your awareness just as fully to The One who wakes you, screeching, in the dark of the night as you do to The One who greets you in the bloom of a morning rose. When we can bear the God of Ultimate Reality—the One so all-encompassing and all-enfolding, so vast as to be infinite and eternal, part of everything that unfolds in the mysteries of life—then we finally enter full spiritual adulthood.

❡

- To believe that God is present everywhere, in absolutely everything, is to throw the doors open to all possibilities about God. God as stalker and stalked, God as predator and prey. God as the natural act of one creature killing another to survive. God seen and heard in the act of hunting. God-as-witness to the death of a rabbit at the jaws of a fox, swiftly breaking the rabbit's neck and carrying it back to its lair. What does it ask of you to become a large enough container, or vessel, that you can hold all of God *with God?*

- Do you, as so many of us have done, deny some parts of God-nature in favor of the parts that please or comfort you? It unsettles us to conceptualize God as the impersonal Primal Mystery as well as a personal Loving Parent. What is there in this possibility that you find unsettling?

- Take some quiet, contemplative time to reflect on how this challenges, alters or expands your relationship with the God of your understanding. How does it challenge your idea of yourself as a participant in that relationship?

- Allow the challenge to live, move, percolate in you. Without shying away from God's primal nature, allow yourself to recall those times when you have encountered it. In what ways were you affected by these encounters? What do you believe they had to teach you?

unlikely places

Go and pray upon a mountain.
Go and pray beside the ocean.
And you'll wash your spirit clean.

Be grateful for the struggle.
Be thankful for the lessons.
And you'll wash your spirit clean.

—Walela

Sometimes, the Mystery we call God shows up in the unlikeliest of places. My living room, for example.

We were enjoying an early spring afternoon, the kind of warmth and fresh air blowing through that only those accustomed to long winter months bundled up in our houses can truly appreciate. The kind of day that causes me to open the windows, even if the screens aren't yet in place, and the doors, so that I can bring the outdoors inside where I'm working.

On this afternoon, my windows were all open and a musty, earthy fragrance wafted through my house. I was elated at being liberated from the constrictions of cold weather. Though delighted by spring's arrival, I was also struggling with a pervasive loneliness that had recently returned to my heart after a merciful absence. My spirits were low and tender, as they had been on and off since the events of September 11th and the awful realization that my dearest people were too far away for me to reach them in a state of emergency. I love the craggy, sweeping beauty of the Maine coast, where I've spent a considerable part of my life, but for months I'd been thinking about moving so I could be closer to those I love.

Perhaps it's better expressed to say that the Mystery was thinking this for me. I wasn't inclined to leave my home, my work, or my friends here, but I'd been aware for over a year—especially when I returned home after being away—that a persistent, annoying *voice* rose up in me to say emphatically: *This is no longer your home. You don't belong here any more.*

I hated this voice. I resisted it as actively as it pursued me. Flying home from a long visit to my daughter's sweet little home in North Carolina, looking onto the ragged coastline below—islands scattered in the sea like children's toys discarded carelessly, shards of diamond-sunlight reflected in the water—I felt a deep sense of peace and pleasure to be home again. I'd just relaxed into that peace when an inner voice began its haunting message: I'm sorry. *This isn't what you want to be told, but you don't belong here now.*

Damn, it was annoying. I wanted to swat at that inner voice like I would swat a mosquito. *Don't bother me. Leave me alone.* I knew better than to expect that tactic to work. When the Mystery is up to tricks in my life, it's up to tricks, and there's not much to do but pay attention.

So that day, as I do many days, I surrendered to the Mystery and waited to see where I would be led next. None of this is easy; I am often lonely and afraid in the period of uncertainty following a wake-up call, and preceding a next set of instructions. I am capable of waiting patiently, but I don't like the waiting period. I chafe. I pace. I wonder and worry. On this spectacularly beautiful spring day, I was restless and anxious, wondering what was coming at me next.

To calm myself, I meditated for a time, breathing into the open and expansive Heart at the center of life, feeling the soft caress of wind blowing through my house, and alert to the sounds of birds returning in great flocks to their summer grounds. It was a sweet, peaceful experience and some of the burden of my uncertainty lightened. But my powerful sense of loneliness did not. When I ended the meditation, I ached just as profoundly as I had at the beginning. *Okay*, I grumbled as I moved to get up from the sofa where I sat. *This loneliness is just going to be my companion for a while. I've lived with it before. Surely I can manage to coexist with it again.*

At precisely that moment, I was struck with an overpowering desire to sleep. To tell the truth, it seemed like someone had hit me with a board and knocked me into unconsciousness. I had only seconds to lay my head on the sofa pillows before I was in a deep sleep, where I remained, out cold, for over two hours. This was not an ordinary sleep. I was aware of being on the sofa. I couldn't open my eyes. I was in that state of unconsciousness where we're temporarily paralyzed, and I was fully cognizant at the time. I was aware that because the doors to my house were open, I'd be extraordinarily vulnerable if anyone walked in.

I was simultaneously asleep *and* acutely aware of my present condition and surroundings. In this altered state of consciousness, I felt rather than saw a person, or a presence, enter my house.

This was a young adult male who entered confidently, as if he knew my house intimately. He strode into the living room to kneel alongside me as I lay sound asleep on the sofa. In the dream, I still could not open my eyes so I sat up and felt for his face. I traced his features until I recognized him. *Oh!* I thought in my altered state of awareness, *it must be Brian.*

Brian, a friend of my son Josh, has never been to Maine or to my home.

The presence responded immediately, though not in words, but in thoughts impressed upon my mind. *You can call me by any name you want,* he said. *I am simply here to love you.* Then he reached out a hand and placed it over mine. Suddenly—though my house is not situated so that sun shines into the front rooms—the room where I was sleeping was suffused with brilliant light streaming through every open window and door. Because my eyes would not open, I still could not see my visitor, but I felt safe in his presence. I lay sleeping yet aware, receiving the love that was pouring into my body from him. In this state, there was no refusing what was happening; I was being infused with a comforting love whether I could take it in or not.

Then another presence entered the room. I was sure this was my son and thought I heard him call out, "Hi, Mom!" I was excited. I hadn't seen Josh since Christmas. He was in graduate school in New Mexico, and it would have been uncharacteristic of him to come home without first letting me know. I jumped up from the sofa, still in the "dream," and went to hug him. Since I couldn't open my eyes, I reached out for him. He held me in an embrace that stunned me with the power of its love. I remained in this embrace for a long time, enough to determine this tall figure was not my son.

Again, I had to find him by touch. I reached out to stroke his hair, long and remarkably silky. I touched his face and felt aquiline features. He was a stranger, yet familiar, who took command of my living room in a way that was simultaneously peaceful and inexplicable. Nothing about the encounter with him made sense to me, not as I slept or as I reflected on it later. The man held me, love cascading out of him and into me like a waterfall, as I felt all my loneliness washing away.

That's all there was, and nothing more. *In my spiritual loneliness, I was simply held by a being of very pure love.*

As abruptly as I'd fallen asleep, I was awake again and sitting upright on the sofa. It was over, whatever "it" had been. I had total recall of my visitors. In fact, they were still so vivid to me that I walked around my house in a daze, looking for them. Something seemed not quite familiar in my house, something seemed unusual, although nothing was out of place and no one was there. The streaming light filling my living room was gone. Perhaps it had never existed.

I cannot explain any more than this. I can only say this wasn't the first visitation by a mysterious presence that comforted me in a time of despair. My living room, Zen-like though it is, is still an unlikely place for a living encounter with the sacred. Yet there was the Mystery: walking through the door, taking me in its arms, holding me long, filling me deeply with love to sustain me in the uncertainty of the times. There's little in this encounter that makes sense.

It seems to me that we're not meant to understand the presence of the Mystery with our logical minds but with our hearts, which *know* when they've been touched by the presence of something holy. Perhaps it's the encounter itself that matters, the experience of human touching Spirit, and not the meaning we try to make of it. *Instead, it makes meaning and purpose of us.*

In each of my direct encounters with Mystery, I found I was

changed in a significant way: my despair was lifted, loneliness comforted, emptiness filled, fear and uncertainty replaced by love. I've learned to measure experiences like these with this question: *Has the experience changed me for the better?*

If I am changed for the better, I accept these experiences for what they are: inexplicable. Always with gratitude. I neither linger over them nor try to understand them. I don't even talk about them to many people. Long ago, in one of those moments of despair we fall into during difficult times, I gave that up. I just decided that I could not know the best path for my life, but somewhere deep in my spirit lived a wisdom born of God. The part of me connected to that wisdom was the only part I could trust to direct me, unerring, toward the right path. I've surrendered my life to that Wisdom many times.

Since then, every once in a while, the visitors come. They stay long enough to put my feet firmly back on the path, and my heart firmly back on the track, which always has to do with restoring love to the places where fear has crept into me and taken love hostage. That mission completed, they depart . . . and I never know when I'll encounter them again.

They leave me with this: a moment of deep, personal experience of the Mystery we call God. They leave me with a sense that my spirit has mercifully been washed clean. I'm always moved by the power of the Mystery to change me for the good, at any time, in any place, and in the unlikeliest of places. Including my living room.

❡

- Take out your journal, or find a pad of paper, to write about the unlikely places or times you have bumped into the Mystery, been visited by it, been touched or held by something you can't explain. Be honest with yourself in a way you may never have been honest with others.

Sometimes these encounters are so unexpected, so mysterious—even if they only last for seconds—that we're unsure what happened and afraid to talk about it with other people. Account for these times in your life. Allow for the possibility they occur in your dreams. Who—or what—was your unlikely visitor?

• Write about times that your spirit has been *washed clean.* Let that mean whatever it means to you. Don't worry about how someone else might interpret it. This is about how the Mystery touches your life. There is no right or wrong about God's unique approach and appearance to each of us.

• If you took these experiences seriously and didn't forget or diminish them, how would this change the way you understand God?

I am who I am

My friend, this body is God's lute.
God tightens the strings and plays its songs.
If the string breaks and the pegs work loose,
this lute, made of dust, returns to dust.

Kabir says: Nobody else can wake from it
that heavenly music.

—Kabir

My friend Katherine is a spiritual trailblazer, a way-shower, and it's her story I want to tell. Kat's a psychotherapist who counseled people for many years before she came upon one of those *holy surprises* I've referred to at other times: breast cancer. She was 45, a single mother in the middle of raising a lovely, lanky, brightly spirited daughter, when cancer handed her its own agenda for the living of her life.

Now, you have to know Kat. She rarely takes life lying down, but more in a headlong, coming-at-you-so-you-better-be-ready manner. She's brave, she's bold, she's beautiful . . . and she didn't like being handed an agenda that threw her so far off the track of what she thought was to be her life. She met breast cancer like a Jedi warrior, and eventually beat it. But cancer changed her in significant ways. One of those ways was the decision to leave her counseling practice and enter seminary for the purpose of becoming a priest. For several difficult years, she explored her call to this vocation, making it singularly hers, often against the opinions of others and unfavorable odds that she would succeed. This week, I heard from Kat that her accomplishments have led to her goal: she has been accepted into the process of ordination that will proceed, in time, to her becoming a priest in the Episcopal Church.

But what kind of priest? That has been Katherine's perennial question since the day she embarked upon this journey. The expectation of the institutional church has been that she would leave behind her work as a counselor to take on the vestments of a priest. More and more, Kat felt compelled to integrate the two roles, and to become all she was created to be—however confusing that may be at times for her to incarnate. Gradually, searching, Kat came to the conclusion that she must embody both, or deny the truth of her own call to serve the Mystery with her particular gifts and skills.

Her struggles came clear one night when, working as a mental health center clinician for enough money to feed, house and educate her daughter, Katherine encountered a woman in crisis. This young woman was from another country, culture, and religion. Because she was far from home and caught in the snare of a demanding academic life, she failed to follow some of the practices of the religious tradition to which she was, under ordinary circumstances, faithful. Her guilt was overpowering. She was afraid that she had violated her religious principles and was destined for the dark fates. Kat, the on-call clinician on the night this young woman struggled, was there to talk with her. She was there in her capacity as counselor. But it was apparent this young woman needed guidance from a spiritual mentor more than a mental health clinician. Gently, kindly, appropriately, Katherine probed the young woman's system of beliefs until they found common ground in identifying a God of *forgiveness and compassion.* Later, Katherine wrote about this: *She talked. I listened, my heart aching with the empathy of knowing what it means to wrestle in the night with God. I found a sister weeping at an empty tomb, and had, with her, slowly turned to see God in a new light.*

When the time came for Katherine to sit in the presence of her ordination committee and she was asked to refine and articulate her vision of priesthood, she told this story as a means to explain the broad range of vision and mission she has been assigned. Both counselor and priest. Not one or the other, but all she is here, trained and at the ready, to embody. The committee's task was to challenge Katherine, until she stood strong and steady on her holy ground. They asked questions: *Wasn't it risky to infuse the role of counselor with her training as a priest?* A good question, a fair question, even a necessary question for Katherine to clarify the call to priesthood. Kat answered, as she described it later, *competently but not fully.*

She explained it to me this way: *I was being challenged to choose an identity, to give up therapist to become priest. I realized I was operating with an understanding from a totally different angle. Priest? Therapist? Photographer? Writer? Mother? Bus driver? Waitress? Friend? Stranger? Patient? I'm blessed with experience that allows me crisp discernment of role boundaries. Certainly in a moment with one as vulnerable as that young woman, I need to know through which portal I am entering, respectfully and competently. But as far as my covenant with God? I am who I am. All of me.*

My role was not the issue. There was no Jew or gentile, no male or female, no Muslim or Christian, no priest or prophet, therapist or chaplain. Just two believers, struggling with what it means to live in the world as such. The work I am given to do in the world takes me into many places of anguish.

My priesthood emerges out of those moments. Any opportunity with which I am blessed to encounter and witness God's Mystery and love, I stand prepared to celebrate and proclaim. To prepare the table, even in the presence of my enemies. That young woman and I returned home in the light of a new day to celebrate the mystery of God's grace through our different traditions. We would seek community in different places. But in the moment of our meeting, God's healing grace waited to be revealed and to be experienced. Waited to be incarnated through each of us.

Many years ago, as I was leaving a marriage that proved unworkable for me or for my husband, I was also giving up home, career, and identity to enter graduate school and start my life over. At the time, it seemed that one life was giving way to another. You've heard me say I endured catastrophic loss, and I faced an unknown future with great trepidation and little support from others. All of this is true, but not the whole of the truth. Here, it's time to tell the rest. What I thought was one part of me giving way to another was, in reality, something I could only understand with the passing of years and the burgeoning of a new perspective. I was not leaving any part of me out to find another. I was expanding into more of me, all of me, the better to be used for the work ahead of me.

I am who I am is a strong statement of individuation and self-definition. It's also a call to become who we are, and no one else. The lute, waiting to be strummed by the fingers of Mystery. The music, waiting to be played through us. The lute player, the instrument, the music, and the whole experience of music being created and played out into the world through my body, through my life, through my love. All that goes before this, preparing us for the moment we will take our stand.

All parts of us, belonging to the whole, and to the holy. Blessed be.

𝔤

- Have you ever believed you had to sacrifice one part of your being so that another could emerge? Is it possible that this sacrifice was unnecessary, even though you were growing into new parts of you?

- What are you able to see now, looking back through the lens of time and maturity, that you didn't know or understand earlier?

- Katherine suggests that we're not intended to be *limited* by role or expectation, but rather *expanded* to find full, authentic meaning and purpose in our lives. Where is the point of greatest meaning and purpose in yours? What do you believe is the highest and best use of your life?

- Are you prepared to become the lute through which the Mystery plays its unique song? If you're not yet ready, who or what might help you in a process of opening all parts of yourself to this expanded version of your life?

Make me an instrument

Whether I like it or not,
I am on this planet
and it is far better to
do something for humanity
while I am here.

—the 14th Dalai Lama of Tibet

One weekend, I threw a party and five good-hearted people came to dinner. To fully understand the momentousness of the occasion, you need to know that I'm not Martha Stewart. I don't throw parties. I hate to cook. I don't entertain at home except when a friend is in distress and I invite her for tea and comfort. My house isn't designed out of the pages of a magazine. It's a little house with a spirit of calm and peace. When I come home, it's after a long day of being with suffering people, and I am ready for the quiet. I sink into it and absorb it like food for my soul, so that—when I go out into the world to be with people again—I'm revivified and have something to give. Think of me as a modern day monastic. The one rule of the house is *no parties.*

But this particular weekend, I had a visitor: my angel friend from the coma in London. We had kept in touch since our first meeting more than two years before. It was time to see each other face-to-face and heart-to-heart. There were certain other friends who had heard about him and were waiting to meet him, and he wanted to spend time with people who were spiritual seekers, so the natural way to bring this about was to gather them for dinner and a circle of conversation.

It's hard to describe what this evening was like for all of us. Words fall short of the experience. Something wonderful *erupted* in our midst. Each of the five people came to the table with an open heart, eager to speak truth and eager to hear the truths of the others. In rapid-fire fashion, stories were told, heard, and held. The *real* stories of our lives, not the ones we tell at cocktail parties. Stories of pain, and stories of love, stories of meaningful connections with others, and stories about ruptures of connection.

We shared deep belly laughter and heartfelt tears. At some point, triggered by something one of us said, we talked about how each of us had, in our separate ways, reached an understanding that we are here on the earth to be used as instruments of, or vessels for, the pouring out of the Divine Mystery.

In the midst of our eager conversation, there was a precious moment of silence. We had all just acknowledged a profound personal connection—unknown to any of the others—with the prayer of Saint Francis of Assisi—*Lord, make me an instrument of thy peace*—when I put on a musical version of that prayer. This is the accompaniment to my nightly meditations. Every person at the table fell silent, closed their eyes, and dropped into their heart of hearts.

When it was over, we continued on with our conversation. What was remarkable about this was that not one person held back the light of his or her full radiance. Everyone shone in the presence of the others, and every one of us got to experience ourselves reflected back in the radiance of a growing, building, emerging collective *light*. Each person looked *beautiful* to me, and they were. The energy of our spinning and weaving of interconnections, truth, story and love grew through the evening until it felt potent enough to blow the roof off my house.

When I was finally tired, I sent them all home. Not because we were finished; it is possible we were just starting. It was because I was too full to absorb any more that night. My friends went out the door laughing and joyous, leaving the "angel" and me behind to fall into our beds feeling much the same way. Every person present for this event would say that something very unusual, perhaps even magical, had happened in our midst.

I wish all of us had dinner parties like this. Places where we can meet with totally open hearts and *find each other again*. The discovery of other-as-self is such a miracle. To see myself fully reflected in another person's loving face or to hear myself in another person's truth is to know the unity of Creation. We can't possibly understand the value of experiences like this if we hold back some, or all, of the light that is our mandate to shine.

On this one evening, in the presence of the great Mystery, we all chose to be seen, to be known, without reservation. No holding back. I know I repeat that phrase many times in my writing, but I believe it's one of our original instructions, long ago neglected: *no holding back.*

In doing this, we created an exponential effect among us that wove a feeling of magic and delight sizable enough to fill a house . . . and beyond. This may have been a once-in-a-lifetime experience, although I think not. I wonder if we don't enter experiences like this more often, simply because we fail to bring our courageous, outrageously beautiful selves out into the open for others to see, to know, and to love.

What if we each made this choice? What if we dared to open our hearts and stand out in the open, ready to be seen and known?

What if we allowed ourselves to acknowledge our common truths as seen in the faces and in the experiences of others, perhaps in the faces of people from another race, gender, economic status, or sexual orientation?

Doing this would spark a spiritual revolution of great magnitude. It would be a point 8 on the Richter scale of spiritual transformation. We could start with making dinner together. No parties. That's still the house rule, though dinner is a definite possibility. Care to participate?

Just come to the table and be willing to serve as an instrument of the Mystery. That's all it would take for us to start a revolution.

ℊ

- This should be fun, so wait until you're in the mood for something to tickle your spiritual funny bone. Sit down with a pad of paper and make a list of the people you would most like to have dinner with, the people who would bring their authentic selves to the table, and break bread with you. Allow your imagination the freedom to picture this event just as you'd really like it to be. Laughter? Tears? Good food? Stories of real people with real lives?

  Sometime soon, hold a dinner party. Invite the people from your list, and wait to see who responds. Ask everyone to contribute something of themselves. Then step aside, and let things unfold as they will. Enjoy yourself. Let go of worry that things have to be "just right," whatever that might be, and simply watch them be what they are.

Could you imagine this might be what Jesus meant when he broke bread with his friends for the last time, and said, "This is my body. Take it, and eat." What if he was not referring to the bread, but to the process where loving people gather and speak deep truth in the presence of the others?

• Now get real for a moment. Where in your life do you serve as an instrument of God's peace? How do you do this, and with whom? Read the prayer of Saint Francis and ask yourself how it applies to the life you are living. Do you want it to apply? Then, get started. Anywhere will do.

Walk in beauty

Beauty to the right of me
Beauty to the left of me
Beauty before me
Beauty behind me
Beauty above me
Beauty below me
Beauty all around me

—prayer of the Dineh people

The audience fell into reverent silence as the blue velvet curtain slowly rose: so sensual, so *scrumptious*, I wanted to wrap myself in it for nothing but the pure decadence of being enfolded by its softness. We were seated, waiting, in the crowded theater at Jacob's Pillow in tiny Becket, Massachusetts. Before us, revealed as the curtain lifted out of sight, stood half a dozen young dancers, men and women, draped in impossible postures as black silhouettes against a brilliant red backdrop. Members of the Hubbard Street Dance Theater in Chicago, they were at Jacob's Pillow for the final performance of the dance season.

This end-of-summer day offered a perfect setting for the artistic gifts we were about to witness. The air was permeated by the crisp scent of incoming-autumn, not too cool, but enough to take the edge off the humidity we suffered through most of July and August.

Everything sparkled and tingled with vibrant life. The trees. The last of the summer flowers, heavy with seed, bobbed their heads lazily in the afternoon breeze. Joyous-spirited people gathered in bright-colored clothing for the final, festive occasion at this theater tucked at the feet of the blue-green Berkshire Mountains. Excited voices became a low, background buzz as people greeted one another and clustered in line for the moment the theater doors would open and the throng would flow inside, a slow-moving river of humanity. And the dancers—*especially the dancers!*— their heads bowed reverently, arms curved ever-so-slightly at their sides. Standing immobile, hushed as stone figures, they awaited the moment when the strains of music would rise above the whispers of the crowd, call out the dance from within their bodies, and propel one, and then another, into ecstatic movement.

Enchanted, I thought: *This moment of utter stillness is the impetus for all authentic movement and action.* No one moved. If anyone breathed, it was lost in the resounding silence.

I felt the heaves of my partner's weeping roll through his abdomen, pressed into close contact with my arm in the crowded theater, before I noticed the tears streaming down his face. He has become a weeper in his elder years, something for which he has no explanation and offers no apology. Elsewhere in these pages, I have called him *the man who cries holy tears,* because those are the words to best describe his spirit: a man touched in unexpected moments by the strangest and smallest of things. The music began to swell, the dancers to break from their frozen postures into movement, a single flow of bodies and sound, all one magnificent endeavor. The elegance of it had opened the heart of my companion, a rolling away of the stone he carried inside for many years without knowing it was there.

His face glistened in the low light of the theater. People in the seats nearby turned to observe the man who wept so forcefully his seat vibrated, and yet there was not a sound emerging from him. He bore the breaking open of his heart with the same silence he bore the stone that burdened and choked him for so many years. No need for others to hear. The *breaking open* was his private epiphany of the power of Beauty to open the way to a direct experience of the Mystery.

The dancers certainly commanded the stage with their grace, but he commanded our section of the audience with his authenticity and emotional courage. He wept simply, openly, honestly, no holding back or hesitation, no embarrassment or apology. His entire body trembled with the force of his heart cracking through its shield, as necessary at one time as it was now a relic of his past. It is for this reason that I love this man: he's not afraid to be broken open. He's seventy years old and looks at life as an opportunity to shed the artifice he gathered earlier as a means of survival. He speaks of a "great letting go" that waits for him, not so far away as it once was, and says that he wants "to practice" for the big experience of dying whenever he has a lesser chance to "drop everything" and just be in the moment. I've become used to the sound of his voice when he's welling up with tears, or the set of his mouth just before the tears fall, or the wet glimmer in his eyes that signals the tears have started to flow. Sometimes we laugh, at other times we weep together. On most occasions, I merely touch his arm to let him know that I'm aware of his tears without needing to ask questions.

At intermission, we met the friends who'd invited us to Jacob's Pillow: a friend from my graduate school days and her husband, neither of whom Bob had met before a brief encounter in the garden as we joined the throngs streaming into the theater. He could barely remember their names. Yet he walked in the garden with Julian, explaining the effect of the dancers on his spirit. I could see that he was weeping again as he told the story. Julian asked him if he knew what the tears were about, and he nodded, choking: "It's about the beauty. About the beauty."

The final dance of the performance was both simple and profound. The troupe, choreographed to move as a single body, started at one side of the stage and crossed to the other. At the midpoint, a solitary dancer dropped away from the line to begin a dance uniquely his or her own—indicating the many parts of the One Body. Each one danced as the dancer's voice reverberated throughout the theater:

. . . My name is Thomas. When I was nine years old, I was diagnosed as hyperactive. I couldn't sit still in class or follow a lesson plan. My parents and teachers were angry with me for something I couldn't explain. Then I discovered dance. From then on, I knew this was what I was meant to do. Once I began dancing, I was never called hyperactive or had trouble in school again . . .

. . . My name is Leah. Both my mother and my father were born deaf. Because they weren't able to communicate with a hearing child, I learned from a young age to use my gestures, my hands, to talk with them. Movement was a natural and easy part of my life. When I was old enough, I took my first dance classes and discovered this was what my life had been preparing me to become. Movement was my first language.

When each dancer completed the individual dance, he or she fell back into the line of dancers moving across the stage as one. Emerging out of and disappearing into a greater whole, they must have rehearsed innumerable times until the complexity of the piece came to look almost effortless to us, the awed audience. Here was the universal story, told through the medium of dance.

We separate from the One at birth and travel along a path that guides us (if all unfolds with its original intention and precision) toward what Stephen Levine calls *the one reason we took birth for.* For a precious time on earth, we inhabit that purpose as fully as possible for as long as possible, and then we return again to the One.

Splendid. The mythologist Joseph Campbell would have been enraptured with it . . . the story of birth, life and death told, not through words, but with movement and vitality and symbolism we might have missed if we hadn't been paying attention. It's so easy to be caught by the spirit's slumbering—the absence of mindfulness—and to miss the cosmic wisdom spread at our feet.

The following night, we had another adventure with beauty. We were at Tanglewood, the home-for-the-summer of the Boston Pops and the Boston Symphony Orchestra. Another perfect night and another final performance. This one featured three women violinists: a classical violinist, a jazz violinist, and a Celtic violinist. The music penetrated my body and I began to tap my feet in rhythm with their soulful strings, then to bounce with joy, and finally, to stand and dance . . . as if I *was* music, and music was me. In their final piece, the three women played their different violins in their different styles as if the instruments were talking to one another. Once the "conversation" reached a crescendo, they turned to the symphony and drew them into the piece. Violin called to flute, who answered and then called to cello. Cello called to oboe, and then to violin, who called to the brass instruments. Music as an exquisite language, communicating beauty as words could only fail to do. Again it was clear that each musician embodied *purpose*. This is who they are on this earth to be: instruments for the music of the heavens.

There was another story. The jazz violinist told of hearing the violin used as a jazz instrument for the first time in many years of training as a classical violinist. She described the thrill that ran through her body, the immediate recognition of her purpose. Here, at last, was *her* music. She couldn't wait to tell her mother, whose quick response to her young daughter's joy was, "Oh, no, baby, that's not what you're going to be. You're going to get a nice job with an orchestra where you'll have benefits and security. You can't play that kind of music. There's no future in it." She went on to say that she *had* followed her heart, her inner knowing, and learned from teachers she never expected to pursue: fiddlers from the mountains of Appalachia, black men fiddling in dark cafes in seedy towns. She was now a world-renowned jazz violinist, a woman who'd created her own music as surely as she had hand-crafted her own life.

The beauty lesson was handed to us one last time, in the form of an eccentric, cantankerous potter with round, tortoise-shell glasses set on his aging face and a stubby cigar hanging from the corner of his mouth. Each of us had been to his studio once—before meeting the other—and remembered him as a highlight of our separate trips to the Berkshires. Unknown to the other, we'd each promised to find him again, which took some navigational talent, and to spend time walking in the beauty of his unusual home. A garden to rival my own. Birds of all kinds, everywhere. A weathered old barn, assaulted by winter storms and dried by the relentless summer sun, now filled with racks and shelves of pots and dishes, plates and bowls, cups and pitchers, floor to ceiling. Colors of every hue: soft pastels, rich earth tones, bright cobalt blues, goldenrod yellows, the reds of Chinese emperors. Following the potter along a path next to the barn, we passed into fifteenth century Japan, removed our shoes at the door, and entered an authentic Japanese Tea House, where we were met with the co-mingling smells of more than thirty blends of aromatic teas.

All the while, the odd little potter talked without stopping, uninterruptible, though neither of us was inclined toward interruption. He's been a scholar of Asian culture for more than

forty years, since an unpredictable turn on his own path led him
from the world of business to a Buddhist monk who instructed
him to become a potter. His pottery now resides in museums and
homes all over the world, at least to hear him tell it . . . and we
had no cause to doubt him. In my home there are four bowls
from which I eat if I want my spirit to be deeply nourished. In
my partner's home, two sets of dishes he chose just for himself.
We weren't alone in our delight with his work. As the potter
talked, we listened for much of an afternoon, while a thunderous
storm swept into the mountain valley, passed through, and the
sun peaked out of the clouds again.

He showed us pictures of the lovely Thai woman he was soon
to marry and her little girl, who would become his daughter. He
talked about growing old and discovering that he wanted the
chance to carry a baby in a pack on his belly before he was
finished with living. He chided my partner about politics and
refused to sell his wares if Bob didn't mend his ways. Bob
laughed and threatened not to buy anything if the potter didn't
change his political course. Sparring as men like to spar, the two
spread elaborate settings of dishes and bowls—colors mixed in
whatever combination appealed—across the worn barn floor as
Bach played, backdrop to the rolls of thunder and cracks of
lightning.

It was another day packed as full with beauty—some delicate,
some savage—as I could stand. Sometimes I just can't take in
any more and have to cry for mercy. This was one of those days.
Everything about it was rich with color, aroma, sound, touch,
even the taste of raindrops on the tongue and pure spring water
the potter offered us instead of tea. Sensory overload, and yet
it was all so beautiful. *Drenched in beauty*, that would be an apt
description. We finally left the studio with a few purchases the
potter agreed to sell if we donated a portion of his fees to feed
children in the Far East who went to bed hungry. We slipped
into a companionable silence until we reached the restaurant the

potter had recommended for our dinner. Only then did we try to cull out of these three events some kind of understanding. Over dinner, Bob began to reflect on the common denominator in each of our encounters with beauty.

"What I found so moving about that man," he referred to the potter, "was that he is himself to the core. There was absolutely no pretense in him, nothing inauthentic. He knows exactly who he is and lives that to the hilt. If you don't like him . . . tough. The loss is yours. He can sell you pottery or not, and it doesn't matter to him. He makes what he loves to make, and you may buy it if you happen to love it too. If you don't, he's just as happy to have you walk out the door and he won't waste a word on you. If you love it too, then he gives his whole self into telling how he became a man who made that particular dish or bowl, and why. He wants you to know the story that flows through his hands to take form in each piece he makes. Everything in that studio is an expression of a remarkable life. I find him, and the pieces he makes, inexpressibly beautiful."

We picked up various parts of each experience, turned them over until we struck on what it was about them that left us *en-spirited,* infused with a sense of "having been touched." It took a while to find the threads, but once we did, they were plain to see. In each adventure—the dancers, the musicians, and the potter—we were privileged to bear witness to fellow human beings who had found the purpose for which they'd taken birth. They developed their purpose until their entire lives were an expression of their *raison d'etre.* Each one of them had become, by choice or by circumstance, artists through whom Ultimate Creation found expression.

Whenever a dancer spun across the stage, a violinist played a concerto, or the potter threw a pot, she or he gave themselves to an act of beauty or creation. They were totally authentic in those moments, truly living the divine template at work in their souls. Each of them fully embodied a truth woven deep into the fabric of their being. Each of them, so clearly *on purpose* or *on path,* was a portal for Beauty to pour into the manifest world ... an opening for Creation to come alive in our midst.

That was what we saw; *that* was what caused my companion to weep: Creation coming fully alive, being fully inhabited or embodied, in our midst. The Mystery, before our eyes, washing over us like cleansing rains during the thunderstorm . . . or the musical conversation between a violin, a flute, and an entire symphony orchestra on a summer's night while butterflies tickled our faces. Each of the dancers was born to dance, each musician born to make music. Even the potter—a scholar by education, a businessman by trade—was born to make beauty that's now enjoyed in the homes of ordinary people like me, as well as in museums and the palaces of kings or queens.

One doesn't have to dance, to call music out of hard-carved instruments, or to throw pots to become an expression of the Mystery. One only has to be what is written in the covenant we carry in our hearts. For some of us, it takes a lifetime to find what that might be, but when we find it, we are challenged to become the living embodiment of it. One woman I know well has spent her career chasing a dream of business success, which she finally accomplished to a notable degree, only to discover that the reason she took birth is to paint. She is an artist, and no amount of success in business gives her the pure delight she feels when she has a brush in her hand, an array of colors on her palette, and a blank canvas in front of her.

Each person, however humble our beginnings or how irrelevant our gifts seem to be, has been perfectly, elegantly designed for a purpose that's assigned to no one else. When we live in full intention with this purpose, we too serve as shining expressions of a living Mystery.

John O'Donohue, Irish poet and scholar, writes these words: *There is a music that keeps your life alive. Within the silent night of your body, the music of your heart never ceases. Though the days come rimmed with sorrow or the nights become anxious with emptiness, the inner music never abandons you. Life is so short. We have remained too long in the limbo of an unlived life. Listen for the music within and your feet become eager for the dance of Spring. The slightest glimpse will free you. As the people of the dawn say: When one flower blooms, it is Spring everywhere.*

So: weep holy tears for the one who has remained "too long in limbo." Weep for the occasional surprise glimpse of your own unlived life, and for the miracle of being awake when that glimpse flashes by. Weep for the self that isn't, and for the Self you have many chances to become. Let your heart be broken open by the beauty of your own divine reason-for-being, and let the music of your soul begin to sound within you. And when your feet jiggle or tap and grow eager to dance, you'll know the Mystery seeded in you from the beginning of time has, at last, begun to bloom.

♫

- Where are you remaining "too long in the limbo of an unlived life?" And for what reason?

- All of us are given glimpses of the life we are born to live. Sometimes we see them passing by, and sometimes we miss them entirely. Take the time to become still inside yourself, and reflect on those glimpses of your true life. You'll know them because they made you weep or laugh with joy. They are sent as mirrors to hold out the sight of you, awakening. What have those glimpses allowed you to see or know about your true self?

- Deep in your spirit, you know the answer to this question:
  What is the one thing you "took birth" for?

Giving thanks

*If the only prayer you say in your
entire life is "thank you,"
that would suffice.*

—*Meister Eckhart*

I'd just come home after a leisurely weekend retreat with
Katherine, who, at that time, had been in divinity school for two
years. In those years, we had only stolen snatches of time to catch
up with one another's spirits. We planned this as a special time
to leave worldly cares behind and simply delight in one
another's companionship. Kat was staying in a borrowed house
snuggled into an old pine forest on the Damariscotta River. She'd
been on retreat for a month, and I was invited to join her for a
few summer days.

We held heartfelt councils by a warming fire, where we
discussed theology, read one another's emerging written work,
watched the skies fill with both drenching sun and drenching rain,

and spent Sunday morning in a radical act of worship neither of us anticipated.

We were awakened that morning by a thunderous downpour of rain on the roof of the elegant little house. We quickly scuttled plans to visit a nearby spiritual center, made the fire roar to keep us cozy, and curled up together on a bank of soft, colorful pillows strewn on a window seat. Kat wanted to read me her recent paper on eco-theology. One of the primary points of her paper was that our incarnated human experience exists in an always changing, developing relationship with the many dimensions of the Divine Mystery, or God.

Several times as we read, paused, discussed, and read further, Kat looked wistfully out the window at the heavy rain making magical splatters and patterns on the still waters of the cove at the foot of the hill just below the cottage. "Oh!" she said, again and again, "I'd love to dive into that water!" I'd been thinking that I wanted to stand out in the rain, naked, open to the heavens washing down on us. After the third or fourth wistful comment, one of us let loose a hearty laugh from deep in the underbelly and said: "What are we waiting for? Let's go!"

What had we been waiting for? We had been gifted with a glorious day of natural wonders in which to worship in any manner we chose. There were no rules but the ones we chose to make in that holy time and place. Cackling with glee, we stripped our clothes and dropped them in a heap by the roaring fire. Katherine dashed for the lower cove, where, a day before, a young river otter had crossed her path while she was swimming. I went to the wooded side of the land and stood, arms wide open to the howling wind and the outpouring of rain, which washed over me for time-suspended minutes and thoroughly cleansed me of my accumulated worries.

There was a small balsam fir in this forest home, blown wildly about in the wind of a surprise summer storm. The tender new growth at the tips of its long branches brushed up and down my body like a caress from the Beloved. The gift of this outpouring of rain presented us with a surprise opportunity to undergo a baptism-in-nature.

The natural world became our temple of worship, and Kat and I gave ourselves completely to our separate acts of devotion. When we finished—purified by the waters of immersion—we met at the house and dressed in silence by the fire. Then we broke bread together: thick, hearty slabs of warm, fresh-baked bread. After a while, when the rains finally stopped, we sauntered up the hill, lingered for a poignant hug, and parted sweet company. Long after I wove my way through the tourist traffic and arrived home, long after I had unpacked and finished my laundry and eaten a simple meal, I sat down to my evening quiet time of prayer and meditation. The words flowing from my heart were simple ones: "Oh, thank you. I love you."

Sometime in the 12th century, Meister Eckhart said: *If the only prayer you say in your entire life is "thank you," that would suffice.*

In his contemporary translation of Eckhart's work, Episcopal priest Matthew Fox wrote: "The creation spiritual tradition that Eckhart preaches is a tradition that believes life itself—its living and dying, growing and sinning, groaning and celebrating—is the creative energy of God, in motion. Eckhart trusted life in general and his own life experiences in particular. As priest and prophet, he taught others to do this as well. As important as knowledge is to our living, still the spiritual way begins with the heart."

Think about this for just a moment. A Dominican priest, who lived eight hundred years ago, believed that God might be as much a verb as a noun: God is living, dying, growing, sinning, groaning, celebrating, raining, swimming, creative energy in full motion. How do we, trained as children to approach God as Father, or possibly God as Mother, come close to an ever-whirling, ever-swirling vortex of motion, sound, color, *energy* and learn to call that "God?"

Eckhart himself wrote: "Where should we begin? Begin with the heart. For the spring of life arises from the heart and from there it moves in a circular manner."

For Eckhart, to be spiritual was to be awake and alive to the mysteries unfolding through all of created life experience. The holiness of creation fascinated him. In fact, creation was his primary sacrament. It's in Fox's translation of Eckhart's writings that we learn, for him, participation in all forms of creation itself was the most sacred way to approach, encounter, and be transformed by the Holy Mystery.

On that rain-soaked morning, Katherine and I chose the sacrament of everyday holiness. We made ourselves ready for God to pour down upon us, to wash over our bodies and souls, and to cleanse us so that we could each return to our full and demanding lives, prepared again to serve those who come to us for sustenance. *Church* was not a destination, but an opening made larger inside our hearts: it was the place within us where we invited the Mystery to enter.

We worshipped in the church of the saltwater river, in the church of the otters, in the church of the old-growth forest, in the church of the soft green tendrils of tree. Our worship was a prayer of gratitude: *Oh, creation, thank you for this beauty, this amazing mystery and wonder, this stuff of life which opens like a treasure before us every moment of every day.*

The realization that God waits for us to know what a thirteenth century mystic and teacher knew more than seven hundred years ago inspires my awe and gives words to my devotion: *Thank you. I love you.*

Gratitude is good medicine for the human spirit. Thankfulness is good for the soul. We practice gratitude when we slow down enough to notice all that is spread before us, the gifts we've been given, the joys waiting for us among the hardships. My friend Bob is a member of a small group of men, all retired or semi-retired, who meet regularly to talk about matters of meaning to them. Their bimonthly conversations involve a little bit of this and a little bit of that: political matters, concerns about terrorism, the rationale for war in Iraq and its aftermath, the ups and downs of an uncertain economy, their children and growing grandchildren.

At one recent meeting, one of the men had prepared a list of things he was thankful for, which he read to the group. My friend, listening to the litany of gratitude, *felt the medicine*—the calming and quieting it evoked in him, and wept. I asked why he thought this prompted him to cry, and he answered in a hushed voice: *"I don't know. It just touched me."*

Gratitude touches us deep in the wellsprings of our spirits. It's good practice to give thanks, and good to receive them. I suspect the Mystery loves to be drenched with gratitude or appreciation.

Summer in Maine, my home, is a mixed blessing of abundant beauty and busy activity. If it's raining, my gardens will be lush. The cedar waxwings will dive into the bush just outside the window where I write to strip it of its bright red berries. The day I returned from my devotional retreat with Katherine, I turned to the window at precisely the right moment to find a hummingbird three feet from me, hovering in midair as it fed on the butterfly bush that had bloomed while I was away. The sweet scent of the tiny clusters of purple flowers filled the air.

Which was sweeter: the bird or the bush? Both provided me with a precious opportunity to experience my gratitude.

Years ago, my children and I read a Leo Lionni book about a tiny character called Frederick the mouse. While Frederick's friends and family were scurrying through the fields gathering food stores for the long winter ahead, Frederick the mouse spent his days resting quietly on a stone wall, soaking in warm rays of sunshine, the beautiful colors, and the delicate smells marking the season of harvest and abundance. The other mice ridiculed Frederick for his laziness, but he let nothing deter him from the task of stilling his spirit and paying full attention to the world around him.

Winter eventually fell, and the little family of mice—including Frederick—huddled close in their nest for warmth and companionship. In time, their stores of food ran out, and they were hungry as well as cold. It was then that Frederick's gifts became apparent. He regaled the others with stories of the sensations of the warm sun beating down upon his small body. He described colors and odors that filled him with appreciation of the world's beauty. Frederick's stories warmed the hearts and the spirits of the other mice. As their spirits warmed, their bodies began to warm too. As Frederick filled their imaginations, so did their empty bellies begin to feel full once more.

In this way, the little mouse helped the others to survive the cold and dark of winter until the change of seasons brought a return of warm weather and abundant food. Frederick knew how to receive gifts of the spirit and how to offer them to others. This is what saved their lives.

Summer is a season for us to fill our spirits with the blessings of a richly outpouring universe. Katherine and I could have spent that Sunday regretting a day of rain and feeling deprived of our plans. Instead, we ran out to meet a raining God on God's terms, and opened our arms to receive the gifts poured on us that day. We found ourselves—each in a different experience of the same opportunity—in two wondrous places, cleansed in an open-air house of worship. No mediator to transact these rituals of devotion for us. No ministers, rabbis or priests to generate a worship event. Nothing standing between us and the Mystery.

It occurs to me to tweak those of us who need reminding—including myself—that the Mystery rises up to meet us in every moment. Sometimes those moments divert our plans or arrive in a form that isn't what we expected. Do we plunge into those moments anyway, offering gratitude, or retreat from them, grumbling that they aren't what we planned? Perhaps a deeper question is this: *Do we allow ourselves to notice and to give thanks for the Sacred Mystery as it displays its living splendor before us?*

Gratitude is healing balm for the soul, especially in the difficult times before us, when much is happening that we cannot control, or even change. The heart of humanity is hemorrhaging, and we can't seem to staunch the flow. There is no better time to practice gratitude than in the small and large moments of our lives. A time for us to look out at the world, or up into the skies above our heads, and to be thankful for the lavish splendor Creation has placed there to replenish our flagging spirits. Gratitude is good medicine. Remember that.

g

- Choose a place of natural beauty and make yourself ready to go there. Prepare in a manner that reflects the sanctity of your intentions. Wrap a prayer shawl around you, gather shells or seeds or even tobacco, as the Native Americans do, to indicate that you come to worship the mystery and magnificence of God-in-Creation.

Walk mindfully into this place and around it, circling it, until you have located the spot that seems to invite you to sit or stand there. Just sense this. Let go of the need for logic or reason. This time is an opportunity for you to move in a sacred manner, toward a sacred place, for a sacred purpose.

Once you are in the spot that draws you, create a prayer or read a poem aloud to the wind, to the trees, to the soft ebb and flow of the tides. Include in your prayer-poem your gratitude for all gifts that are given to you: beloved family and friends, experiences that have shaped you, events that support you on your spiritual path, gifts of the natural world which sanctify your life.

When you are finished and ready to leave, offer your gifts in return to the spirits of this place, to the changing of tides, to the rustling of trees, to the pouring out of sunshine or cleansing rain, to the washing clean of your spirit. Remember the words *thank you.* They are a prayer, and they will, in the words of Meister Eckhart, *suffice.*

Seize the moment

Accept. Then act.
Whatever the present moment contains,
accept it as if you had chosen it.
Always work with it,
not against it.
Make it your friend and ally,
not your enemy.
This will miraculously
transform your whole life.

—Eckhart Tolle

I heard two stories this week that caused the hair on the back of my neck to stand up. Both tell more about the wild unpredictability of life unfolding. Both of them have jolted me—they will jolt you too—into heightened appreciation of that unpredictability. Stories like these happen to fall our way on occasion . . . and command our attention. I learn from them: necessary lessons, hard lessons, awe-filled lessons. They always change me.

Prophet and mystic, theologian and teacher, priest and writer, Meister Eckhart instructs us that the wild, unexpected nature of *life living itself* is the process—not the person—that is God. I've quietly come to accept this as true. For that reason, I prefer to call God by the name I use in this book: *Mystery*. If we insist on naming God's holy nature, I've come to believe this is the closest description of what God truly is: mystery emerging, unfolding, revealing itself, mystifying us. It appears that the deepest heart of God-nature is, and will remain, ever-revealing, ever-expanding, ever-transforming mystery. In this way, God is like a flower. Just as it's encoded in the nature of a flower to bud, blossom, and die back to bud and bloom another season, it's simply the nature of God to be *god-ing* . . . or *happening*. God is not controlling its process of emergence any more than the flower controls its seasons of blossoming and dying.

Just as it falls to us to appreciate the flower in bloom, it's ours to appreciate the activity of God-happening in our midst. This brings me back, in a wide loop of thought, to the two stories with something to tell us about God-happening.

The first story is this. A man I met briefly, passing in a driveway of a friend's home, was injured several months ago in a single car accident. Severely traumatized. Brain-injured. It's possible, as much as we know now, that he won't survive this insult to his brain. If he does survive, it will be in a very compromised condition. Life as he knew it . . . is gone.

I heard about this because the man had been seeing a woman I know, and though the relationship had apparently cooled, she cared about him as a friend, and his family wanted her to know that he was near death. She was more than a thousand miles away from the hospital where he'd been airlifted; she was struggling to decide if she would travel to be with his family during his crisis, or stay home and support them from a distance. I don't know which she'll choose to do. Either way, it's a difficult decision.

What I do know is that when we are suddenly ripped from each other, with no warning, there's usually much left unsaid and unattended. A lot of unfinished emotional business. Days before I heard about this accident, I was boarding a plane to visit my daughter when I was struck with an overwhelming impulse to write a beloved friend, someone with whom I had not been in contact, just to tell him what he means to me. No reason I could understand, but a strong inner prompting to do this. I followed through on that impulse. Hours later, my connecting flight was held on the tarmac in Philadelphia, and the pilot came on the speaker phone to tell us that our take-off had been delayed because all communication was down in the air space over Washington, DC.

In a time of widespread, random terrorism, this was frightening information. An audible gasp spread like a wave of fear throughout the cabin. In that moment it seemed possible that we were in another wave of suicide plane attacks. I was profoundly grateful I had taken time to write that letter. I wouldn't have wanted to die without telling him how much I loved him.

I was lucky. Whatever it was that shut down communications over Washington was not an act of terrorism. I reached my daughter safely, and made a safe return trip home. Not everyone reaches his or her destination safely. Nearly three thousand people did not safely reach home on September 11th. The man I briefly met in a driveway did not arrive home safely on April 4th.

Rachel Levy, an Israeli teenager, died in her neighborhood store, on a shopping errand for her family, as she walked into the market at the same instant a Palestinian girl blew herself up as a human bomb. How many words remained in their hearts—never spoken—or in the hearts of the people they left that morning?

The second story is a much gentler and sweeter one, though it no doubt carries considerable pain leading up to this moment.

A friend of mine attended Easter morning services at a church—not of her religion—that she visits only on the few occasions each year that her son is a violinist in the service. She took with her a friend who had never been to that church in her life. The women had difficulty finding a place to sit in the crowded congregation, but finally they were seated and ready for the service to begin.

Just before the service started, my friend's friend felt a tap on her shoulder, and looked up in shock to see her former husband, who lives hundreds of miles away. They'd struggled with an edgy relationship since their divorce. He too never attended this church. It "just happened" that he was there to see their son for the Easter holiday and randomly decided on that church as the place they would meet for services. He made a decision to be somewhere he had never been, on a morning she also, unexpectedly, came to be there. The struggling former spouses had a brief, warm and healing encounter that neither could have planned or foreseen.

My friend told me the story with awe. She described sitting near as her friend wept tears of gratitude through the entire service. She thought this was a special story that ought to be spread to others, and brought it to me. I bring it as a gift, in turn, to you.

For me, the message is this: life is simply too brief and precious for us to wallow in hurt or resentment toward the ones we love, tempting as that sometimes is. We can't predict what will come around the next corner. It could be an ordinary, uneventful day. It could be that tragedy lurks just out of sight. It could just as easily be grace, waiting for us to arrive. For me, the lesson is to *be ready*. To take the time, when the inner voice prompts me to stop, to listen and to follow instructions. I might grumble and doubt my sanity, but I won't have regrets.

Moments come and moments pass in which the Mystery is

happening. We catch some of them; others slip through our fingers like water through a sieve. I think of the distraught face of Rachel Levy's mother telling newscasters she knew her daughter was dead the moment she heard the bomb explode near her neighborhood. I think of her little brother leaving the family's telephone number at her unmarked grave so Rachel would remember to call home. I think of two women: One who has to bear terrible news of an accident that changed, and could quite likely end, her friend's life . . . and another who felt a tap and looked into the face of a man from whom she had been estranged far too long.

What would they want us to learn from their encounters with the unpredictable nature of God? That it's real. That we may never know when God's Mystery will brush against our lives in a sudden, unexpected way. Therefore, each moment is to be cherished, noticed, appreciated, and put to good use. Remember Don Juan, the Yaqui Indian who taught Carlos Castaneda to walk in the world as if death was always riding on his left shoulder. Elemental wisdom: *Stay awake. If you are asleep, you may miss your life. Notice everything for it's too quickly gone. Stay in the present moment with as much awareness and intention as possible: there are surprises waiting for you.*

As I write this, there are surprises waiting for me. I'm looking out at a nearly perfect early spring day in Maine. The sky is a bright azure blue, the clouds are plump and luscious, a tiny titmouse sits in the bush beneath the window where I write. This isn't a day I want to think about death riding my shoulder. But I'll give these stories a little room to roam around in me, some time to tinker with my heart, before I get on with the business of my life. I will think about the beloveds I want to call or want to write, just to say, "I love you." I'll slip away to my gardens and measure the green shoots erupting from the rich-smelling earth to see how much taller they are today than they were yesterday.

I'll turn toward life. Beautiful, wondrous, terrible, splendid life.
I will seize the day, seize the moment. I will, in the words of
spiritual teacher Ram Dass, *be here now.* There is no other place
with so much to teach me. I'll do this more aware of the fragility
of life and the mystery of God-happening, and more grateful
because these stories remind me of how precious life is . . . and
how precious we are to each other.

℈

- Eckhart Tolle writes in *The Power of Now* that we must
  accept whatever the present moment contains. That we must
  always work with it, not against it. That we must learn to
  make the present moment a *friend and ally, not an enemy.*
  If we do this, even for short periods of time, he assures us
  that this spiritual practice will *miraculously transform our
  whole lives.*

  What does he mean by this? How does it change you to
  bring your attention only to the moment in front of you,
  and to stay there, fully present?

- A friend recently wrote me to say that she was in a period
  of great darkness, that grief was leaking out of her very
  pores, and that she was unable to stop crying from the
  sorrow and overwhelm of her life. She was totally present
  to her grief. Difficult as it was, she seized the moment and
  allowed it to be as awful as it was. No masks. No attempts
  to be someone she could not be. Only authentic grief,
  pouring from her in rivers of tears. In your understanding,
  where is God *happening* in this period of her great
  darkness? And where, or how, does God *happen* in yours?

- Take an uninterrupted hour, or day, to do nothing but be
  present to everything the day presents to you. The world,
  your life, your family, can live without you for a while.

Leave that all behind for just this one hour or day, and watch with full attention for what waits to be revealed.

Stay awake. Notice everything. Be there with as much intention as possible. What are the surprises, small and large, that plunk themselves before you for your delight or sorrow? Everything, absolutely everything, that comes to you is God-Life-Love-Mystery wanting to dance with you. Tell me this: will you dance?

worth the risk

The time is now, now,
now, NOW.

—Bob Whalen

Over two nights, I had back-to-back dream encounters where I was in a sizeable gathering of Native American people who were singing, praying, and burning sage to cleanse the heart of humanity of hatred and evil-doing. There were vast numbers of them, traveling from the far corners of the earth to gather on mountainsides and buttes, wherever there was a holy place from which to send up a cry to the heavens. Both dreams were startlingly similar, an odd dream experience for me. I haven't ever dreamed the same dream two nights in a row. In both dreams, I was a witness, not a participant, as if I was there to remember what the "first peoples" have never forgotten.

I write a lot about the imperative *to remember* what was coded or imprinted in our souls at the time of our incarnation. To remember *what we already know.* This brisk, bright fall day seems a good time to reflect on what I'm remembering and how this *remembering* reveals itself to me. It isn't a cognitive process. Nothing like that. It is more a cellular one, in which I gradually become aware that something is nudging its way up from the depths of my unconscious to my awakened self. First, these back-to-back dreams, and then a song that has been pursuing me.

The song is a contemporary hymn, one with a comforting melody and simple words:

> *Peace is like a river flowing,*
> *flowing out to you and me.*
> *Peace is like a river flowing,*
> *setting all the captives free.*

Several days ago, I noticed that I was humming the melody, then singing one line, and another, and finally, the whole refrain. I sang in the shower, I sang while I was doing my laundry, I sang while I knit and while I shopped for groceries. I am still singing: the song has held my attention for days. What is this song *remembering* and teaching? What is God *revealing* through the song and through my singing?

The night before these dreams, I watched a news clip of the memorial service held the previous weekend at Ground Zero for the families of the victims of the World Trade Center attacks. As prayers from many religious traditions were spoken and songs lifted to the skies, the cameras panned the crowd of several thousand people. I saw the faces of Americans from many nations, races, religions, and cultures, holding placards with photographs of their loved ones: written on them, their last words of love. They were weeping opening and unashamed in their terrible grief. It was a profound grief to witness. My own heart cracked open at the sight of their broken hearts, and I too wept openly and without shame.

Then, not by accident but—I suspect—by design, the news segued to a village in Afghanistan that had been bombed by American planes not long before the news cameras arrived on the scene. The villagers were frantically digging in the rubble, using only their hands, for the bodies of those who were killed in the bombing, hoping—as we were hoping just weeks before— for survivors. At the edge of the scene, almost out of camera range, nearly unnoticed in the urgency, a young Muslim woman buried her face in her hands, leaned against a bombed-out building for support, and slid to the ground in slow motion. She wept, unashamed, for her people, her family, her neighbors. This too was a terrible grief to watch.

What am I remembering? That we are not, even in these times, despite all appearances, enemies to each other, but brothers and sisters under the skin. The grief is no less terrible in Afghanistan than it is in Washington or New York. The murderous rage unleashed in the world—wherever it began and whatever the reasons for perpetuating it—is causing a terrible grief. A grief that will take many generations to heal. Almost certainly, I will not see this wound healed in my lifetime.

I have little power over these events. I'm not a world leader in a position of policy or decision-making. I don't understand the long string of events throughout the centuries that bring us to this place. I am just a student of human nature, sometimes a teacher when the moment presents itself. This hatred and rage we hold for one another is beyond my understanding. I'm not sure I want to understand how the human heart has become so hardened that acts like these are the only way to announce that rage or pain to the world. It is not an easy task to live with this powerlessness and still maintain some equanimity.

In my better times, I'm grateful for years of spiritual practice and the anchor they provide when all else fails. In the worst of times, I lay awake endless nights, tending to my dread as well as I am able, praying as best I can, for both the innocents in this unfathomable tragedy and for the terrorists: *Sustainer of all life, I say, be present to the suffering of innocent people of all nations, races, ages, religions. Help them to heal from their unimaginable grief. Be present to those who perpetrate these crimes against members of their own families, for they too are captives and are suffering.*

These prayers offer me some measure of comfort. But what really helps me rise above feelings of powerlessness is to open my heart, as wide as I possibly can, and throw my love out into the huge vacuum of need that exists right now. I send love to the people who work shoulder to tired shoulder at Ground Zero, and to the woman slowly dropping to the ground in Afghanistan. I send it to my friends, worn as they are from managing the anxiety and despair that is growing daily in our hearts. I send it to strangers far over oceans and mountains and deserts. And I sing to them: *Peace is like a river flowing, flowing out to you and me. Peace is like a river flowing, setting all the captives free.*

We are all captives of this time in human history. This is not a moment we'll look back on with any pride, but it is a moment where we can—if we will—rise to the occasion and throw our love out into the world. The alternative is to generate fear, hatred, anger, and pain; and there's enough of that to last us long into the next century. If I allow *peace* to flow through my heart— just this one heart over which I have some influence—then I'm no longer held captive by events beyond my control. My only task, as a woman who set off, somewhat naively, on a quest to find the Holy Grail, is to remember that the grail is a metaphor for what lives in my spirit. I am the one who gives, or denies, access to it. If I fall hostage to fear and rage, then I have lost the grail. If I maintain peace of mind, peace of heart, peace of spirit, and I send it through my meditations and prayers to those all over the world who need it as much as I do, I possess the grail. It can never be taken from me.

This is what I'm *remembering*. Perhaps it is better said, *what is trying to remember itself through me.* I have only one heart with which to respond to world events. I have little influence over what will happen next, but the choice I do have is a potent one.

I can open my heart, meeting uncertainty with compassion and fear with outrageous courage, or I can close it. I alone make the choice. Examined against the amount of darkness in the world, my one choice seems small and insignificant. But if you choose too, and then another of us, until we are standing together as the people of my dreamscape stand—praying, singing, doing our part to throw good out ahead of us—perhaps we can turn the tide, after all.

Consider this: it may be all we can do to stand together and pray or sing, adding to the good, but that's a powerful *something*. And it's almost certainly worth the risk.

ℐ

- More than any time in history, we are at grievous risk. And, more than any time in history, we have the capacity to realize every one of our actions has a corresponding consequence. Making anger, generating fear, hurting another, I contribute to the *harm* that is increasing in the world. But generating peace in my own spirit, against all temptations to do otherwise, I contribute to a growing experience of peace for others. Grandmother Twyla Nitsch, a Native American spiritual elder, asks the seekers who come to her door: *Are you contributing to the good, or to the harm of the world?* Which contribution are you making?

- One day recently, I stopped at the nearby hospital to have a routine blood test. I'm there monthly so many of the lab technicians know me by face, if not by name. This day, there was a new person in the lab, and she was assigned to draw my blood. As she was preparing my arm for the imminent prick, she asked if I was a therapist. I told her I was, and asked how she thought to ask that. "Oh," she told me, "I notice there's always a calm, or a peace, around therapists. You're a granola-type people. You're the ones everybody wants to hang out with because you're so calm about things."

I thought about this long after I left, and decided that what she noticed is the quality of equanimity that grows out of *listening*, all day for many years, to many kinds of pain and all kinds of joys. We learn that nothing lasts for long, and everything passes in time. I'd never thought of my work as a spiritual practice, but now I can see that possibility and appreciate that, in fact, I do have what I need to be alive in these times. So do you.

What spiritual qualities has your life led you to develop, whether you were paying attention or not, to help you rise to the needs of our times and toss your love—or peace, or calm—into the world?

Hummingbird

Count me in forever.

—*Katherine Stiles*

There's a perennial garden directly below the window of the room in which I write. In fact, there are gardens ringing my house in a full circle. In this one garden there's a plant called *crocosmia* or *Lucifer's Tongue*. This is an elegant, long-legged plant with curved tips filled with bright red, trumpet-like flowers. I plant crocosmia—though it doesn't winter well in the harsh climate of the coastal Northeast—because it is a hummingbird's dream. Of all the birds and butterflies to visit my gardens, hummingbird is my favorite visitor. Its fragile beauty instantly connects me with the mystery at the center of all Creation.

In bad times and in good, close by and far from home, the hummingbird has appeared to me in the most surprising moments. High in the Sierra Mountains of northern California, where I sat for three days and nights on a solo vision quest, praying for my grief to be cleared and purpose to be revealed.

In the Rocky Mountains of Colorado, where I had gone for a training week that issued me a personal epiphany, making it possible to return home and make a very difficult decision. On tiny Isle au Haut off the coast of Maine, where a friend graciously offered me shelter in her miniature house through a period of necessary reflection. In each place, the hummingbird came to visit me. I gradually came to think of hummingbird as my personal totem. She even appears, on occasion, in my dreams.

One day last summer, while I was writing, the hummingbird came to feed at the crocosmia. This was nothing unusual; hummers love red flowers. I suspect she was there many times a day in her search for nectar to fuel her tiny body. But something happened this day that was far beyond the usual. The hummingbird, having had her fill, lifted eight feet into the air, well above the trumpet-flowers of the crocosmia, and hovered— at eye level with me—outside my window. For several breathtaking seconds, the hummer and I looked one another in the eye. We were separated only by glass, no more than three feet apart.

Eye to eye with a hummingbird. Astounding enough to steal my breath. I might have missed the moment if I hadn't looked up at the instant she hovered, briefly, for me to encounter. I watched, struck with awe, at the thousands of times her inch-long wings beat in figure-8 rhythm to sustain her temporary holding pattern. Then she was gone, this spectacularly beautiful creature, present for a small fraction of time. A glimpse of the Mystery, and then . . . no more. I'd been blessed by a visitation from a tiny emissary of the Heart of Creation.

I was still telling the story of my hummingbird visitor when, the very next day, at the same time in the afternoon, she came again and repeated her movements of the earlier visit. She drank her fill of nectar, lifted into the air just high enough to meet my eye, and hovered once more, three feet and one window beyond my reach. In the few delicate seconds we faced each other, I was once again eye to eye with one of God's most beautiful creatures.

After establishing this *connection*, the hummingbird flew away. I may not see her again for several years. Perhaps I'll never see her again. Once, maybe twice, in every lifetime, a moment such as this.

There is no doubt in my mind that this was a direct encounter with the Mystery that we call God. One of many such encounters in the course of my plus-fifty years on the planet. Some have been difficult encounters, where I was stripped of all that thinly laced me together. Others—magically imbued with the elements of mystery—were uplifting and inspirational. All bore a thumbprint of awe and wonder. They're the little slips of paper dropped upon the path, either left unnoticed, or, if I'm paying attention as they drift by, caught and slipped into the pocket for later use.

I'm grateful to have been given the gift of *noticing*. Even in the most painful of times, I attempt to notice where the Mystery is at work, and I discover—not a surprise!—it's always at work, in all situations, and in all places. There is nowhere that the Mystery of God is absent.

God is never the variable: I am. I'm either conscious, watching for evidence of its presence, or I am asleep. I'm either noticing, or failing to notice. My life is wealthy beyond measure when I'm awake, aware . . . and noticing.

Oh, I've had my share of quarrels with God. I haven't always liked much of what's happening on the sometimes arduous trail through holy ground. Some time ago a colleague warned me that the more real a relationship I developed with the Mystery, the more I was willing to see and hear and taste and know God for what God really is—beautiful, complex, unnamable, baffling and often infuriating Mystery—the more deeply I would find myself falling in love with the Beloved. This has been true.

Once again I was in conversation with my friend Katherine about how we locate and take our spiritual stands when times are especially trying. In the wish to comfort me, she wrote just the right words: "I love the way the circle gathers round when we're most in need. Count me in forever."

Katherine's words jumped off the page and struck me, a direct hit, in the heart. *Count me in forever.* Those are my words to the Sacred Mystery, which has taken me in its firm embrace countless times, regardless of whether I'm surrendering or kicking and screaming . . . and holds me.

My relationship with the Source of All Creation is one enduring constant of my always-changing life. I love God's mysterious, changing, expanding nature ferociously . . . and also despair of ever fully grasping all that's attempting to become conscious in my life because of, and through, this Amazing Mystery of Mysteries. I am thankful for each visitation, whisper, or delicate touch that rouses me from my spiritual stupor to infuse me with a renewed aliveness and appreciation of the complex, beautiful River of Life in which I am, and you are, immersed.

Eye to eye with a hummingbird. Oh, Mystery: wondrous, complex puzzle that you are, born in us anew every moment, I stand in awe before you. *Count me in forever.*

ℂ

- Recall a time when a butterfly landed on your shoulder, a bird or a deer fed from your hand, a hummingbird visited you eye-to-eye, a whale breached with her calf for you to witness her greeting to the human family.

- Once, in a dream, a giant monarch butterfly flew directly

into my heart, and exploded. In what ways have you been surprised by something inexplicably mysterious and holy? What has been revealed to you about "God-happening" through these encounters?

• What are the events in your life—large and small—that invite you to fall in love with the complexities of God's mysterious nature, and prompt you to say, *Count me in forever?*

• Where in your life is there evidence to support the statement that *the more real a relationship we're willing to develop with the Sacred, the more willing we are to see and hear and taste and smell and know all of God's essential nature, the more we fall in love with the Mystery we call God?*

Root of all things

Holy Spirit,
giving life to all life,
moving all creatures,
root of all things,
washing them clean,
wiping out their mistakes,
healing their wounds,
you are our true life:
luminous, wonderful,
awakening the heart
from its ancient sleep.

—*Hildegard of Bingen*

This time the heavens lived up to their promise. Even the meteorologists hedged their bets, telling us that the skies are so unpredictable we might not get to see this once-in-a-lifetime display of heaven's magic. But the fates were with us, at least with me, and here I sit—at 5:40 on a very cold late fall Maine morning—in a state of indescribable awe and gratitude for what

I have just witnessed. The heavens opened . . . and gave us glimpse after glimpse of unimaginable beauty.

It was too early and far too cold when I got up at 4 am to try for a peek at the promise. I am less of an early morning person as I age. I like the comforts of my bed. Yet, though I set the alarm to wake me, something whispered through my sleep to rouse me before the beeping of the alarm had a chance to clip my sleep short. I opened my eyes in gentle acknowledgment that it was time to step out under the canopy of night sky for whatever was there to be seen and experienced.

It was already happening without me. Before I stepped to the window leading to my back deck, I saw the first brilliant shooting star. By the time I put on my heavy socks, bundled into a coat, and found my mittens, I had seen dozens.

I stepped out into the sharp sting of the night air. I heard the creatures of the night rustling in the trees just at the edge of the woods. It was probably best that I didn't see them, or they me. This heightened my sense of being one creature among many to witness the Opus Magnificat of the universe. Other than my neighbor, alone on his small porch, there was no human activity to be seen or heard. But in the realm of the heavens, first dozens—and then hundreds—of shooting stars streaked across the black velvet pre-dawn sky. The shooting stars came in great bursts of brilliance or in puffs and wisps of light, some green or blue, some streaking across the paths of other shooting stars, one double burst. On and on, the mystery of creation revealed itself for these few early risers to see.

I thought of September 11th and its aftermath of terror and war. It almost seemed as though there was one shooting star for each innocent life lost in those difficult days, and perhaps this was true. I had lost count too soon to determine. It certainly seemed believable that this too-brief moment in a lifetime was one sign that we are not alone in this great murky and mysterious cosmic soup. It was hard, if not impossible, to disbelieve. Borrowing a phrase from Michael: the Mystery was *God-birthing* all wonder and awe, bounty spread before us, for our witness. Here was God, its magic and mystery, just *happening*.

Those who were awake, saw it. Those who remained asleep, did not.

On that magnificent morning of shooting stars, I realized it was time for me to stop waving my arms, to stop clamoring for people to awaken, and to drop down into deep quiet once again, listening for wisdom to be born anew in my spirit. The instructions had come in the midst of that wondrous night of shooting stars, and they were clear. After a long period of writing and issuing pleas for us to become conscious of what we're doing and how we're living, the seasons of my own life were turning, and it was time to become quiet and reflective again. It was time to wait for the next steps to be made known. Time to wait until the next scraps of paper fall on my path.

It is in that deep space of quiet that we'll keep our spirits bright and strong during this period of uncertainty in which we live. Let us remember the dancers, and the lesson of the dance: it's only from the point of utter stillness that we make the next, authentic movement or take the next true action. We must pay attention to this as though it is the most significant act of our lives, which it may well be. Attend to the still point in you where the Mystery abides, and I will do the same.

May the Mystery that is the "root of all things" reveal itself through each of our beautiful spirits. And may our prayers, our hopes, our dreams continue to illuminate and enlighten the hearts of the family of earth.

§

- We are each given the choice to rouse out of our slumber (to become consciously embodied partners with God in creation) or to remain asleep (and unconscious). Waking up, we see. Asleep, we miss the chance to experience the Mystery that is God exploding throughout the universe. That choice is in my hands, and yours. What will you decide?

Everybody has his or her own possibility
of rapture in the experience of life.
All one has to do is to recognize it and then
cultivate it and get going with it . . .
It's important to live life with the experience,
and therefore the knowledge, of its mystery
and your own mystery.
This gives life a new radiance, a new
harmony, a new splendor.
The big question is whether you are going
to be able to say a hearty yes to your own adventure.

–Joseph Campbell, in *The Power of Myth*

Thoughtful reading

Anderson, Sherry Ruth and Hopkins, Patricia. *The Feminine Face of God.* New York: Bantam Books, 1991.

Baldwin, Christina. *The Seven Whispers.* Novato, California: New World Library, 2002.

Baldwin, Christina. *Calling the Circle.* Newburg, Oregon: Swan-Raven & Company, 1994.

Chittister, Joan D. *Heart of Flesh.* Grand Rapids, Michigan: Wm. B. Eerdmans Publishing Company, 1998.

Chodron, Pema. *When Things Fall Apart.* Boston: Shambhala Books, 1997.

Chodron, Pema. *The Places That Scare You.* Boston: Shambhala Books, 2001.

Cooper, Rabbi David A. *Entering the Sacred Mountain.* New York: Bell Tower, 1994.

Dillard, Annie. *Holy the Firm.* San Francisco: Harper & Row, 1977.

Douglas-Klotz, Neil. *The Hidden Gospel.* Wheaton, Illinois: The Theosophical Publishing House, 1999.

Dwinell, Michael. *God-Birthing.* Ligouri, Missouri: Triumph Books, 1994.

Dwinell, Michael. *From Within the Heart of God.* Philadelphia: Xlibris, 2003.

Flinders, Carol Lee. *At the Root of This Longing.* San Francisco: HarperCollins, 1998.

Fox, Matthew. *Meditations with Meister Eckhart.* Santa Fe: Bear & Company, 1983.

Gibran, Kahlil. *The Prophet.* New York: Alfred A. Knopf, 1923.

Glassman, Bernie. *Bearing Witness.* New York: Bell Tower, 1998.

Harvey, Andrew. *The Direct Path.* New York: Broadway Books, 2000.

Hillman, James. *The Soul's Code.* New York: Random House, 1996.

Hull, Akasha Gloria. *Soul Talk: The New Spirituality of African American Women.* Inner Traditions, 2001.

Kelsey, Morton. *Set Your Hearts on the Greatest Gift.* Hyde Park, New York: New City Press, 1996.

Kidd, Sue Monk. *The Secret Life of Bees.* New York: Penguin Books, 2002.

Kornfield, Jack. *A Path with Heart.* New York: Bantam Books, 1993.

Kornfield, Jack. *After the Ecstasy, the Laundry.* New York: Bantam Books, 2000.

Lamott, Anne. *Traveling Mercies.* New York: Pantheon Books, 1999.

Markova, Dawna. *I Will Not Die an Unlived Life.* York Beach, Maine: Conari Press, 2002.

Martin, William. *The Parent's Tao Te Ching.* New York: Marlowe & Company, 1999.

Martin, William. *The Couple's Tao Te Ching.* New York: Marlowe & Company, 2000.

McNair, Wesley. *Talking in the Dark.* Boston: David R. Godine Publishing, 1998.

Muller, Wayne. *How, Then, Shall We Live?* New York: Bantam Books, 1996.

Nouwen, Henri. *Life of the Beloved.* New York: Crossroad, 1992.

O'Donohue, John. *Anam Cara.* New York: HarperCollins, Cliff Street Books, 1997.

Oliver, Mary. *New and Selected Poems.* Boston: Beacon Press, 1992.

Palmer, Parker. *Let Your Life Speak.* San Francisco: Jossey-Bass, 2000.

Richo, David. *Shadow Dance.* Boston: Shambhala Books, 1999.

Sardello, Robert. *Freeing the Soul from Fear.* New York: Riverhead Books, 1999.

Sinetar, Marsha. *Ordinary People as Monks and Mystics.* New York: Paulist Press, 1986.

Smedes, Lewis. *A Pretty Good Person.* San Francisco: Harper & Row, 1990.

Spong, Bishop John Shelby. *Why Christianity Must Change or Die.* San Francisco: HarperCollins, 1998.

Teasdale, Wayne. *The Mystic Heart.* Novato, California: New World Library, 2001.

Tolle, Eckhart. *The Power of Now.* Novato, California: New World Library, 2001.

Walker, Alice. *The Temple of My Familiar.* San Diego: Harcourt Brace Jovanovich, 1989.

Wall, Steve and Arden, Harvey. *Wisdomkeepers.* Hillsboro, Oregon: Beyond Words Publishing, 1990.

Weiss, Brian, M.D. *Messages from the Masters.* New York: Warner Books, 2000.

Whyte, David. *The House of Belonging.* Langley, Washington: Many Rivers Press, 1999.

Wood, Nancy. *Spirit Walker.* New York: Bantam Doubleday Dell Publishing Group, 1993.

Wood, Nancy. *Sacred Fire.* New York: Bantam Doubleday Dell Publishing Group, 1998.

Thank you for buying this book. We trust it enhances your understanding of the ways in which the Mystery is uniquely alive and at work in you. Please consider reading it with your friends or your book group, encouraging your local library and bookstores to carry it, and giving it as a gift to family or friends. In this way, you help small organizations like ours to reach those interested in our work.

Rogers McKay is a non-profit spiritual educational organization co-founded by Meredith Jordan, a psychotherapist, and Ellie Mercer, a United Church of Christ minister, with the intention to support women and men embarked on a path to expand a personal relationship with the Sacred Mystery. Their programs are designed for seekers from all faith traditions. Meredith Jordan is available to facilitate retreats, workshops and groups in spiritual development. She is also a presenter at spiritual or religious conferences and events.

In addition to publishing *Embracing the Mystery* as a resource for spiritual seekers, Rogers McKay has produced *Be At Perfect Peace,* a CD of inspirational guided meditations to help deepen one's connection to the healing presence of Spirit, or God. To order additional copies of *Embracing the Mystery,* cards and posters of the ETM cover art, and the *Be At Perfect Peace* CD, please call 207-283-0752 or go to the Rogers McKay website at *www.sacredportals.org*.